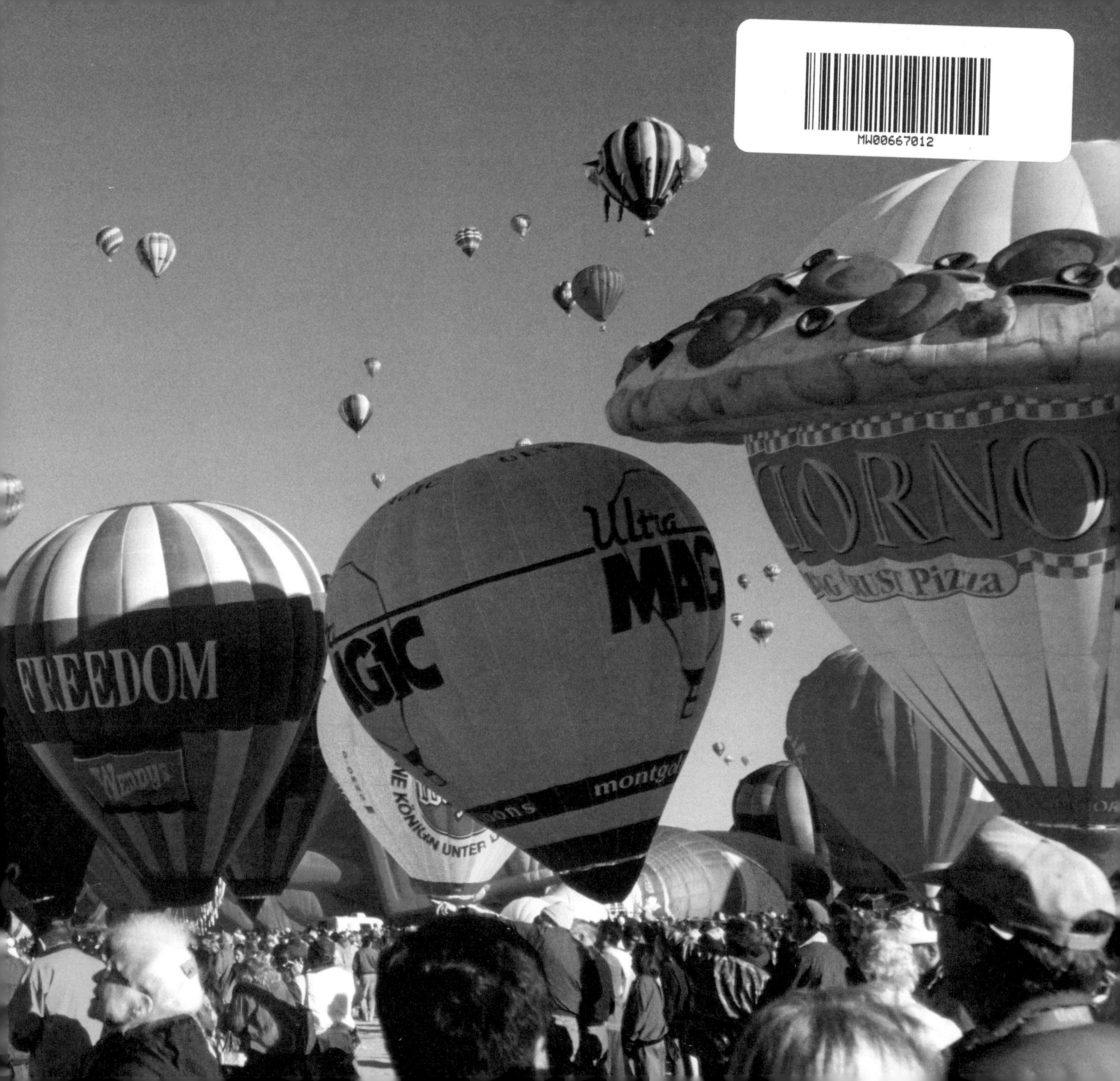
FREEDOM
Wendy's
Ultra
MAG
montgol
KÖNIGIN UNTER
ORNO
Pizza

From: Kent & Karen - Christmas 2018

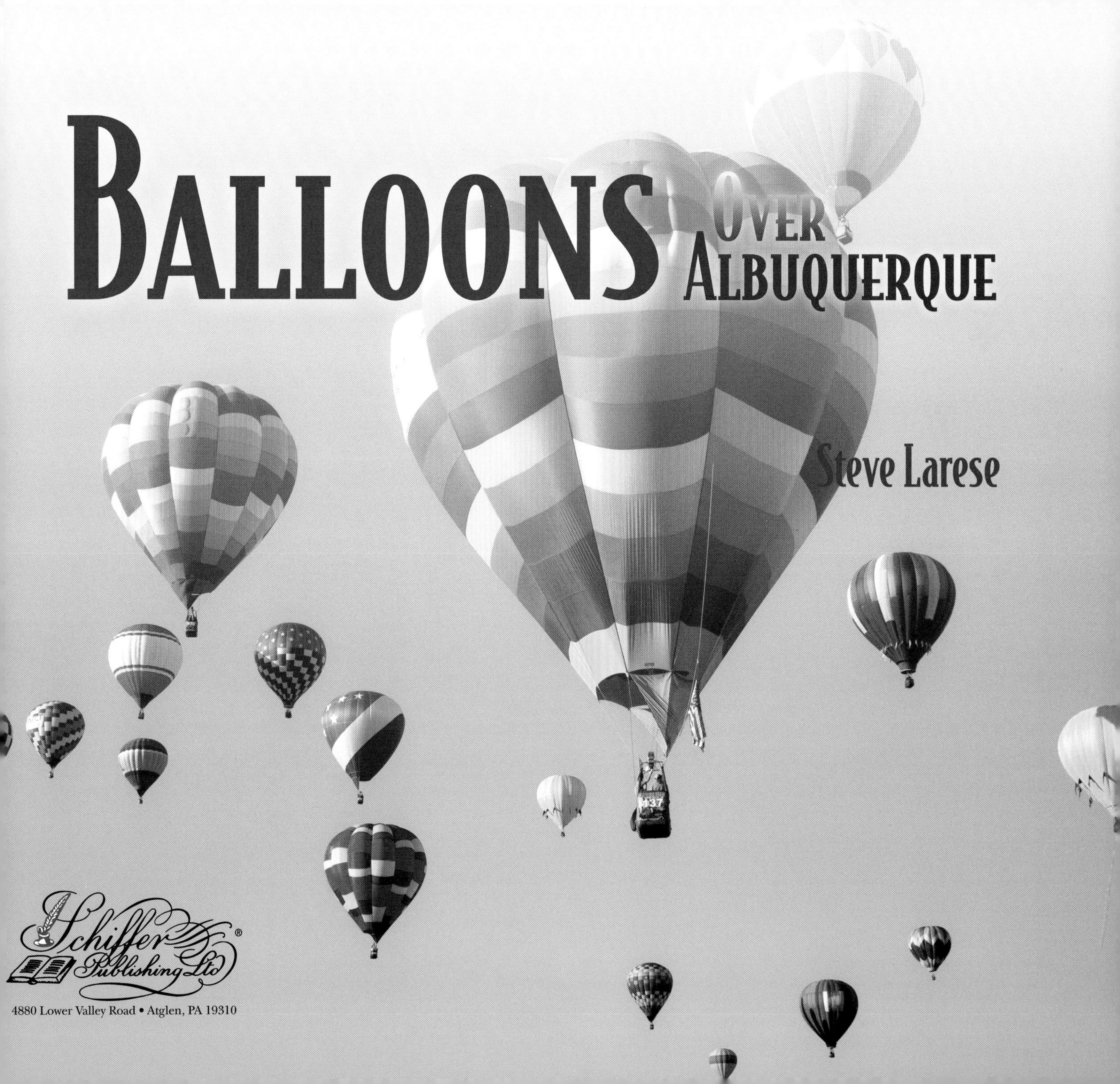

Balloons over Albuquerque

Steve Larese

Schiffer Publishing Ltd
4880 Lower Valley Road • Atglen, PA 19310

Other Schiffer Books by the Author:

Durango Perspectives, 978-0-7643-3337-8, $9.99
Santa Fe Reflections, 978-0-7643-3653-9, $24.99
Southwest Reflections: Grand Canyon & The Four Corners, 978-0-7643-4093-2, $29.99

Library of Congress Control Number: 2014943444

Cover and Interiors designed by John Cheek
Typeset in Bodega Serif/GoudyOlSt BT

ISBN: 978-0-7643-4794-8
Printed in China

Published by Schiffer Publishing, Ltd.
4880 Lower Valley Road
Atglen, PA 19310
Phone: (610) 593-1777; Fax: (610) 593-2002
E-mail: Info@schifferbooks.com

For our complete selection of fine books on this and related subjects, please visit our website at **www.schifferbooks.com**. You may also write for a free catalog.

This book may be purchased from the publisher. Please try your bookstore first.

We are always looking for people to write books on new and related subjects. If you have an idea for a book, please contact us at proposals@schifferbooks.com.

Schiffer Publishing's titles are available at special discounts for bulk purchases for sales promotions or premiums. Special editions, including personalized covers, corporate imprints, and excerpts can be created in large quantities for special needs. For more information, contact the publisher.

It all began with one balloon....

Every October, Albuquerque's brilliant turquoise sky swirls with a kaleidoscope of color during the annual Albuquerque International Balloon Fiesta. People from across the planet watch mesmerized as hundreds of hot-air balloons dot the desert sky during the largest annual balloon gathering in the world. Throughout the week, an average of 500,000 people attend the early morning launches and evening balloon glows.

Beyond its size, say Fiesta officials, what makes Fiesta special is that it's one of the few where people may walk onto the field and interact with the balloons and crews. People become part of the event, not just observers on the sidelines. The cold pre-dawn sky gives way to flares of propane as balloon crews test their burners. Crowds gather around the baskets to warm themselves, sipping hot chocolate and nibbling breakfast burritos. Fans roar to life, and balloon envelopes billow on the ground. Finally, as the sky begins to lighten and stars fade over the Sandía Mountains, burners roar and heat the trapped air, causing the balloons to tip upright amid cheers.

The Balloon Fiesta began, appropriately enough, with a party. Sid and Bill Cutter's mother, Virginia, was celebrating her birthday in 1971, and the brothers wanted to throw her a bash.

"I decided to go with a World War I theme," Sid Cutter told me in 1994. Cutter passed away at 77 in 2011 after careers as an Air Force pilot and with his family's business, Cutter Aviation. "I rented Snoopy and the Red Baron costumes, thinking I would be the Red Baron and my brother would be Snoopy, although he got to the Red Baron costume first and I had to be Snoopy. But what I really wanted to do was get an old airplane for the hangar."

After realizing a vintage airplane would be difficult and expensive to get, Cutter was encouraged to rent "one of those new balloons."

"In 1971 there were maybe 50 balloons max in the U.S." he said. "They were just being 'rediscovered.' " So I thought, 'Well, they used balloons in World War I, and I can float it outside my business for advertising after the party.' That shows you how much I knew about balloons back then."

So Cutter—who went on to be awarded the Montgolfier Diplome, the highest honor in the world for ballooning and was twice the national hot-air balloon champion in 1978 and 1986—ordered and received his first balloon, a patriotic red, white, and blue one with gold trim that Cutter looked at as a nifty $5,000 party decoration for his mother. Stuffing it into the hangar, Cutter hit the gas and left it burning all night to keep the balloon inflated.

"So here I am in my Snoopy costume with my brother dressed up like the Red Baron," Cutter said. "Everybody was having a great time, and the booze was flowing. Some of it flowed into my brother, and he began telling people he and I were going to fly that balloon in the morning."

Cutter figured that if a hangover didn't thwart his brother's plan, the lack of propane would. But at six the next morning, the Red Baron was at Snoopy's door.

"I told him we'd used all the gas keeping the balloon inflated last night, but he had gone to the truck stop and got some more," Cutter said. "He had to save face and was determined to fly that thing. So I thought we'd just have some people hold on to the rope, learn the burner and take Mom up for a little bit afterward, and that would be that. But we forgot to tell the ground crew to hold onto the rope, and the next thing my brother and I knew we were 300 feet up and heading toward power lines."

Cutter attributed the fact that wasn't his first and last balloon ride to a perfect flying day. The brothers managed to miss the power lines and landed in the rough at University of New Mexico Golf Course. While this was happening, the trusty ground crew was getting breakfast at an International House of Pancakes. But plenty of other people noticed the Cutter brothers' jaunt.

"When we landed, there were 5,000 people and five police cars waiting for us, but no ground crew," Cutter said. "People loved it. Balloons were a pretty rare sight then."

But what is considered to be the first Albuquerque Balloon Fiesta didn't take place until KOB Radio, looking for a unique way to celebrate its fiftieth anniversary in 1972, contacted Cutter.

"KOB (a local radio station) heard about my balloon and gave me a call, asking if I could fly for their fiftieth anniversary," Cutter said. "I said, 'Why don't we do it big and have a balloon race?' They said, 'Great, what's a balloon race?' and I said, 'Hell if I know.'"

Cutter found out. He contacted twenty-one ballooning teams from across the country to attend the ballooning "happening." Thirteen made it, and while newly elected governor Bruce King and Slim Pickens were slapping each other on the back down below at the KOB shindig at Coronado Center mall below, the first Albuquerque Balloon Fiesta was being born above.

"This was just a radio anniversary, but 20,000 people showed up at six in the morning to watch thirteen balloons take off," Cutter explained. "It was something else. Albuquerque was trying to find something to hang its hat on. The city had tried a couple of chile cook-offs, but nothing compared to this. Looking at the numbers and the demographics, the city felt balloons would put it on the map."

The city was right. Cutter organized the next two Balloon Fiestas until it grew too large for him to manage, and the City of Albuquerque took over in 1974, creating a nonprofit Fiesta organization, the way it remains today.

Today, the Fiesta begins the first Saturday of October through the week until Sunday morning. Weekend mornings see mass ascensions of all balloons, followed by evening balloon glows and fireworks. The Wednesday morning balloon glow begins at 6:30 a.m., followed by a mass launch of balloons representing an average of twenty nations. On Thursday and Friday mornings, only special shapes such as Belgium's Darth Vader launch, and those evenings nearly one hundred special shapes inflate again for the Special Shape Glowdeo. Throughout the week, ballooning competitions —such as attempting to hit targets on the ground with bean bags and grabbing a key that starts a new truck—are scheduled.

After the balloons land for the day, Albuquerque offers plenty more to do. The Anderson-Abruzzo International Ballooning Museum next to the launch field takes visitors through the history of ballooning with interactive displays (www.balloonmuseum.com). See the lights of Albuquerque from the top of 10,378-foot Sandía Mountain via the 2.7-mile-long Sandia Peak Tramway. Historic Old Town is a must-visit for Southwest dining and shopping. Albuquerque has many excellent museums, including the Albuquerque Museum of Art and History, New Mexico Museum of Natural History and Science, and iExplora! Science Center and Children's Museum. The Albuquerque Zoo and Biopark are perfect places for families in between ballooning events, where sharks, sea turtles, jellyfish, and gardens will make you forget you're in landlocked New Mexico. And New Mexico's famous chile-based cuisine can be found in restaurants throughout city.

Visit **www.balloonfiesta.com** for complete information about Balloon Fiesta, and hopefully the following pages will inspire you to visit and see for yourself the greatest ballooning show on earth.

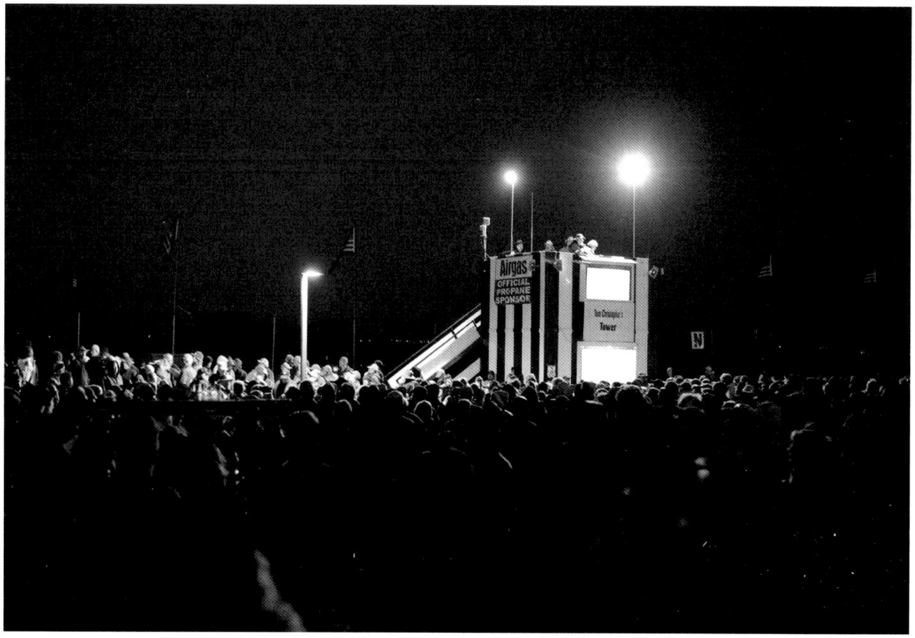

Every morning before a mass ascension, balloon pilots gather to hear weather reports, event news, and watch small helium balloons launch to assess wind conditions.

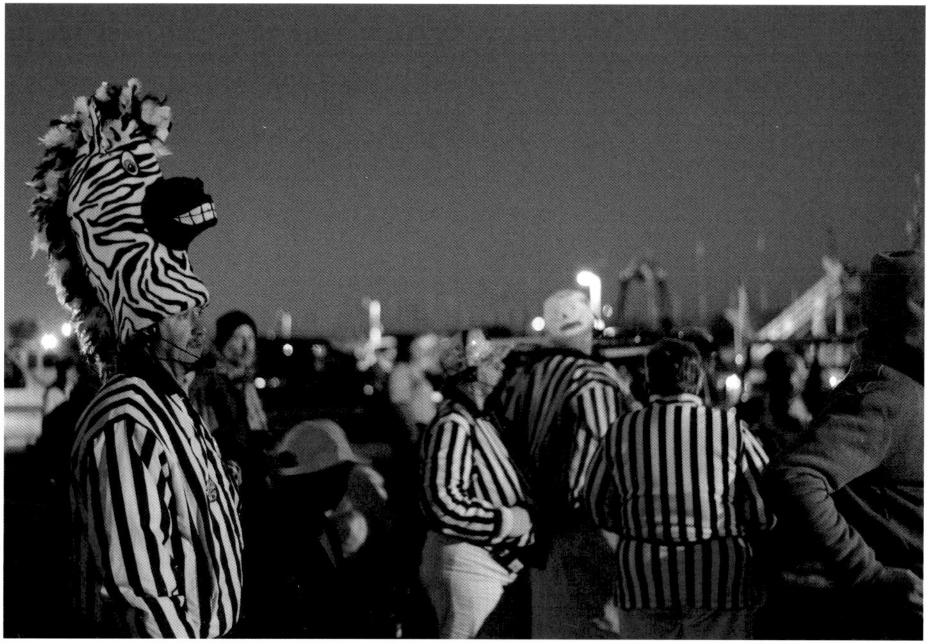

Zebras—volunteers who clear balloons for launch and handle other safety issues, listen to the morning briefing. They wear black and white striped clothing—often with humorous zebra motifs—so that they can be quickly spotted by pilots among the thousands of spectators.

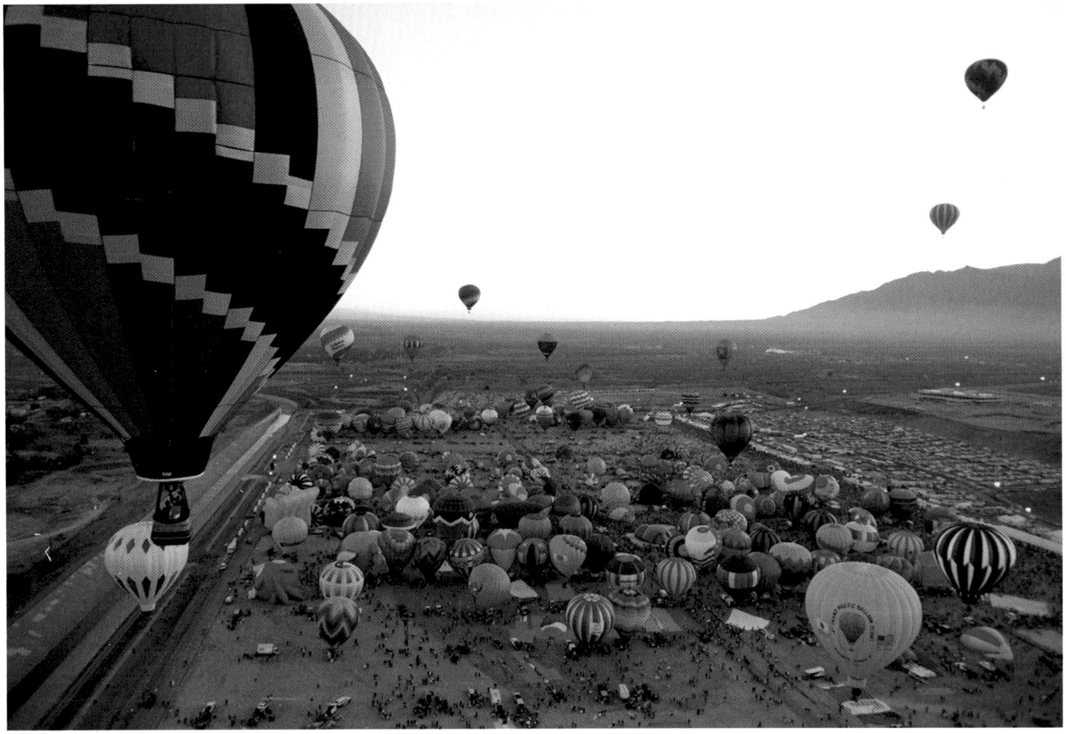

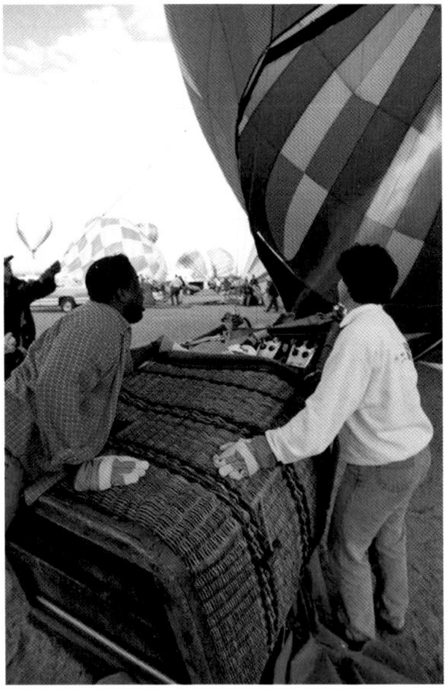

The air in its envelope heated, a balloon is set upright for launch.

With the sun not yet breaking over the Sandía Mountains, the first wave of balloons launches. Typically there are two waves with an average of 350 balloons each.

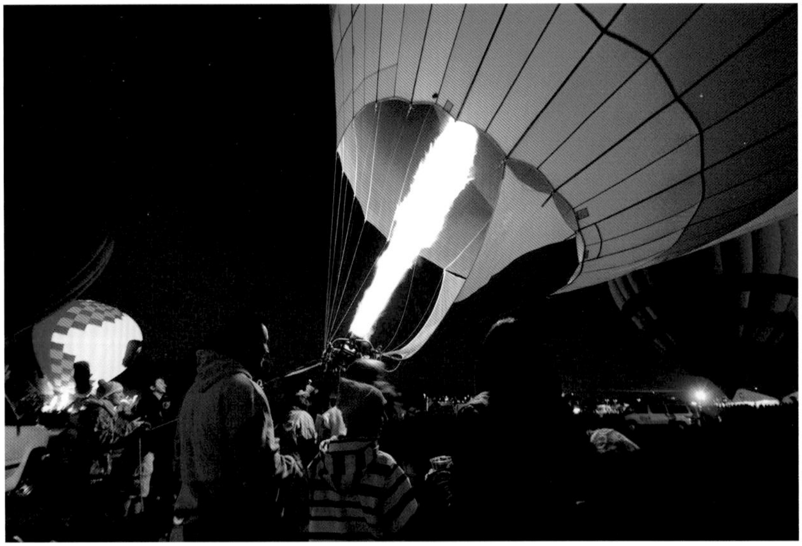

Balloons inflate at dawn after receiving a favorable weather forecast for the morning.

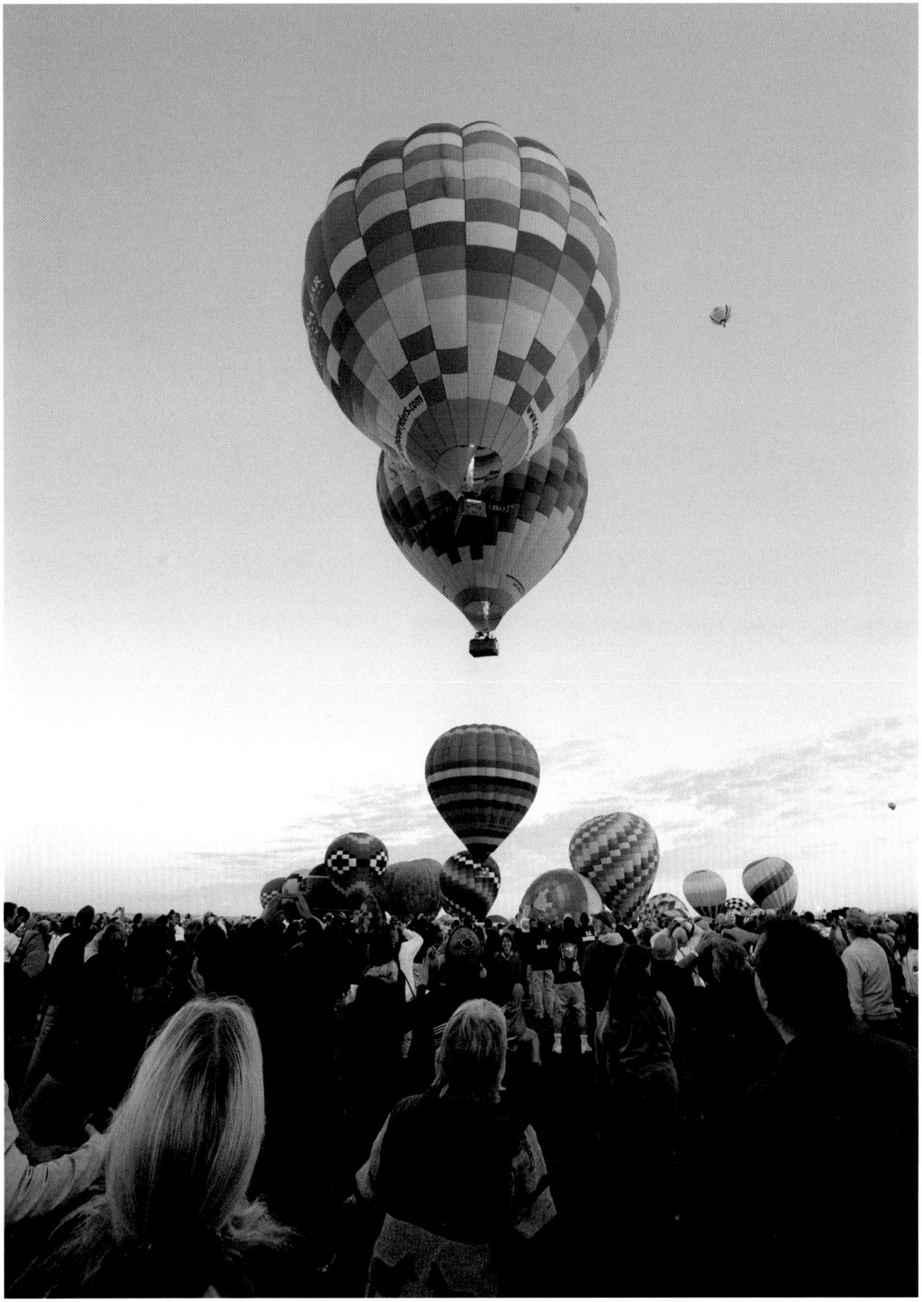

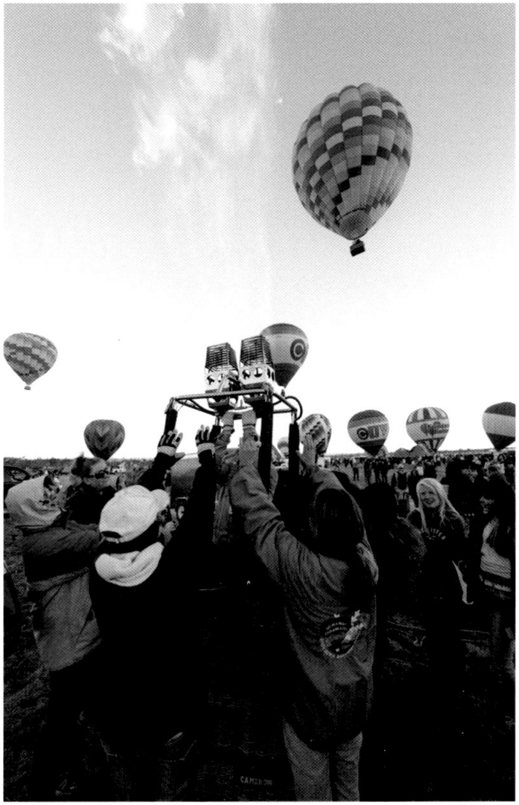

Crew and visitors warm their hands as a balloon pilot tests his propane burner before assembling the balloon envelope. October temperatures in Albuquerque can approach freezing in the morning and quickly climb into the 70s during the day. Visitors should dress in layers.

Balloons soar to the cheers of thousands below.

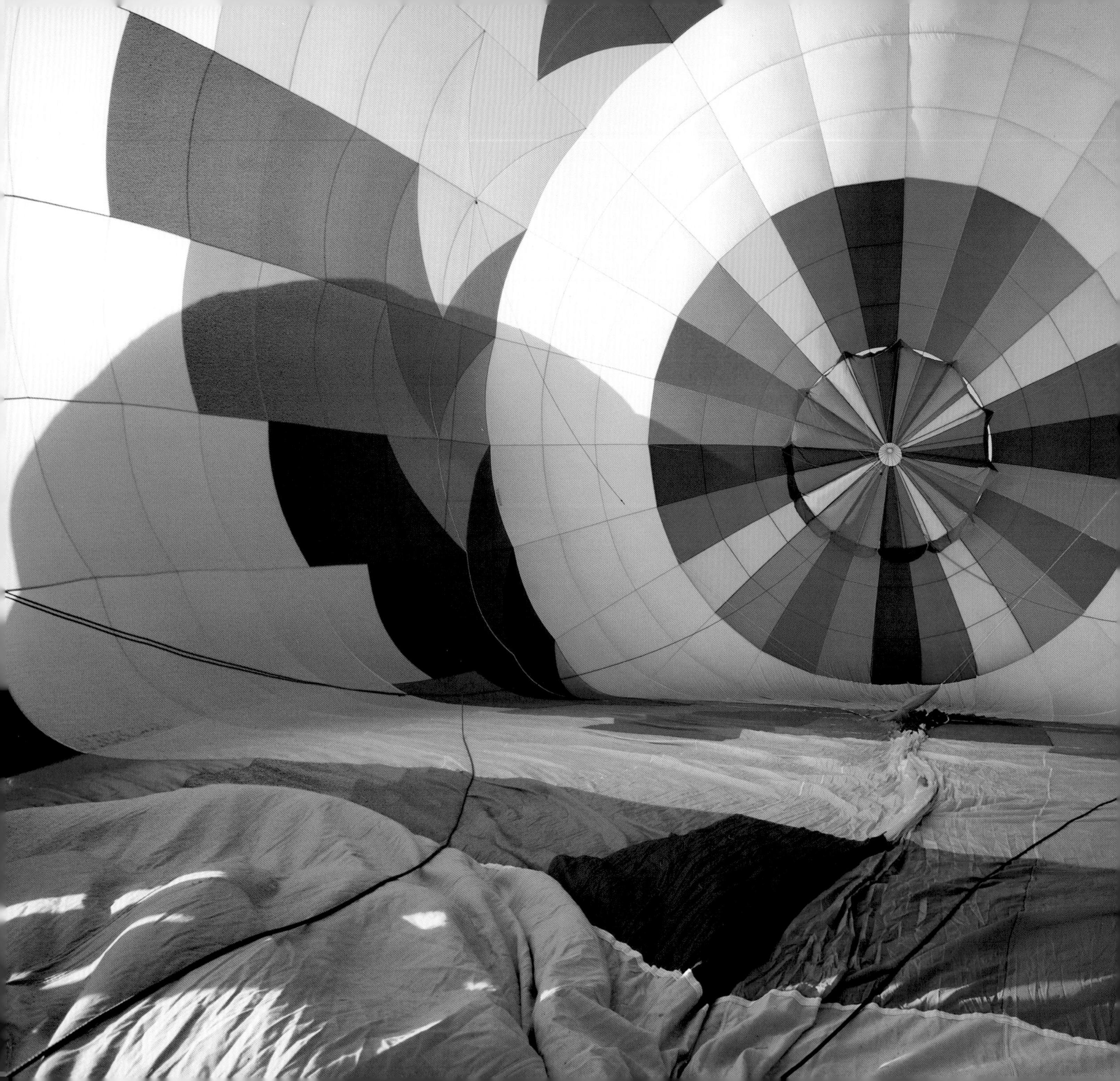

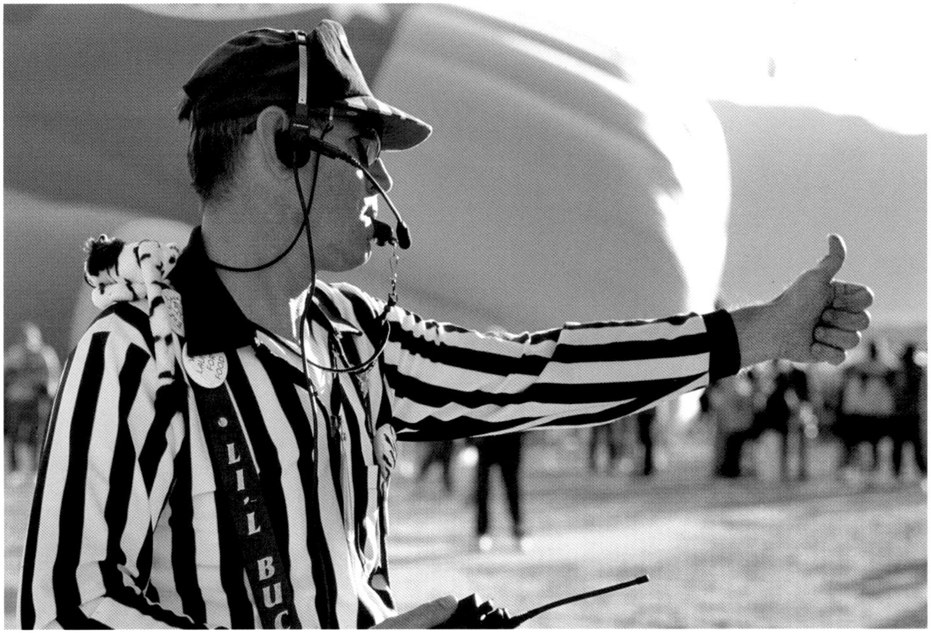

A zebra gives the thumbs-up to a balloon for lift off.

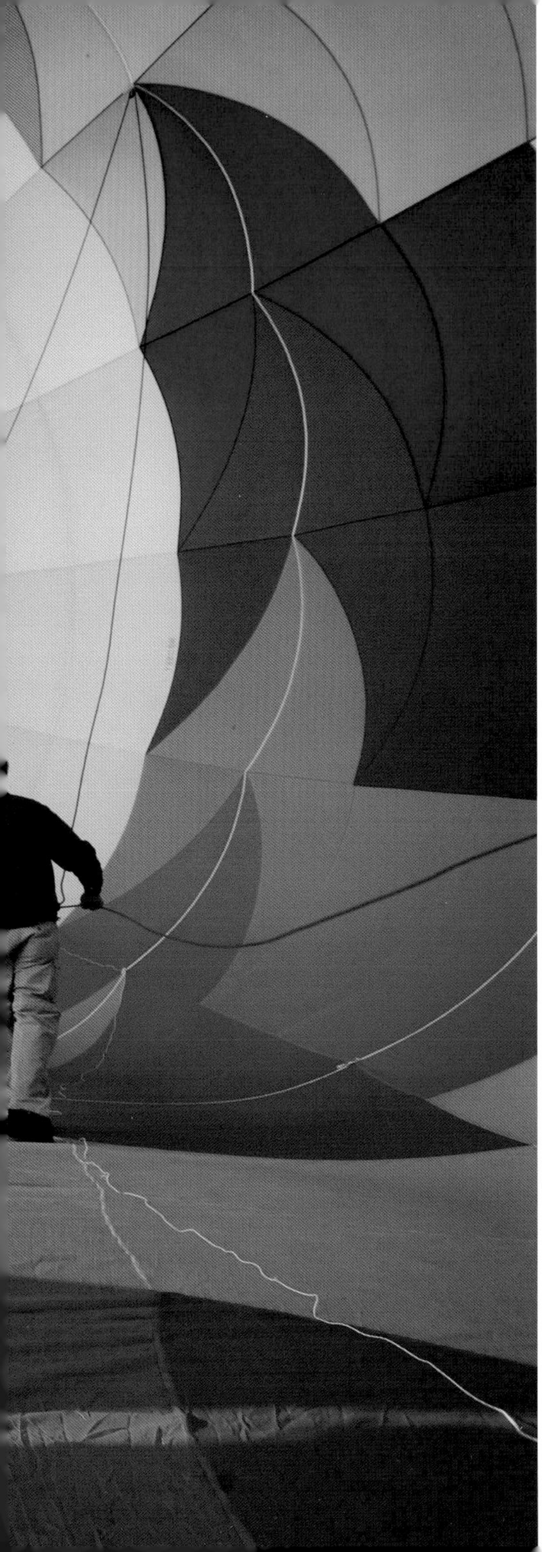

A pilot inspects the interior of his balloon that has been cold-filled with air using a fan. A burner will then heat the air, making it hotter than the outside air and causing the balloon to lift.

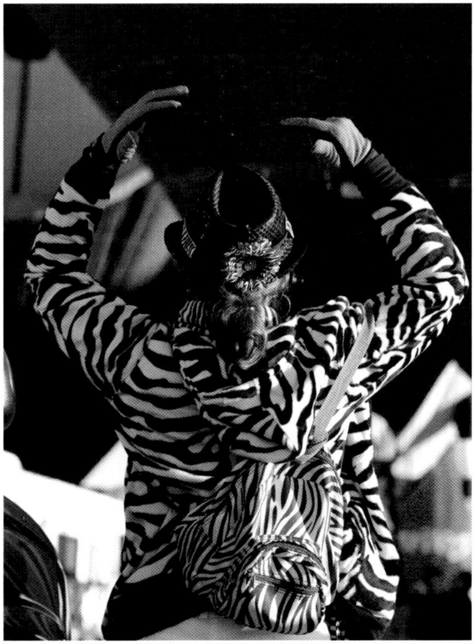

A ready signal before launch.

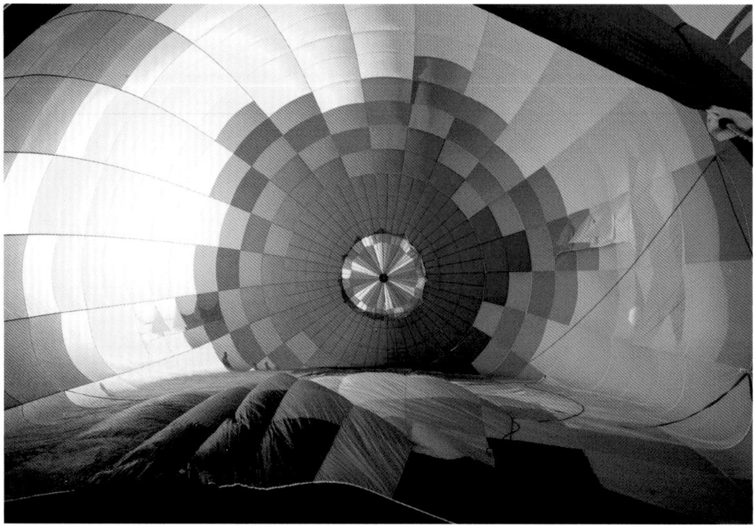

The envelope fabric is usually made of ripstop nylon, then coated with a sealer to make it impermeable.

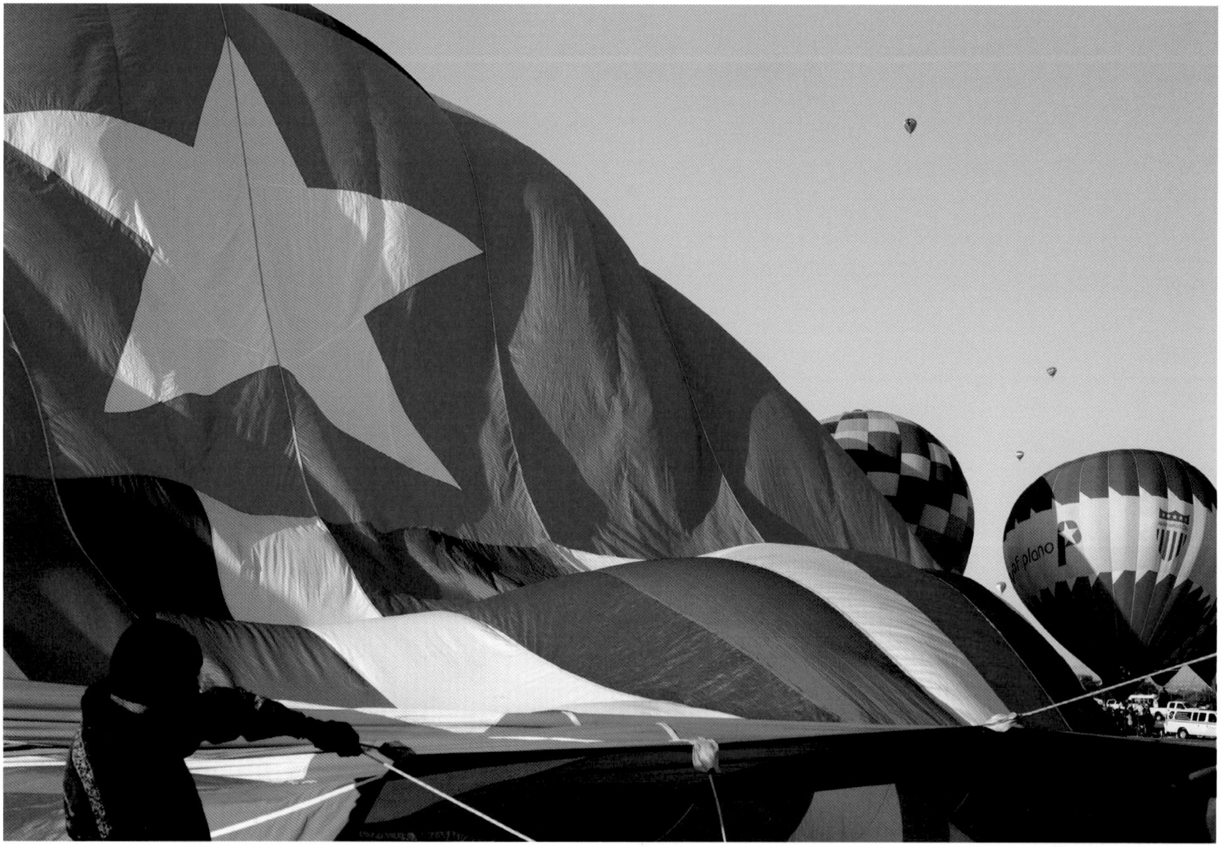

Stars and stripes wave as a balloon is readied for take off.

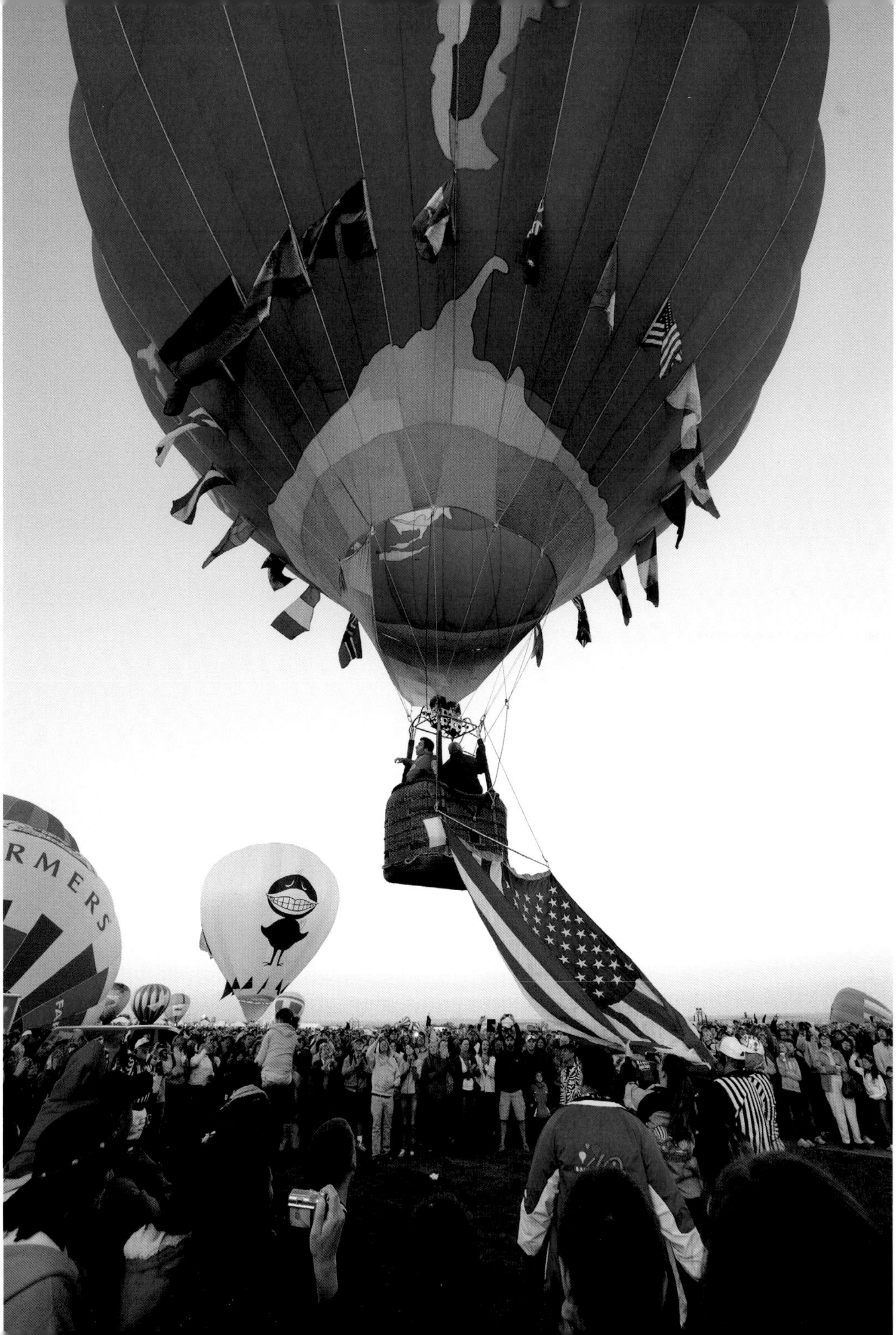

The United States flag unfurls during the Flight of Nations mass ascension by the World Balloon. World Balloon, Inc., a balloon tour company, was started by the Albuquerque International Balloon Fiesta's founder, Sid Cutter, who passed away in 2011.

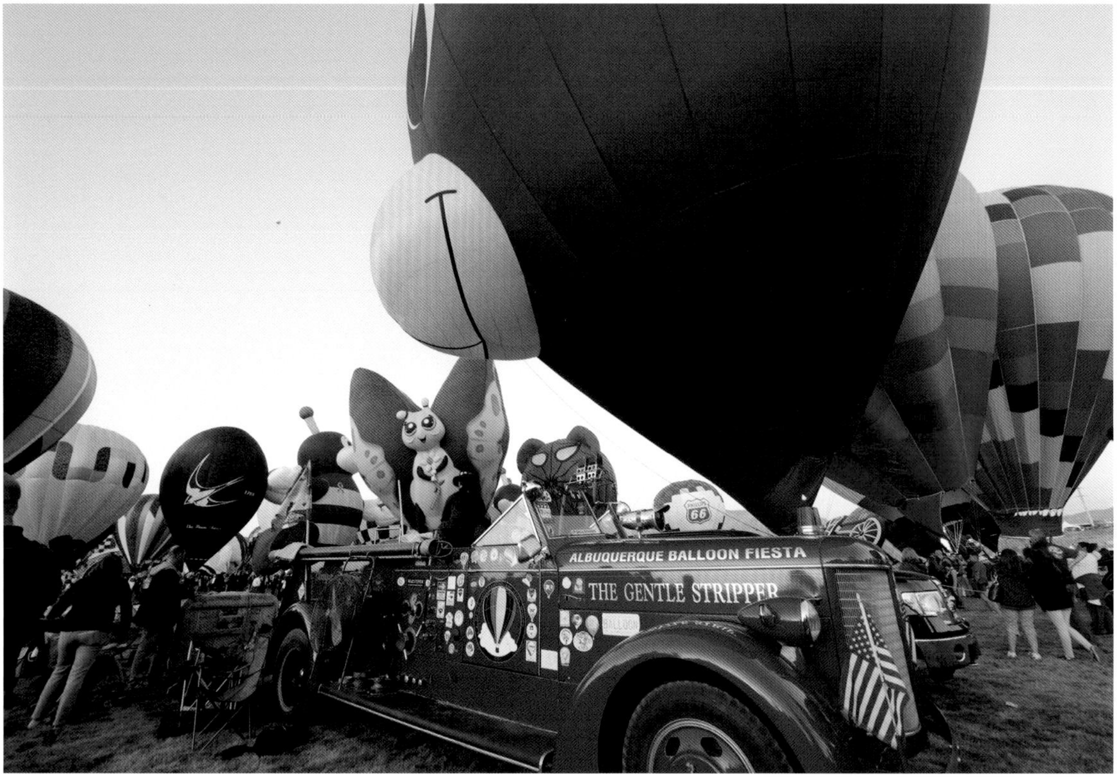

An antique fire truck has found a new life as a balloon chase vehicle. After balloons launch, support crews load into chase vehicles and track the balloons to their landing sites, which are never completely known in advance.

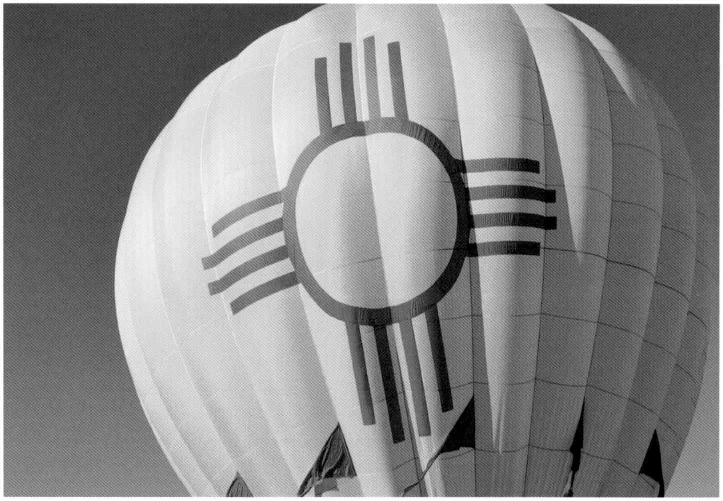

The Zia, the state symbol of New Mexico found at Zia Pueblo, adorns a balloon.

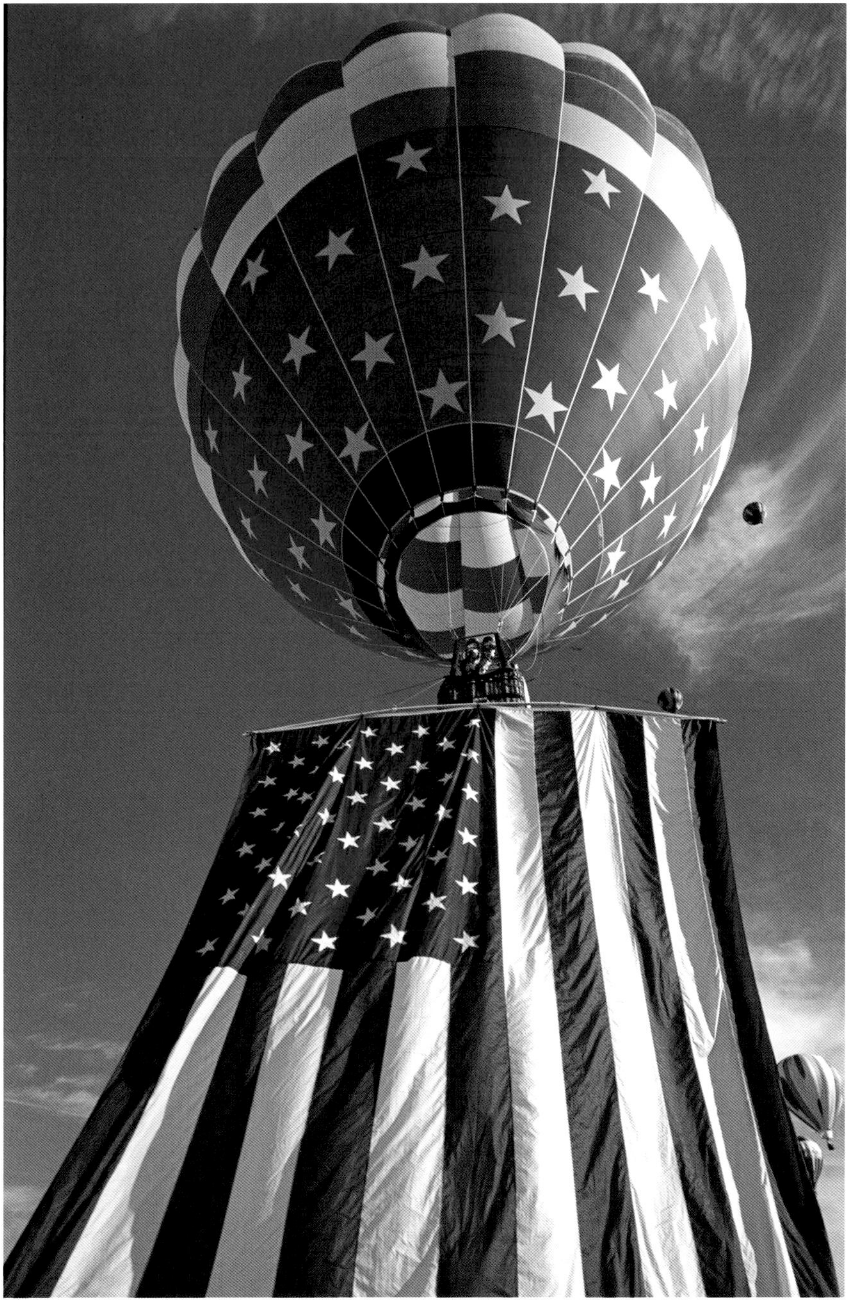

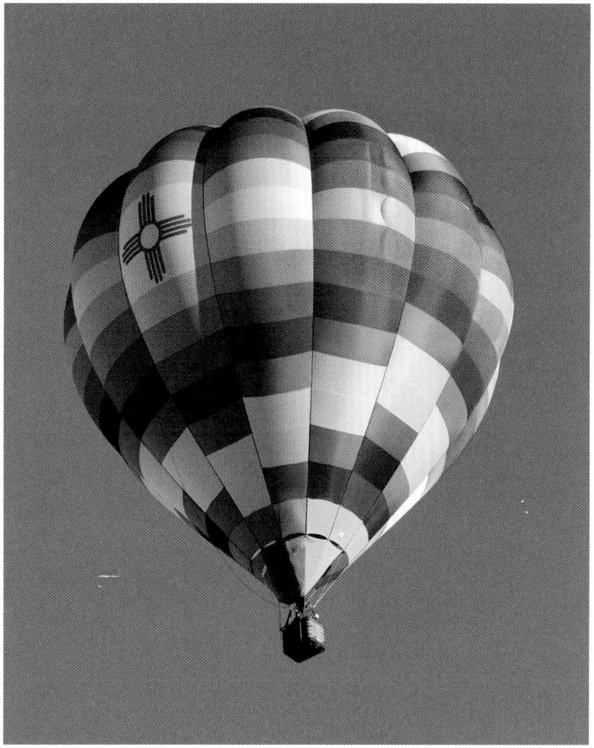

A New Mexico-themed balloon drifts above the field.

The United States flag rises during a mass ascension. Pilots often fly their countries' flags during take off, underscoring the truly international aspect of Fiesta.

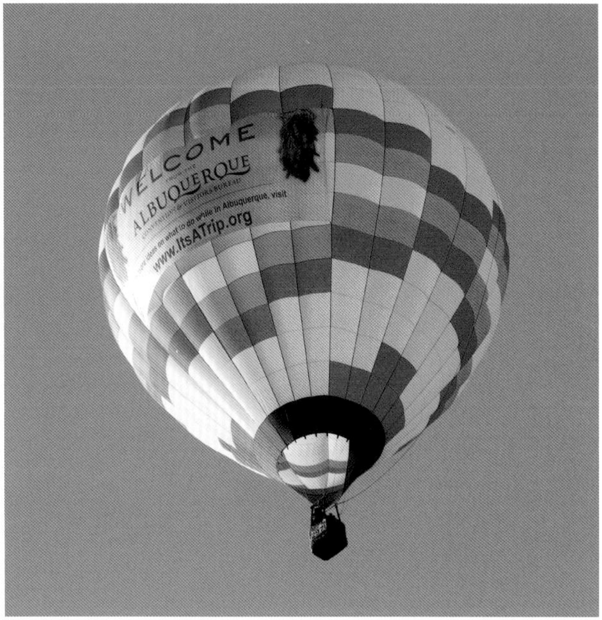

The Albuquerque Convention and Visitor's Bureau balloon advertises the It's A Trip website (itsatrip.org), which lists many activities to enjoy in Albuquerque after the festival.

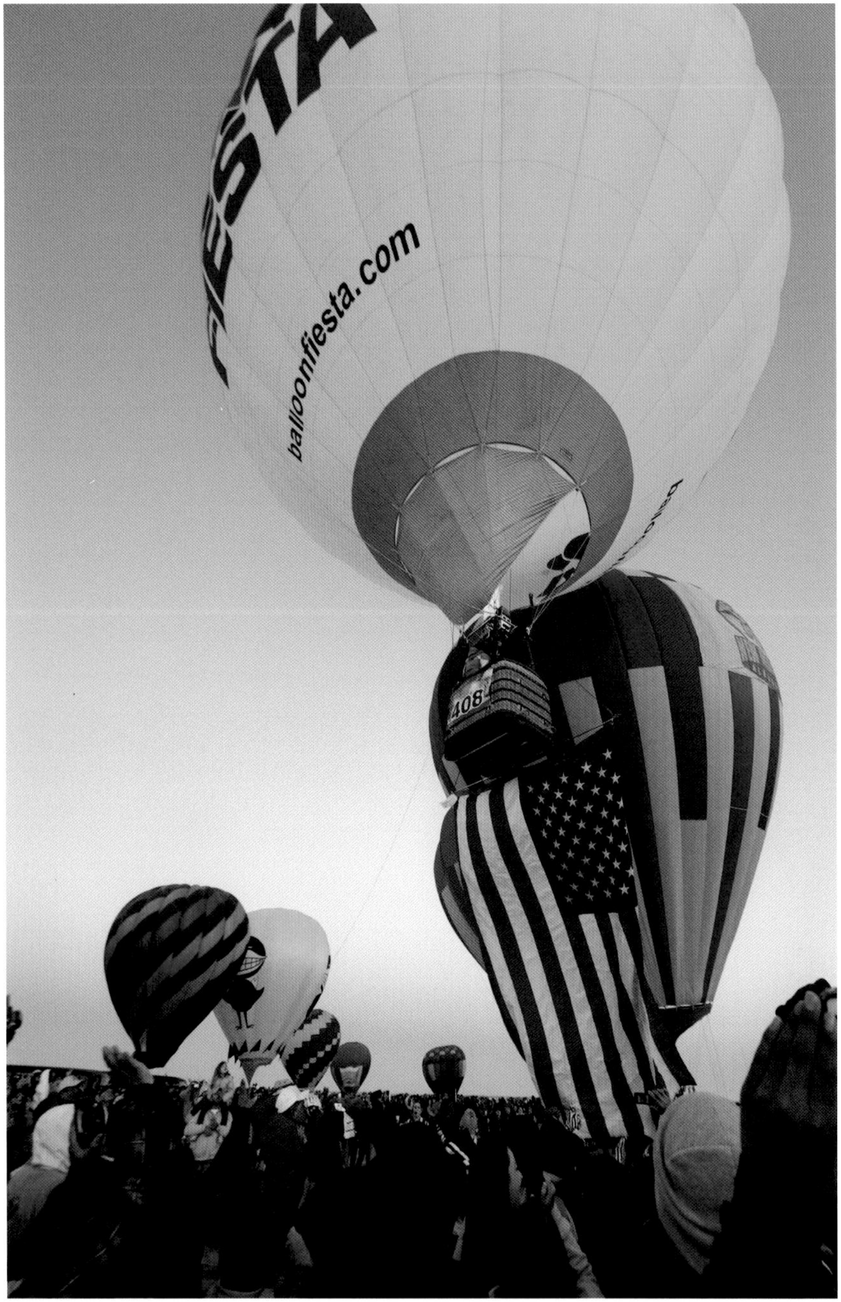

The official Fiesta balloon takes off, leading the way for the morning's mass ascension.

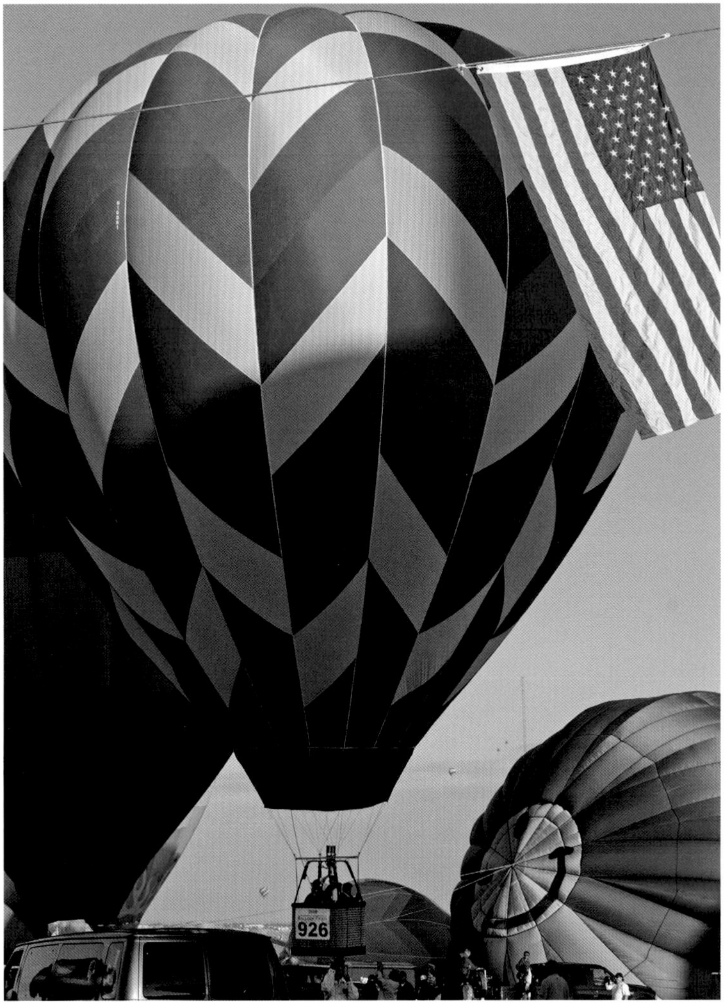

Lift off, as the morning sun finally reaches the field.

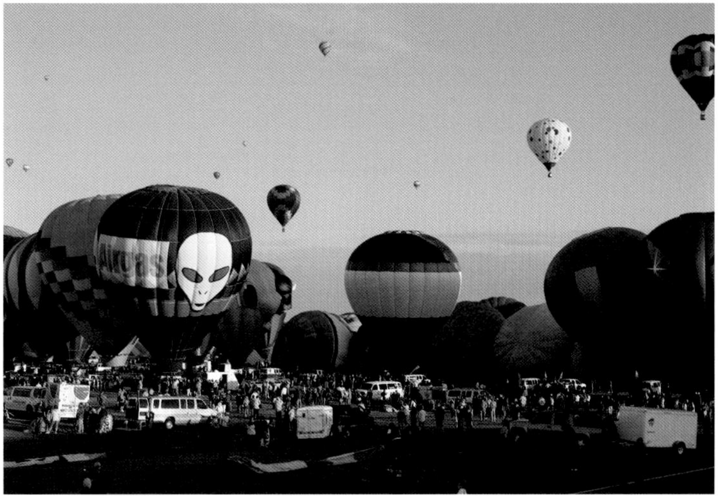

An alien watches over the balloon field. New Mexico has long been associated with space alien lore.

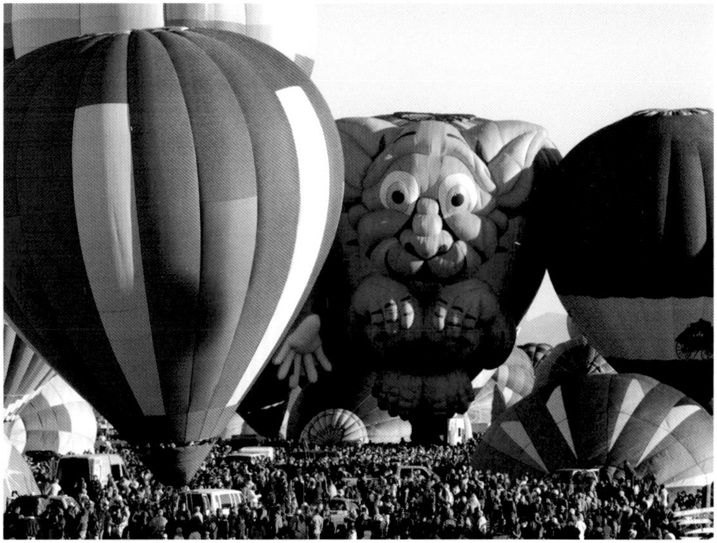

"Gizzmo" is a gremlin special shape balloon from Wichita Falls, Texas.

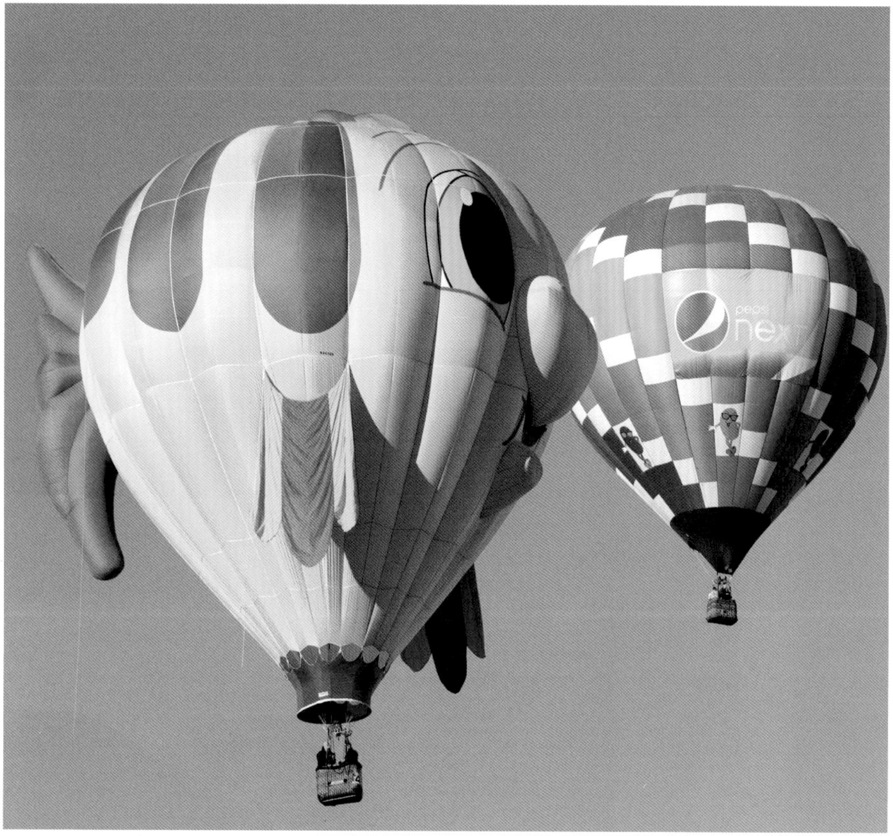

"Gus T. Guppy" from Burnsville, Minnesota, weighs 400 pounds and is 60 feet long.

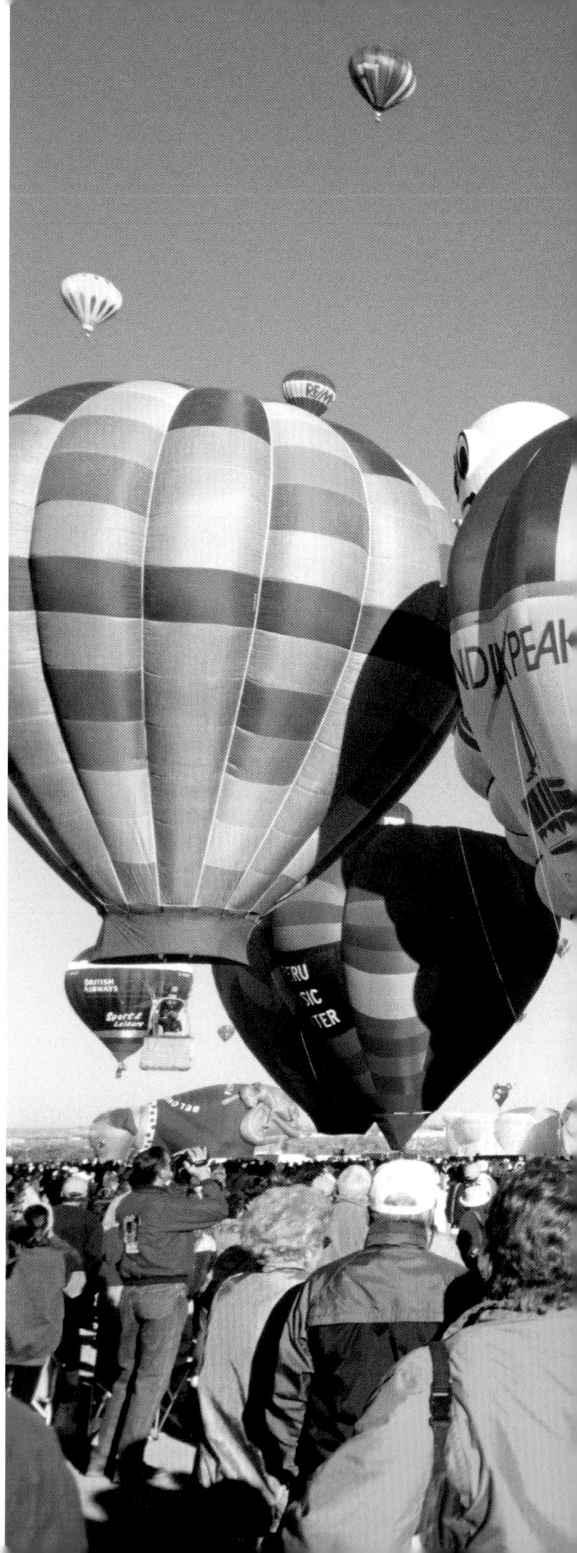

More than 1,000 volunteers donate their time each year to helping with Balloon Fiesta. Many use their work vacation days.

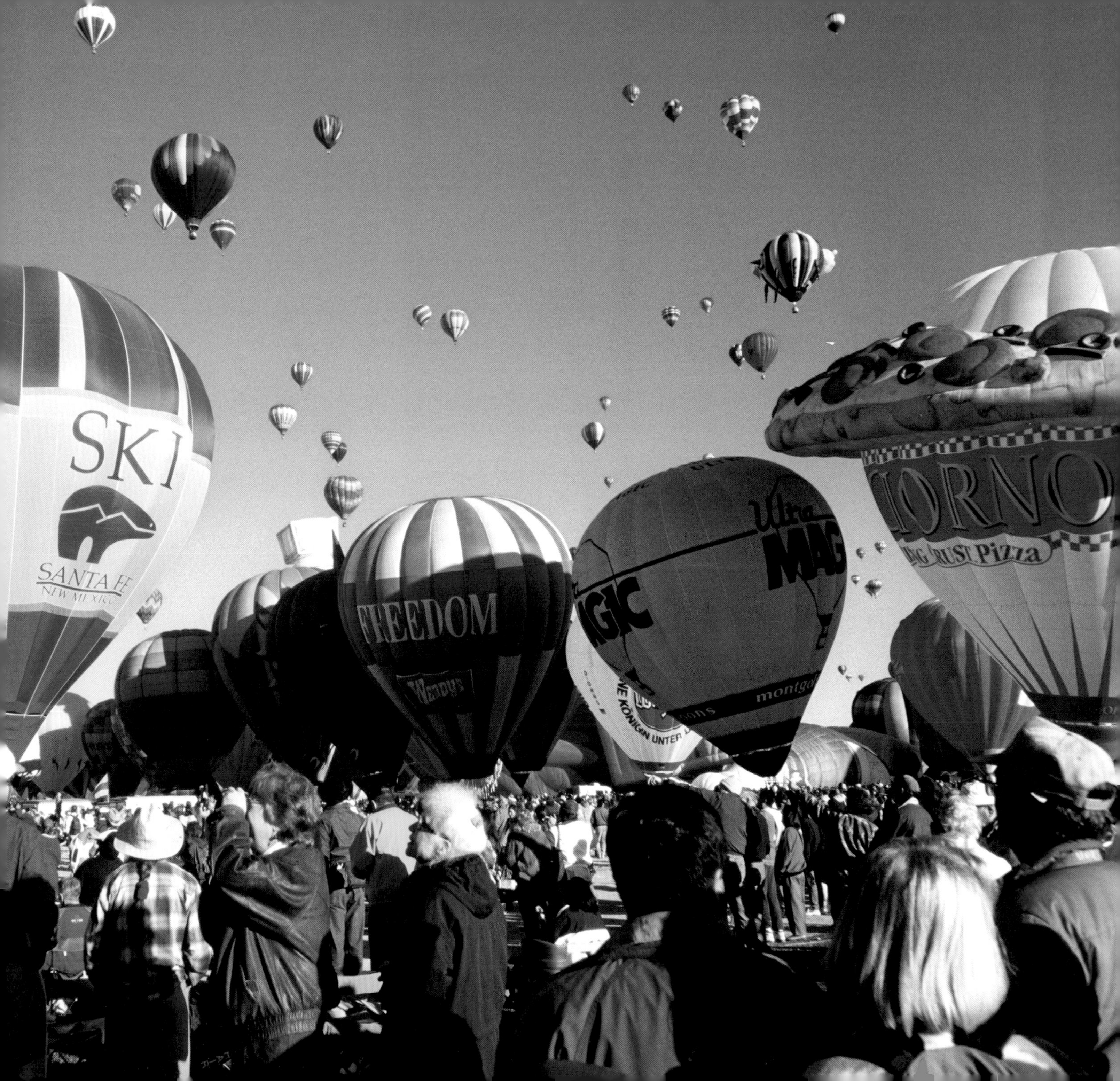
SKI
SANTA FE
FREEDOM
Ultra MAG
Pizza

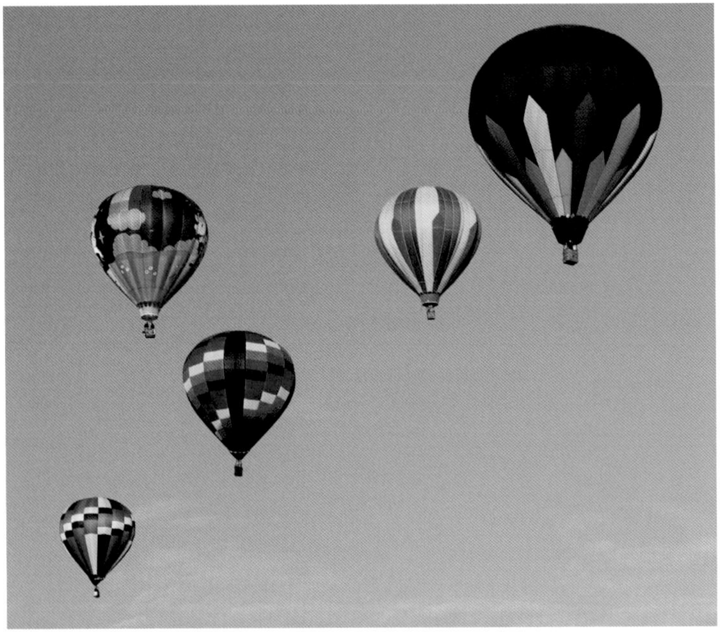

Balloons drift together against the Albuquerque sky.

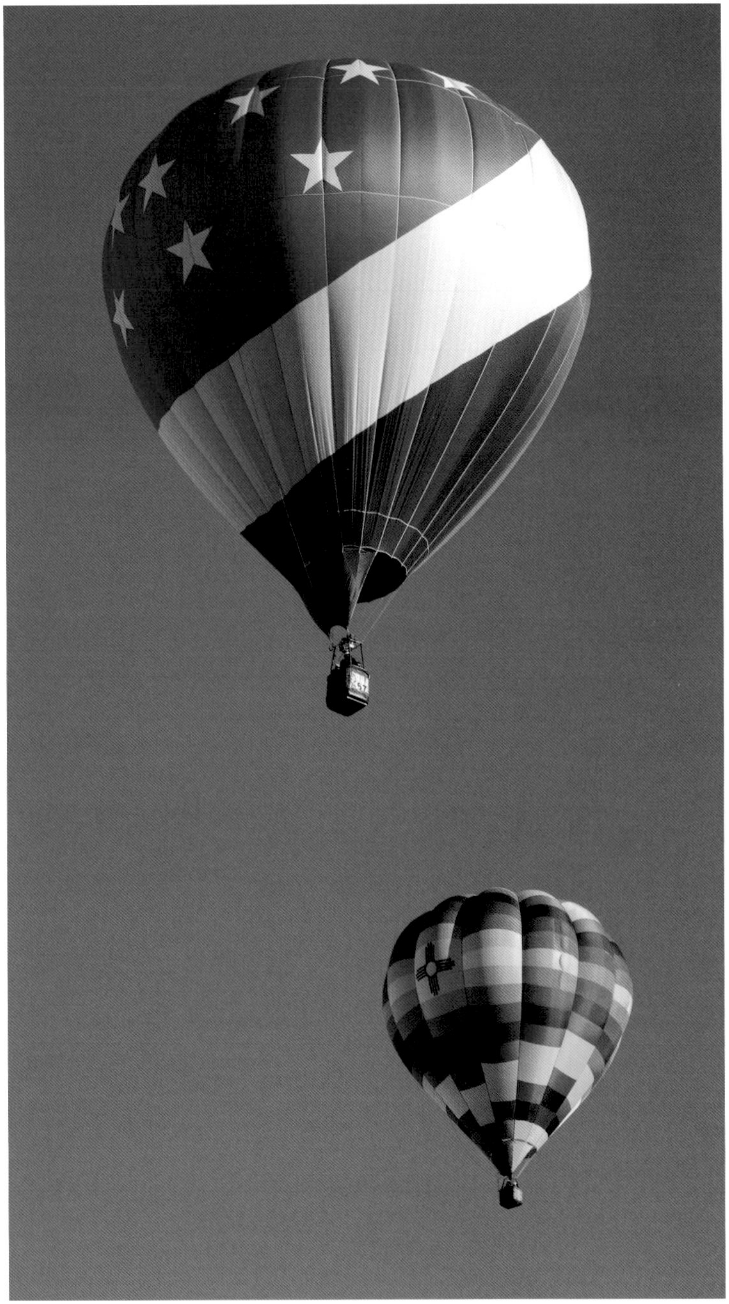

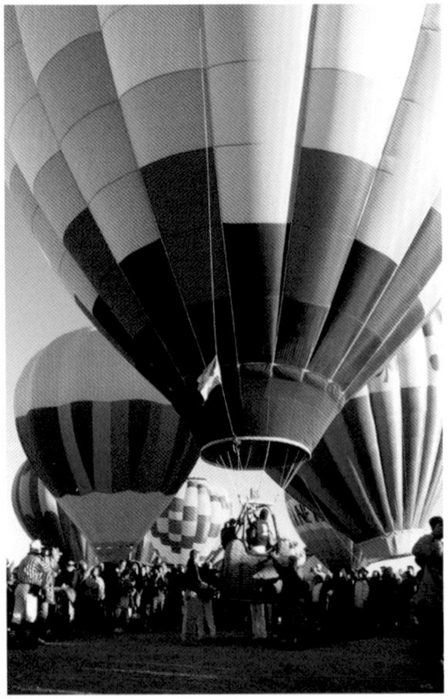

Helpers hold a balloon down as the crown makes way for take off.

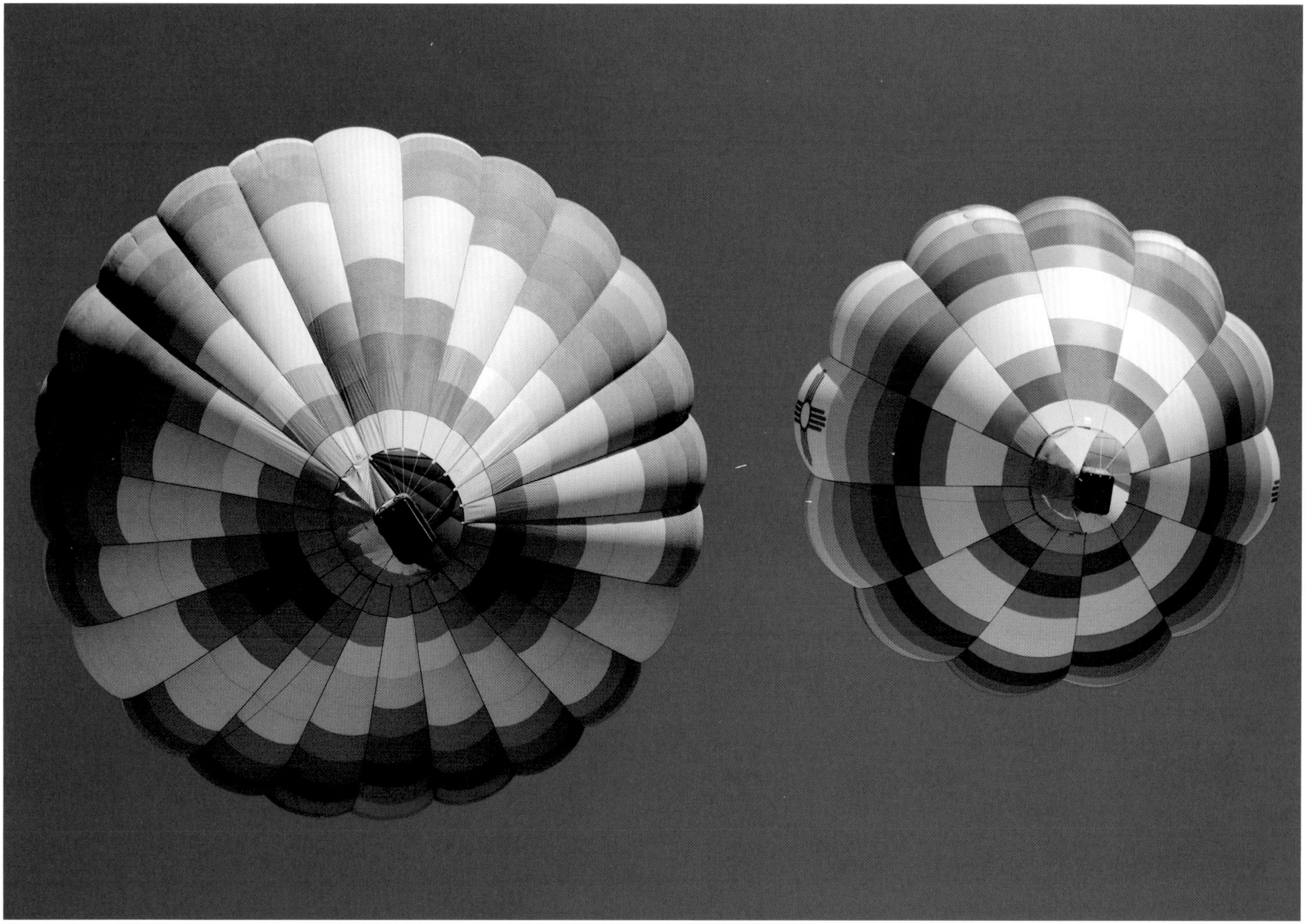

Albuquerque enjoys an average of 310 days of sunshine, though the Fiesta is at the mercy of October winds and weather.

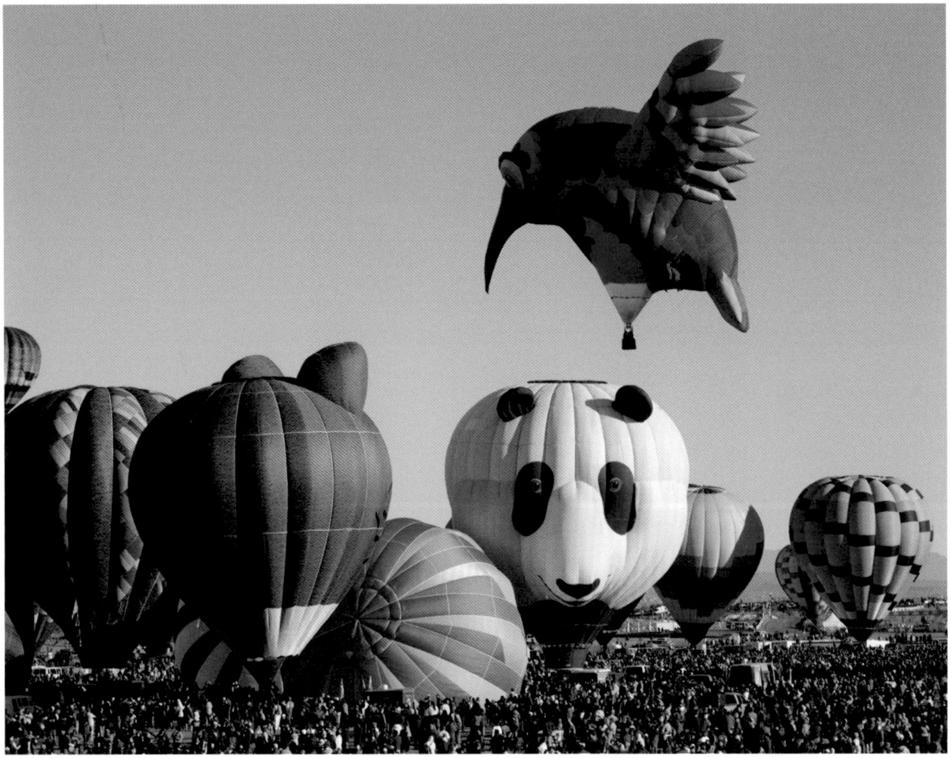

"Hummingbird" from Brazil rises above "Party Panda" from California.

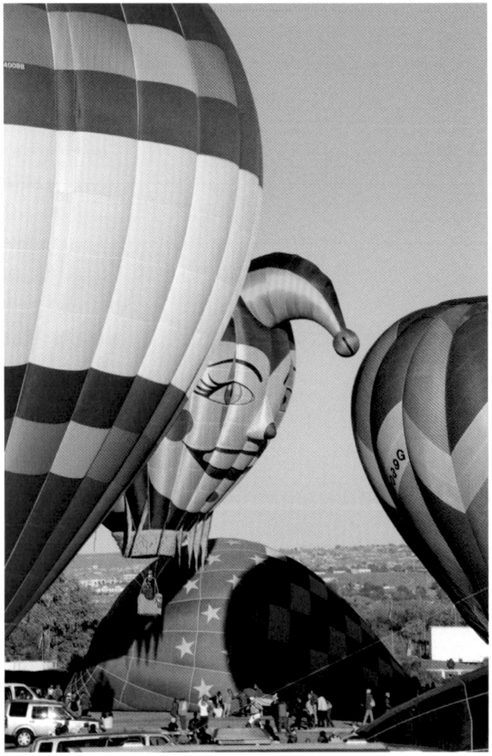

"Lady Jester" from Albuquerque begins her ascent.

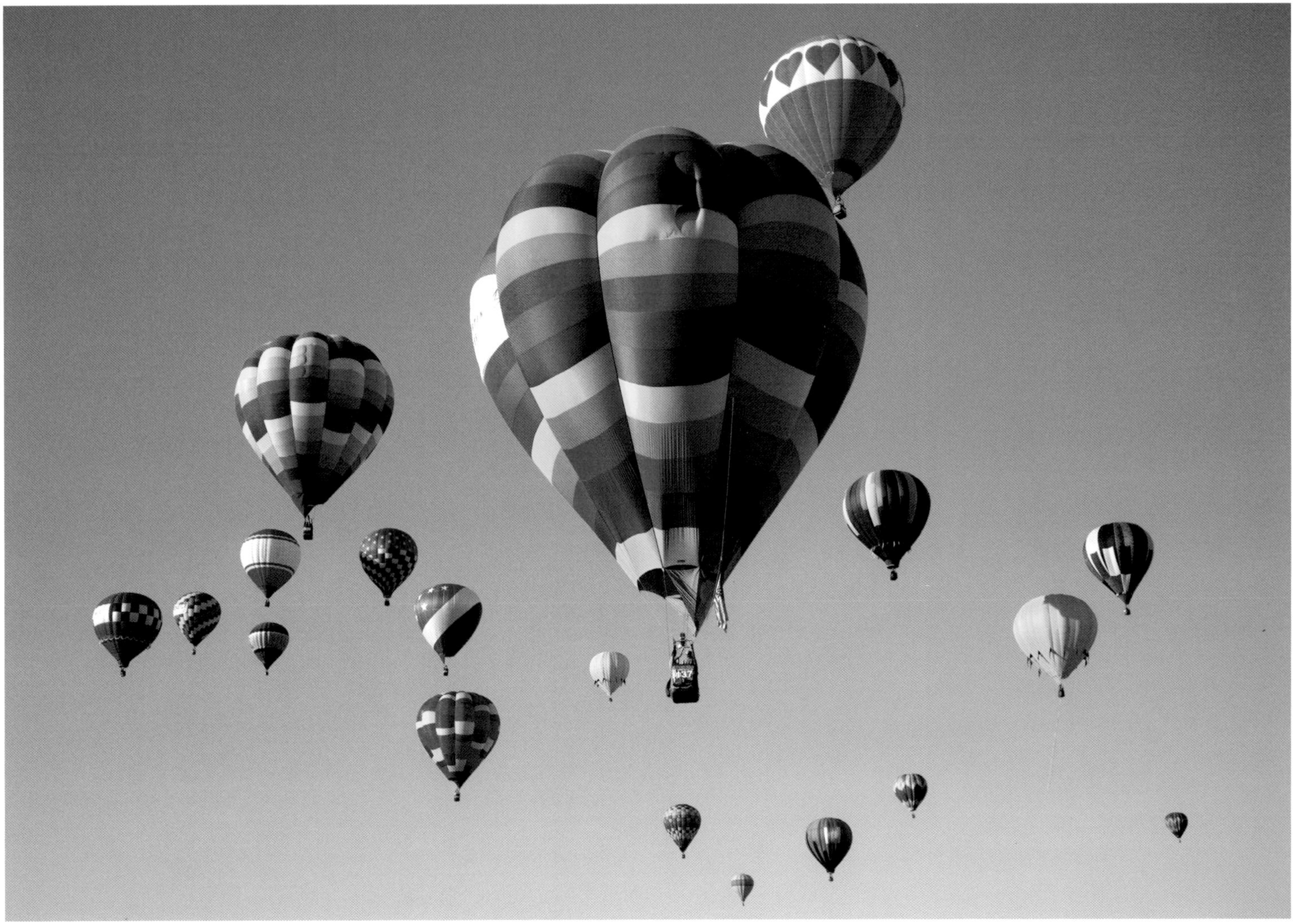

The "Albuquerque Box" is a wind pattern that occurs in the fall, caused in part by the Sandía Mountains. When conditions are right, air currents create a predictable "box" pattern that allows pilots to take off, fly, and return close to their starting point.

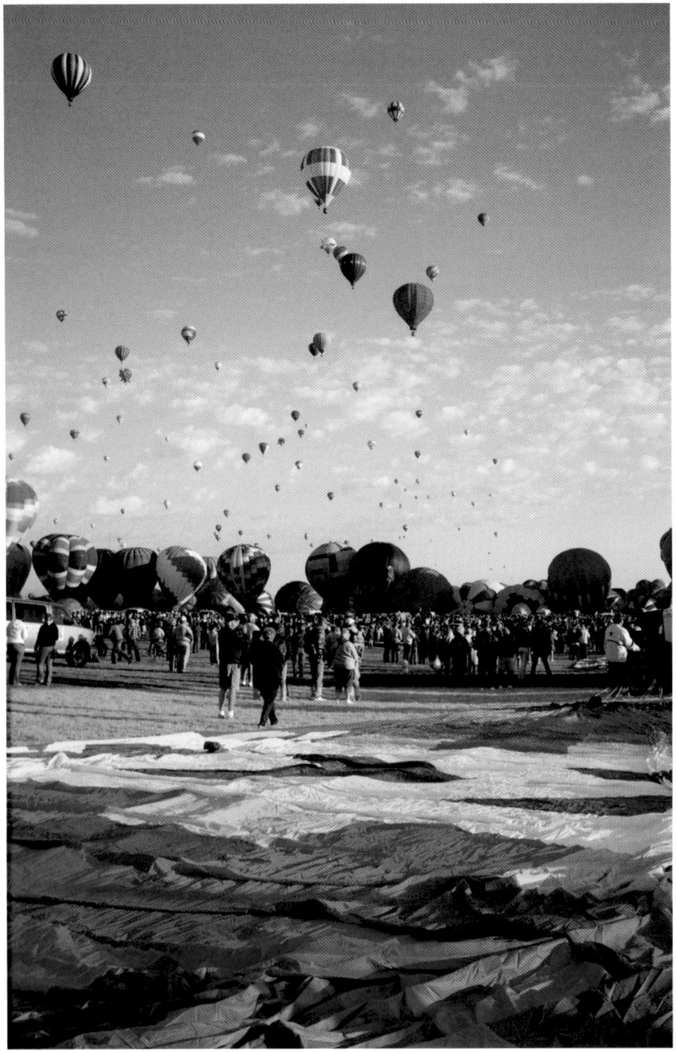

A balloon envelope blankets the ground, awaiting cold inflation via fan.

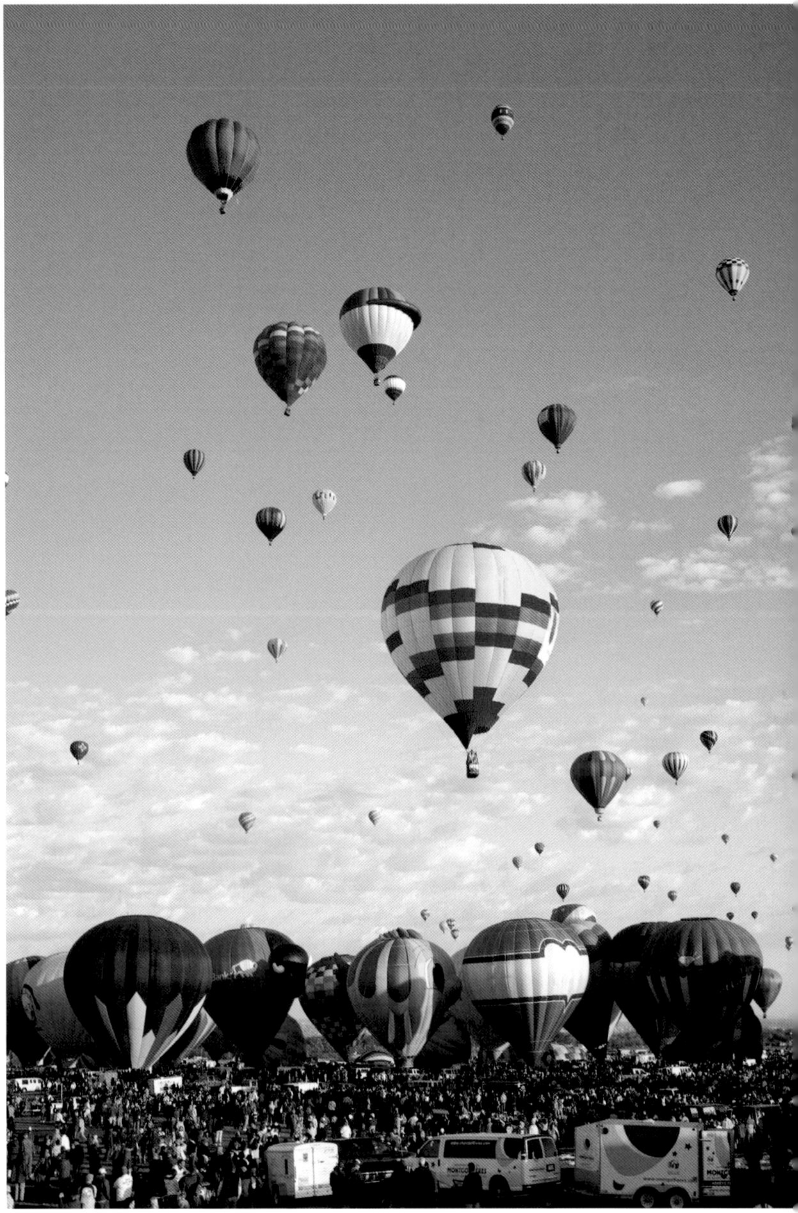

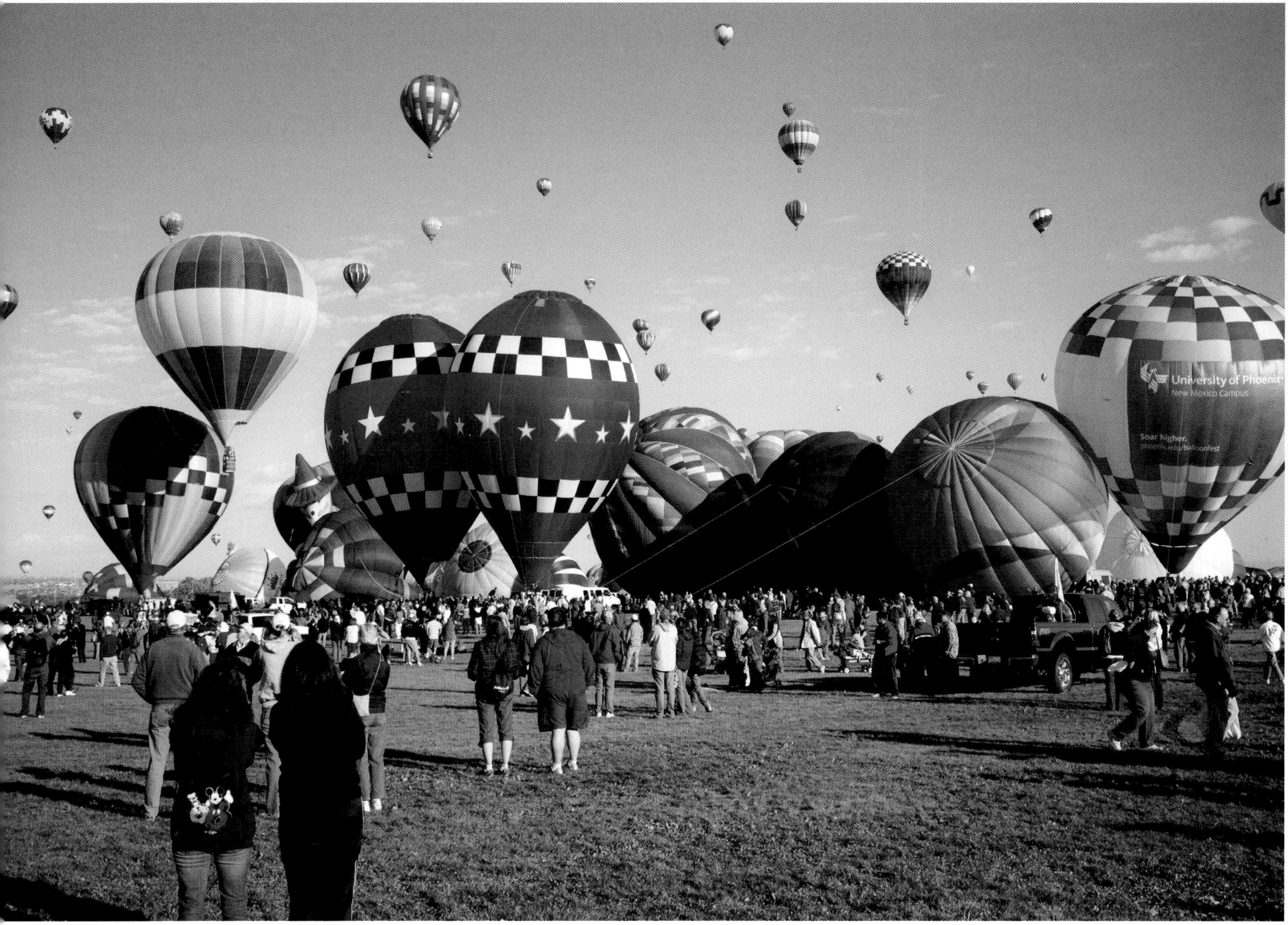

Between 500,000 and 750,000 people on average visit attend the Balloon Fiesta annually.

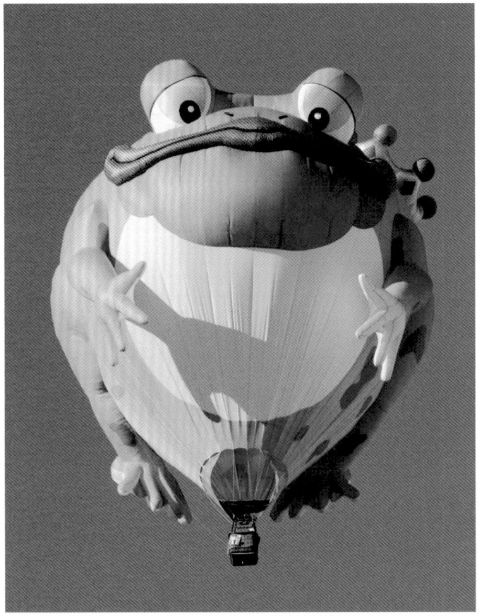

"Hopper T. Frog" of Wichita Falls, Texas, leaps into the air.

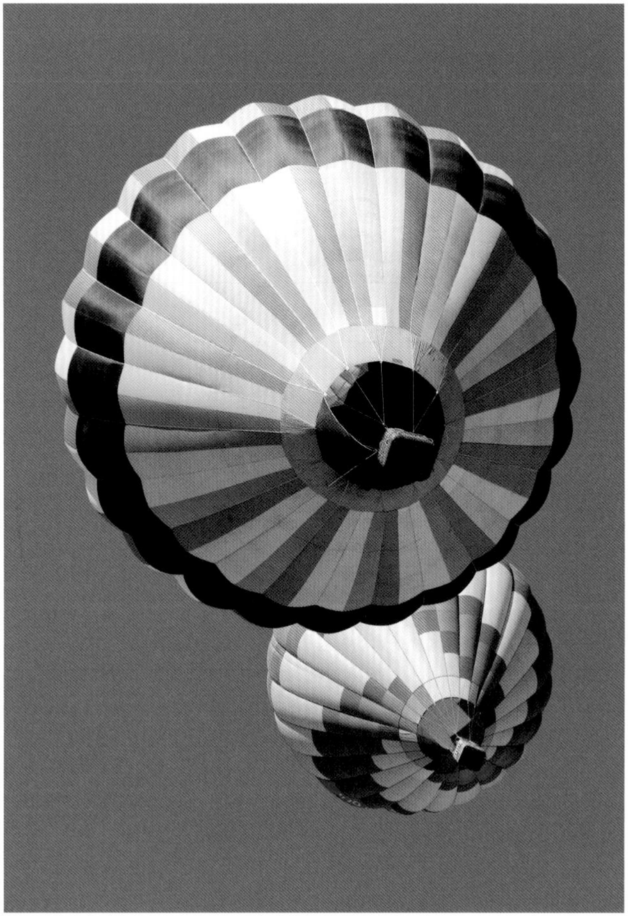

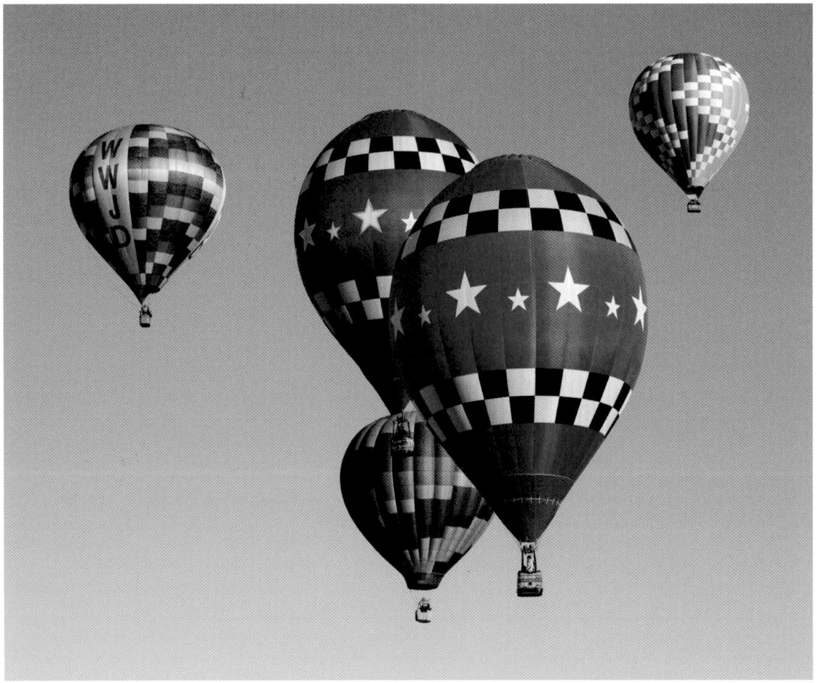

The first balloon flight took place in France in 1783 as a demonstration for Louis XVI and Marie Antoinette in Versailles. Not sure if humans could survive at these new altitudes, a sheep, rooster, and duck were the first test pilots. The balloon flew tethered for eight minutes at 1,500 feet before being brought down. The animals were unharmed.

The first human balloon pilot was to be a condemned criminal (in case something went wrong), but at the last minute scientist Jean-François Pilatre de Rozier and nobleman François Laurent d'Arlandes decided the historic event was too auspicious and went instead. The twenty-minute flight on November 21, 1783 was a success, and history was made.

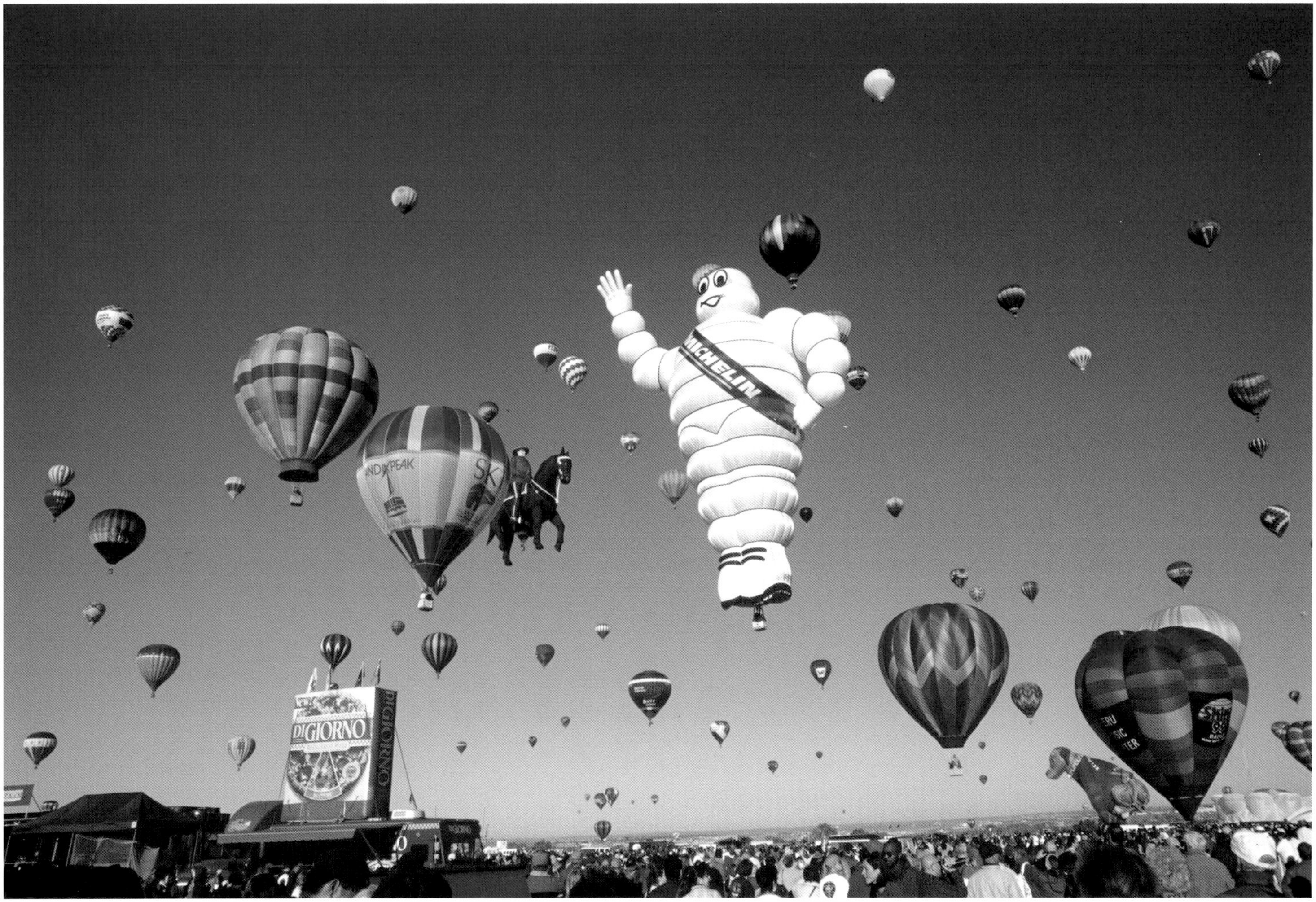

"Bidendum," commonly known as the Michelin Man, first flew in 1998 to commemorate the French company's one-hundredth anniversary. The balloon is 150 feet tall.

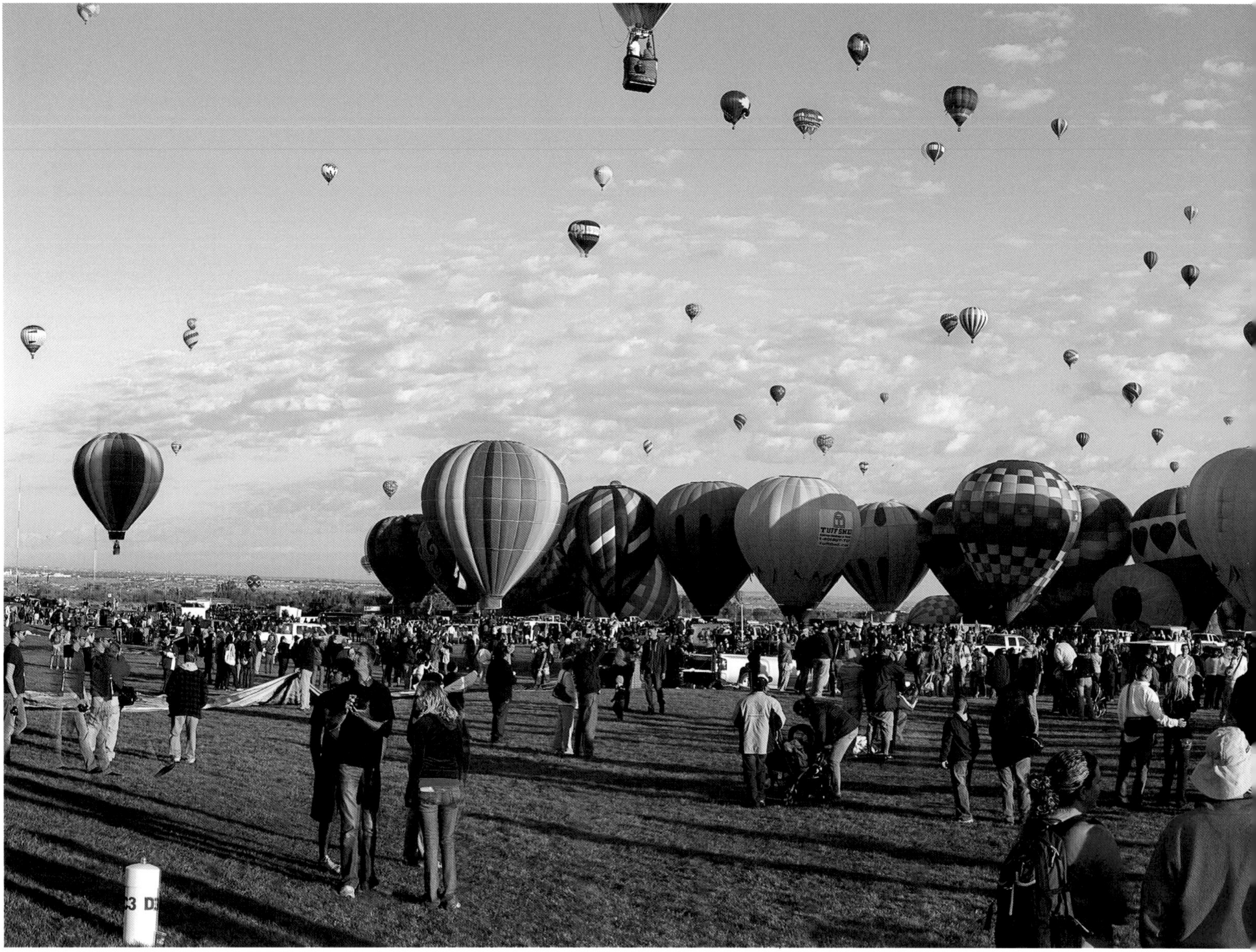

The balloon field is seventy-eight acres.

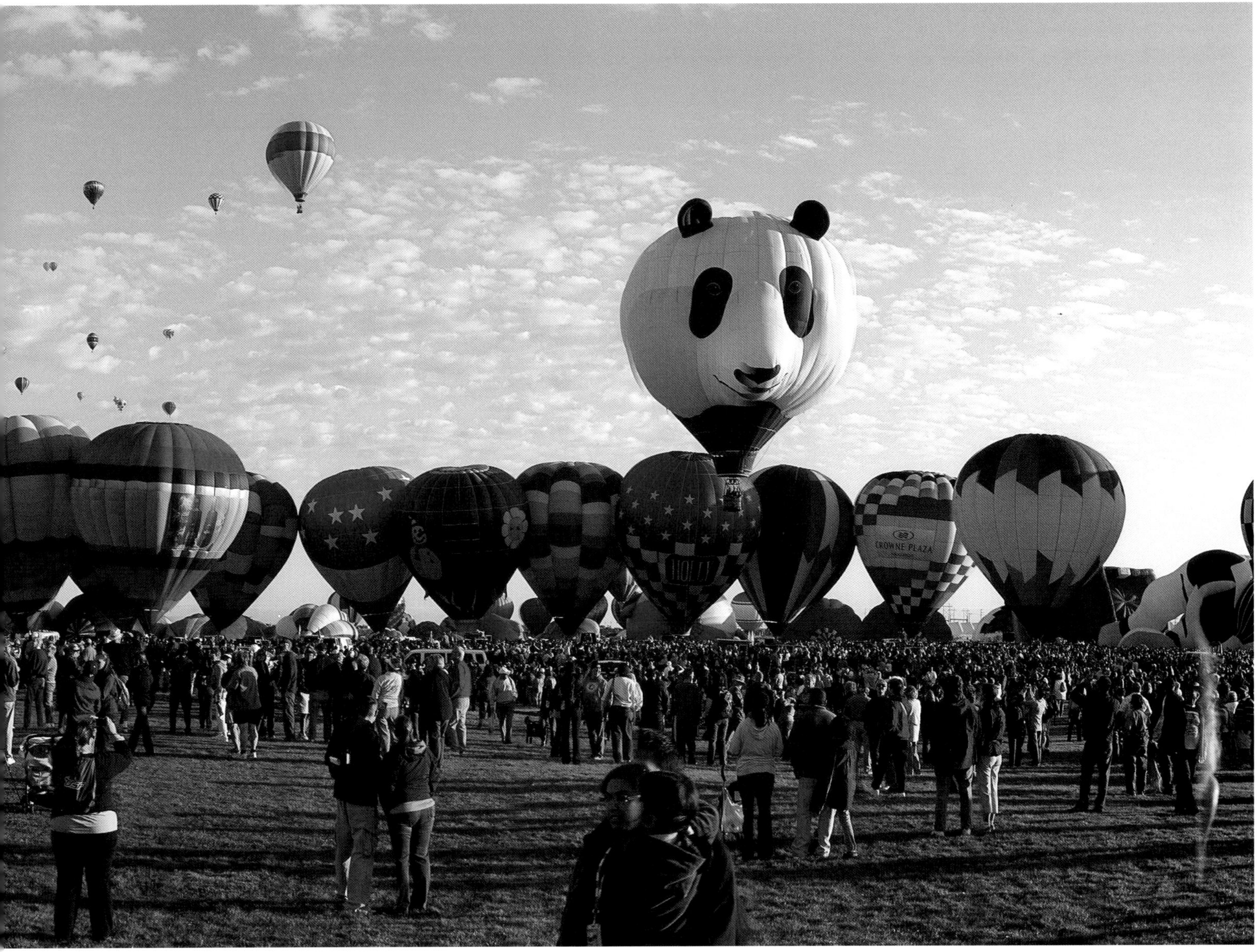
CROWNE PLAZA

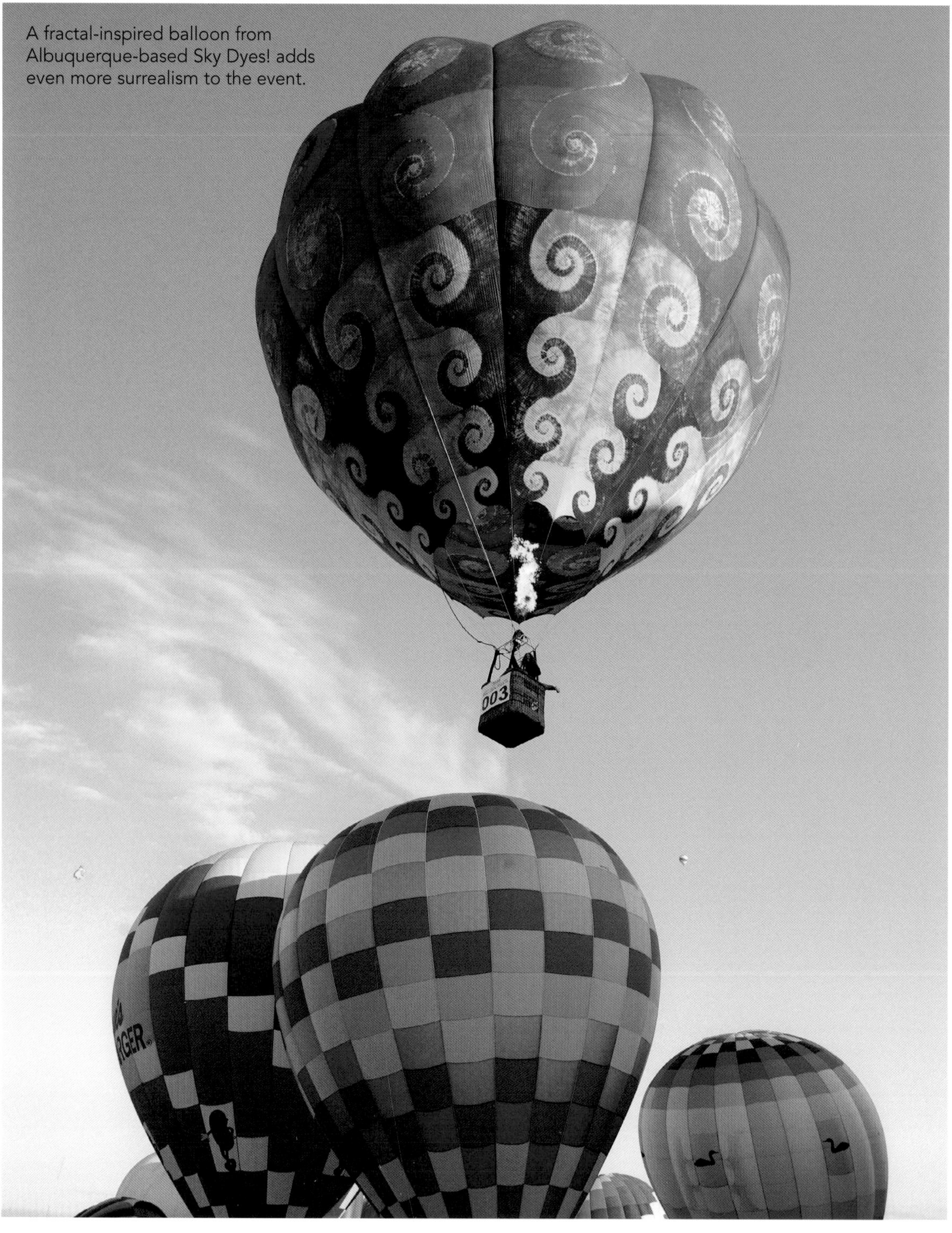

A fractal-inspired balloon from Albuquerque-based Sky Dyes! adds even more surrealism to the event.

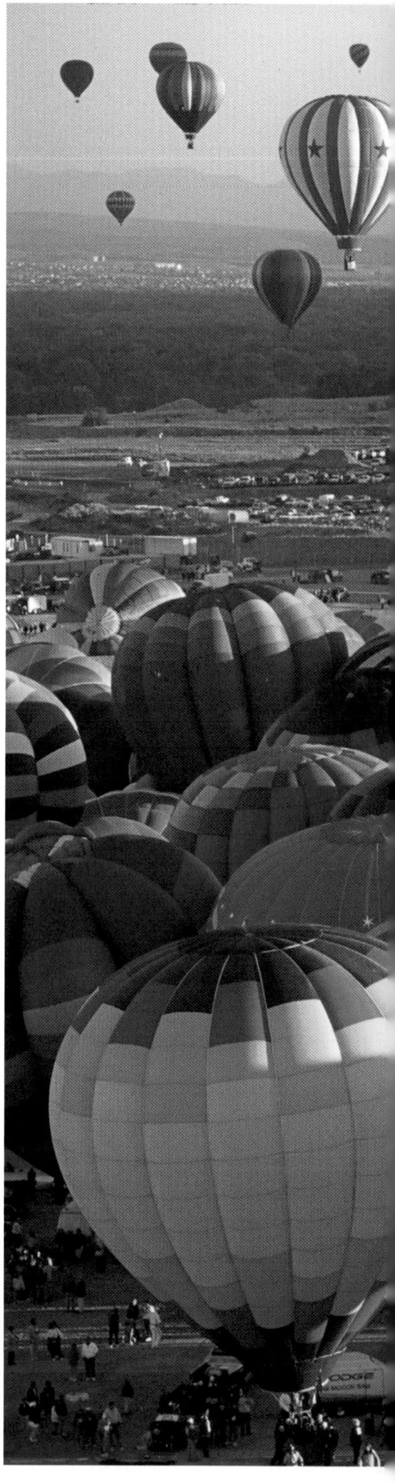

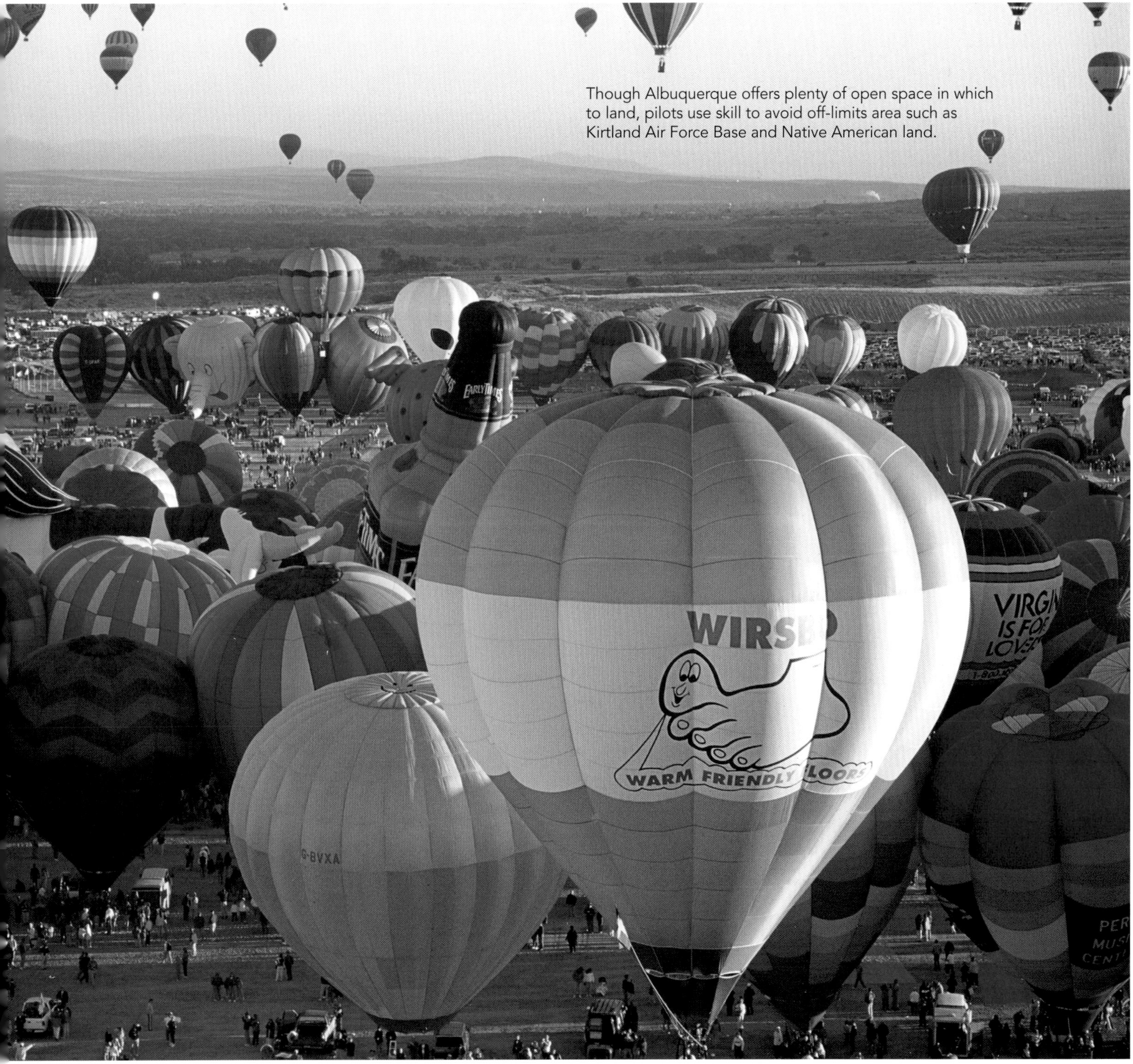

Though Albuquerque offers plenty of open space in which to land, pilots use skill to avoid off-limits area such as Kirtland Air Force Base and Native American land.

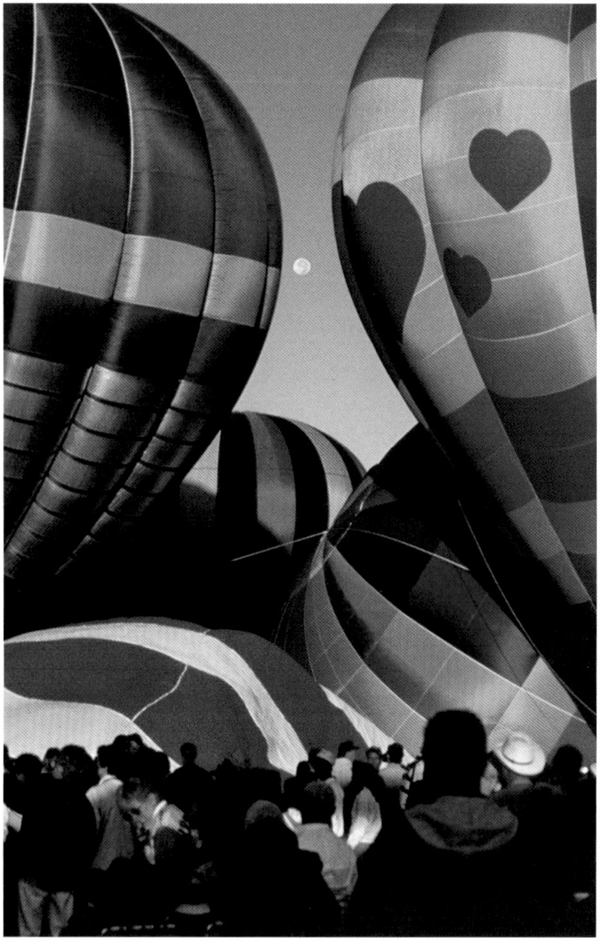

A waxing moon peeks between two lovely balloons.

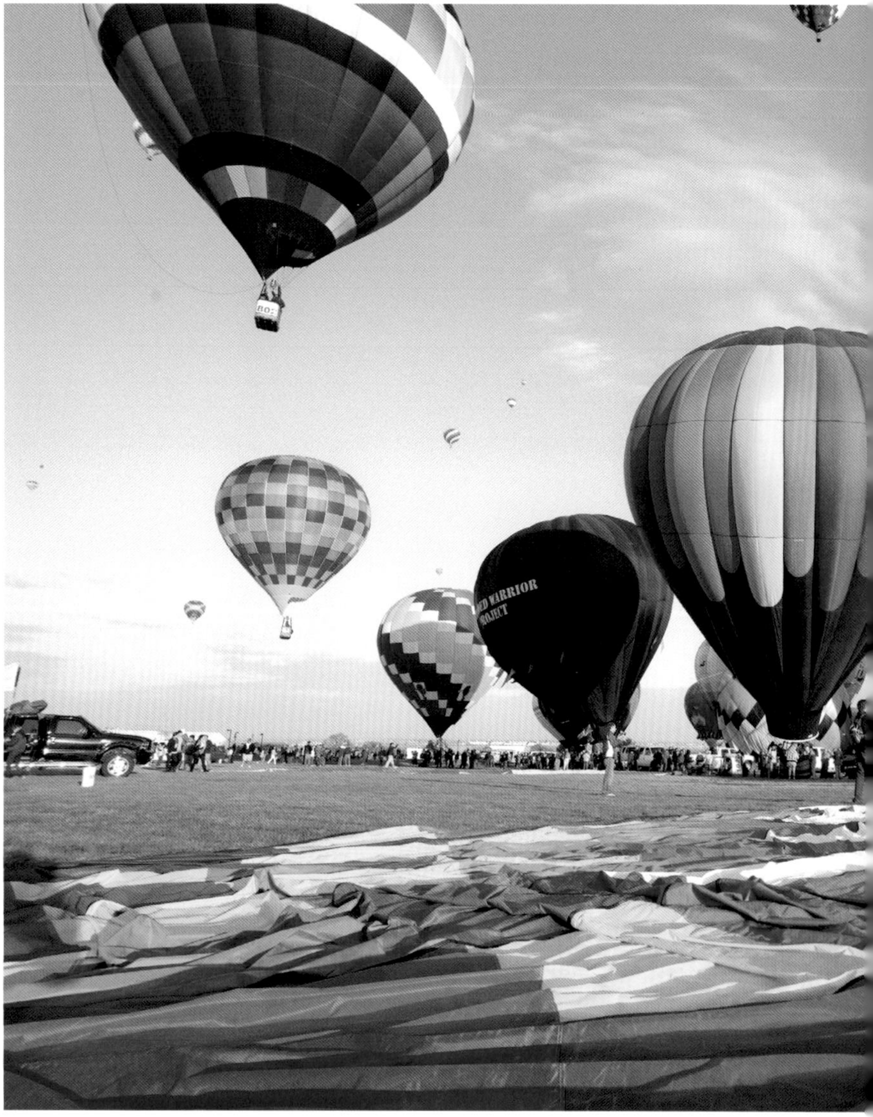

It takes approximately two hours for all balloons to launch during a mass ascension.

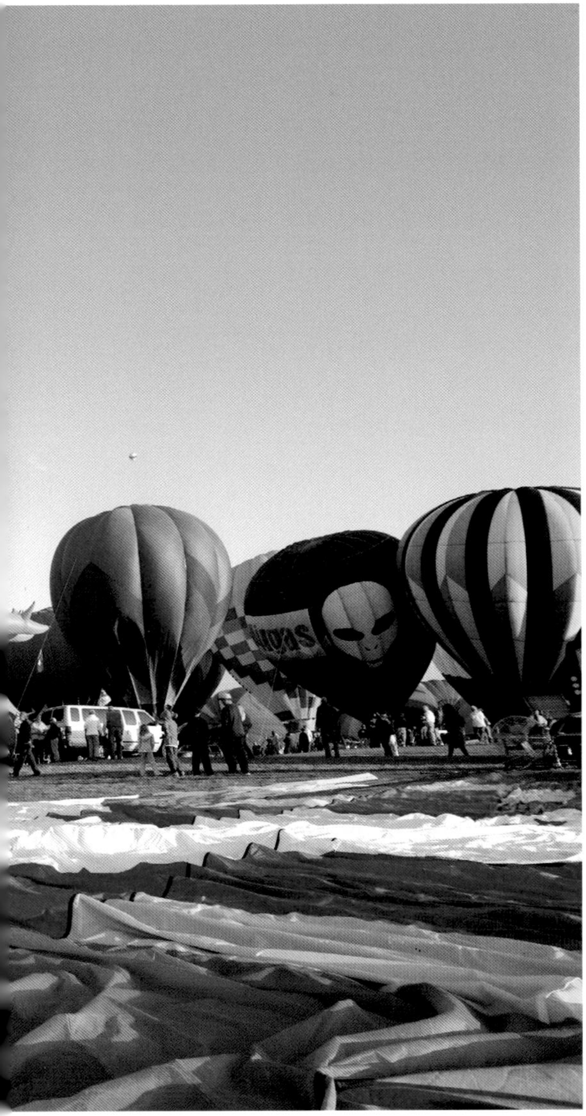

The Albuquerque International Balloon Fiesta takes place the first full week of October, from the first Saturday morning to the second Sunday morning of the month.

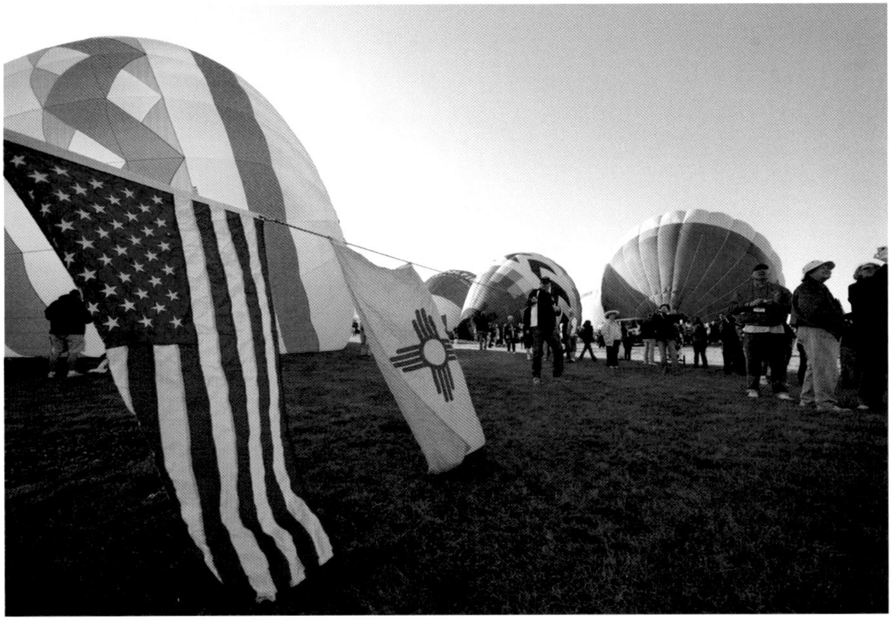

Lines attached to the top of balloons steady the craft while they inflate horizontally. When the air temperature is hot enough, the balloons are righted into launch position. Flags help spectators see the lines for safety.

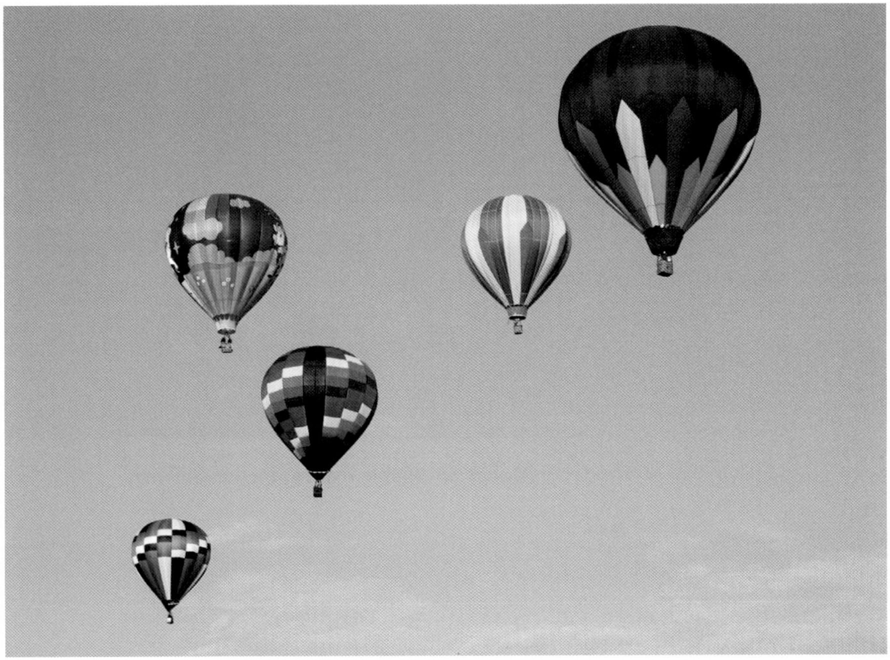

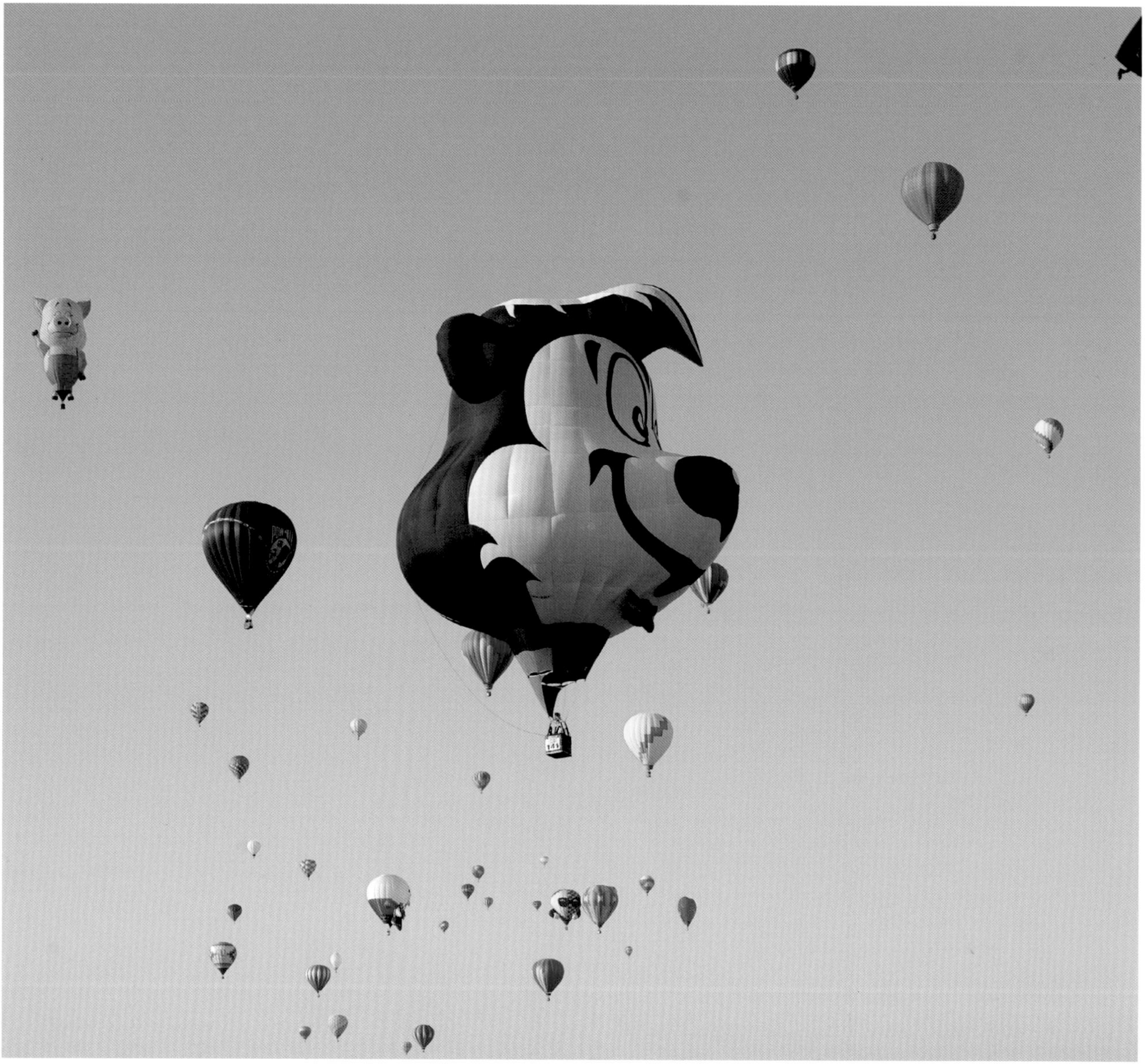

"Spunky" of Menlo, Georgia, has no trouble making friends at Fiesta.

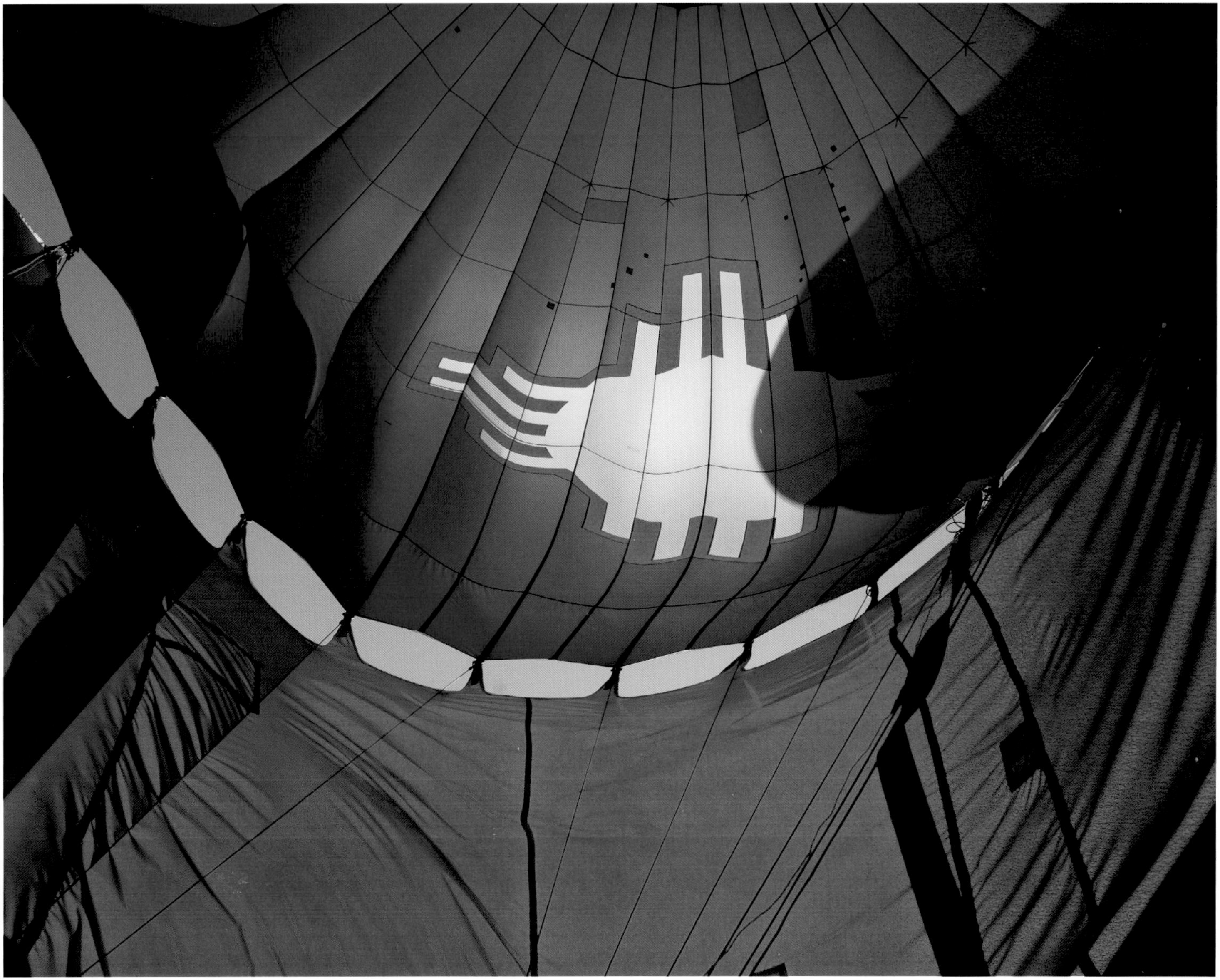

Vents built into envelopes allow pilots to release trapped hot air to deflate the balloon.

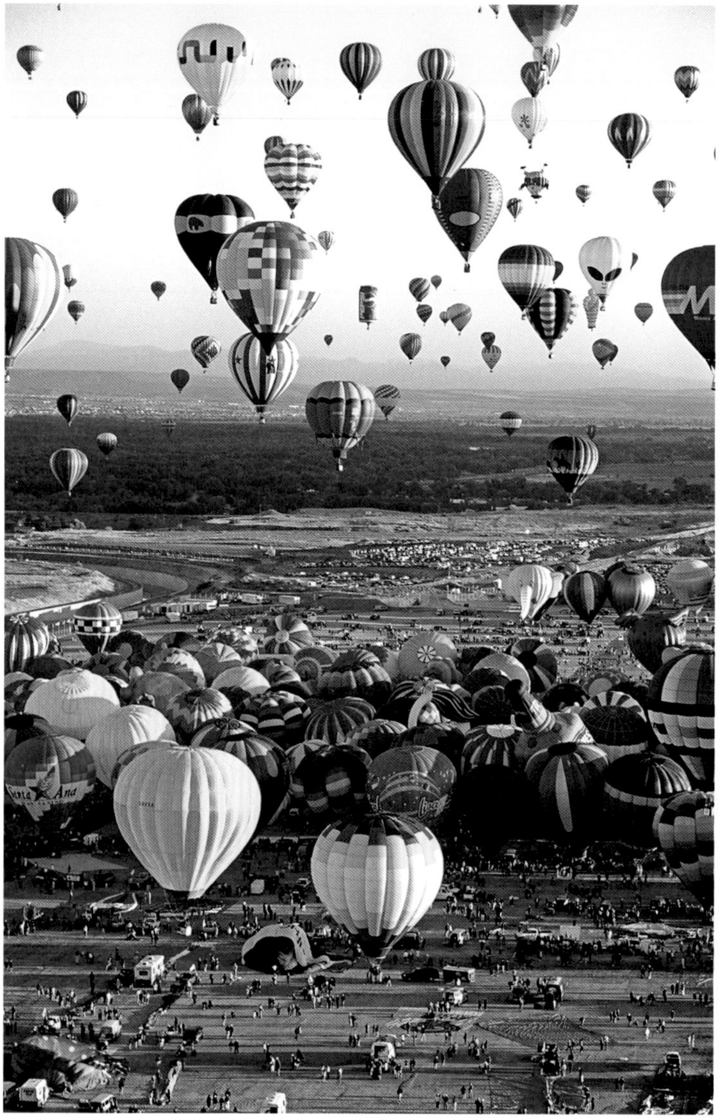

During mass ascensions, balloons launch in two waves starting at about 7:15 a.m.

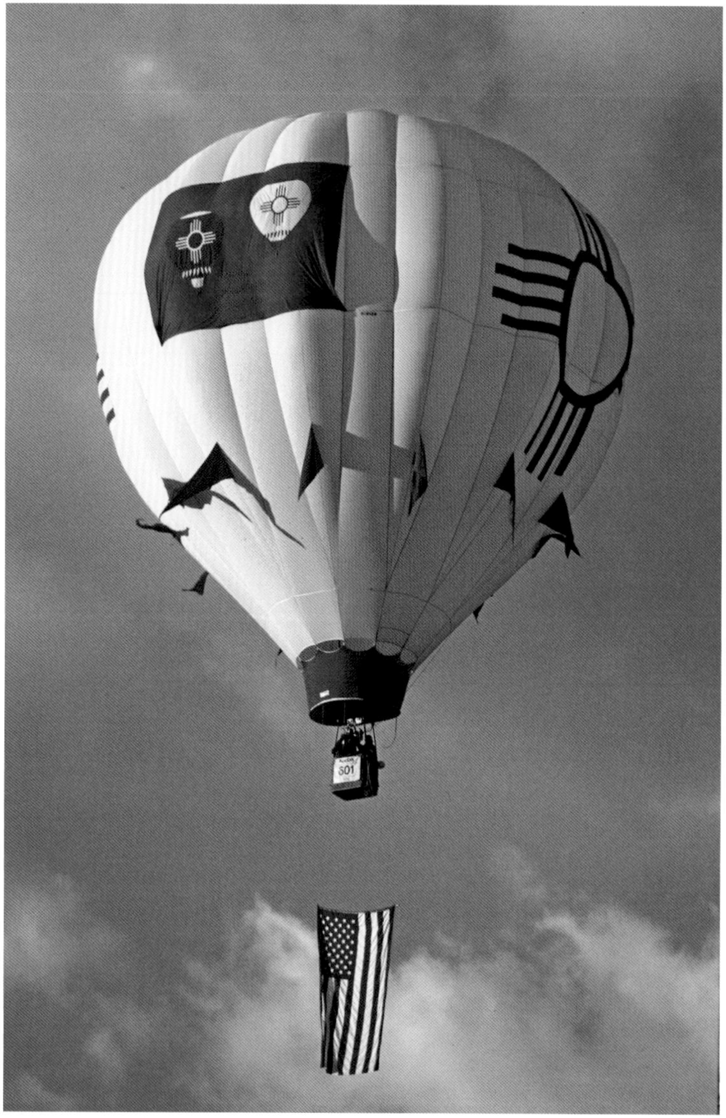

"The Star-Spangled Banner" is played as the first balloon lifts off to begin the day.

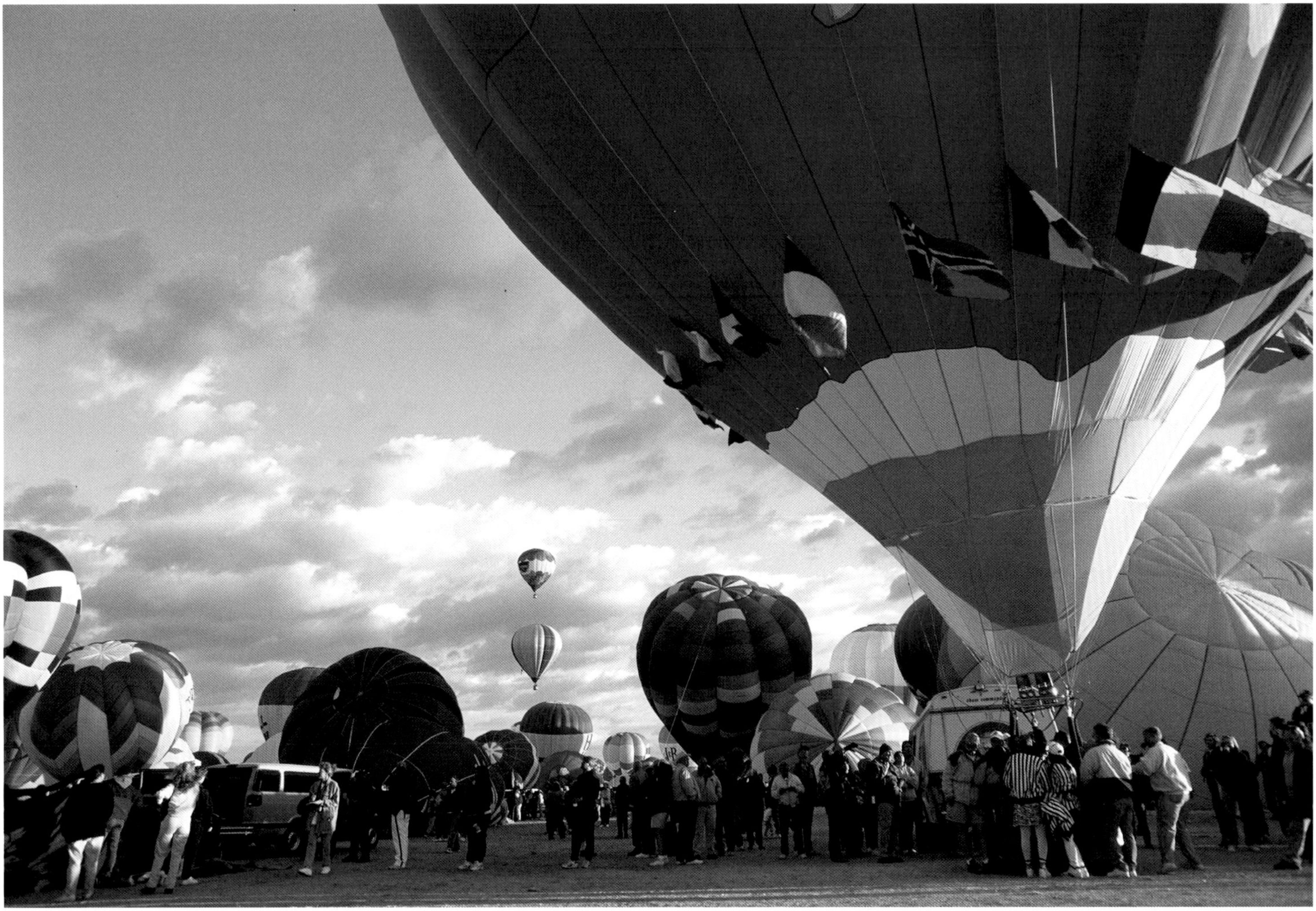

The first gathering of thirteen balloons in 1972 was held in the parking lot of Coronado Center mall in uptown Albuquerque. The following year, thirteen countries took part in the "First World Hot Air Balloon Championships," held at the New Mexico State Fairgrounds. By 1978, Albuquerque was playing host to the world's largest ballooning event (with 273 entries).

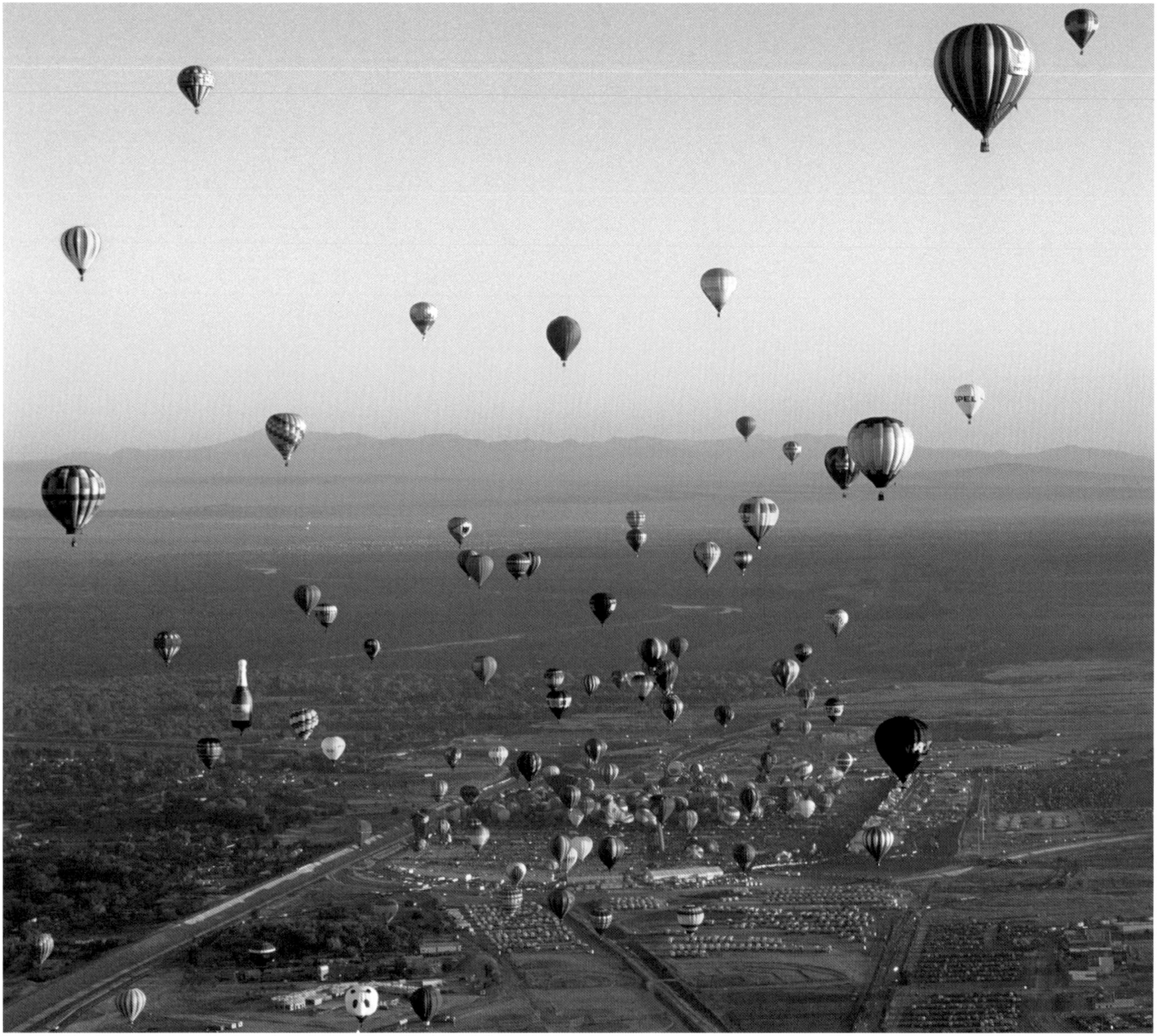

The Fiesta earned the Guinness Book of World Records designation in 2011 for the greatest mass ascent of hot air balloons, when 345 balloons were launched in one wave on October 1.

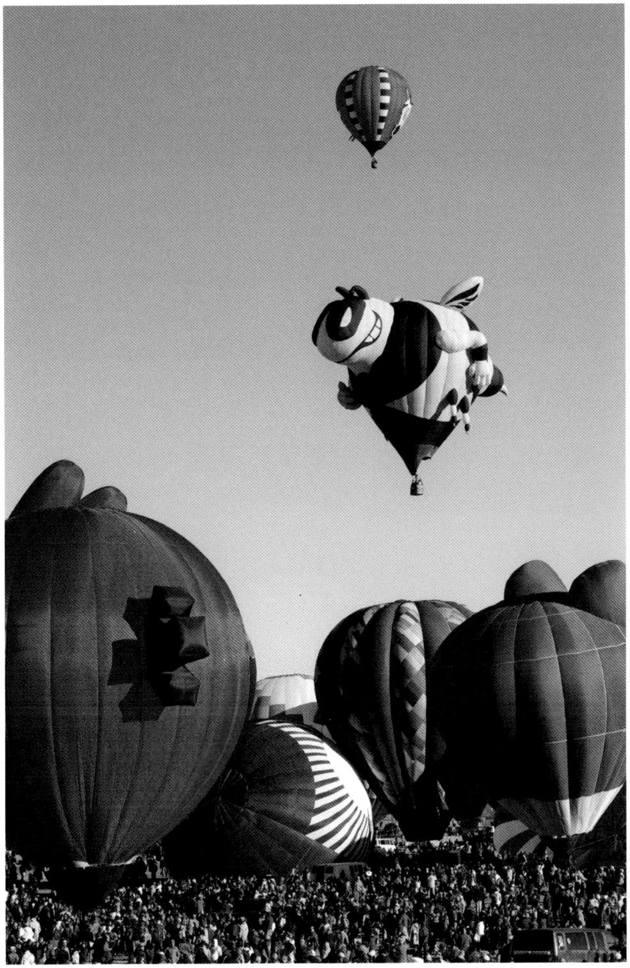

"Yellow Jacket" from Brazil always creates a buzz when launched.

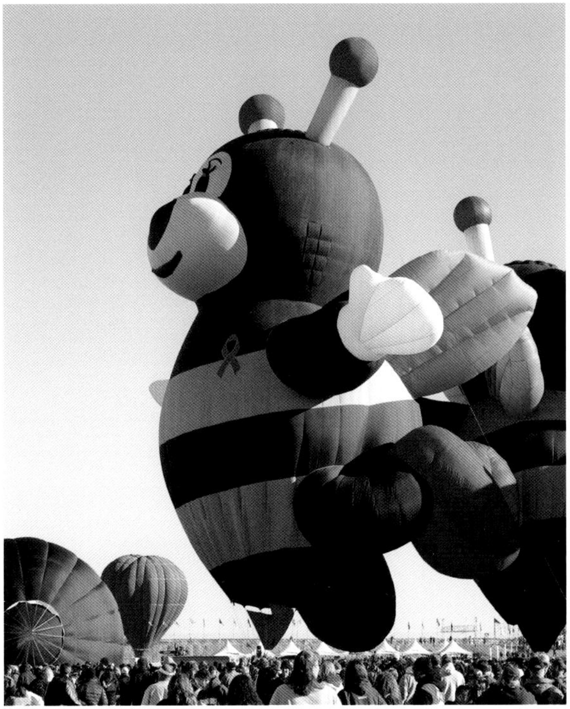

"Little Bee Lilly" from Arizona is a crowd favorite.

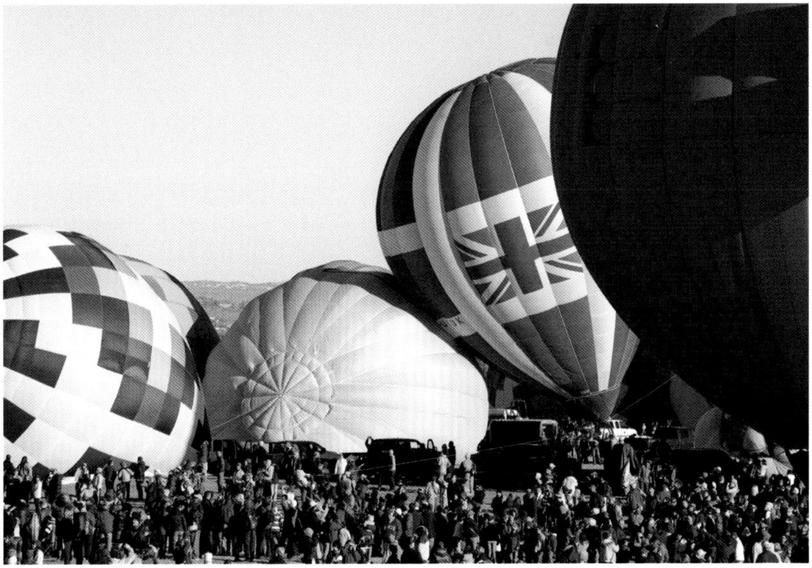

The Union Jack prepares to represent the United Kingdom in New Mexico's brilliant blue skies.

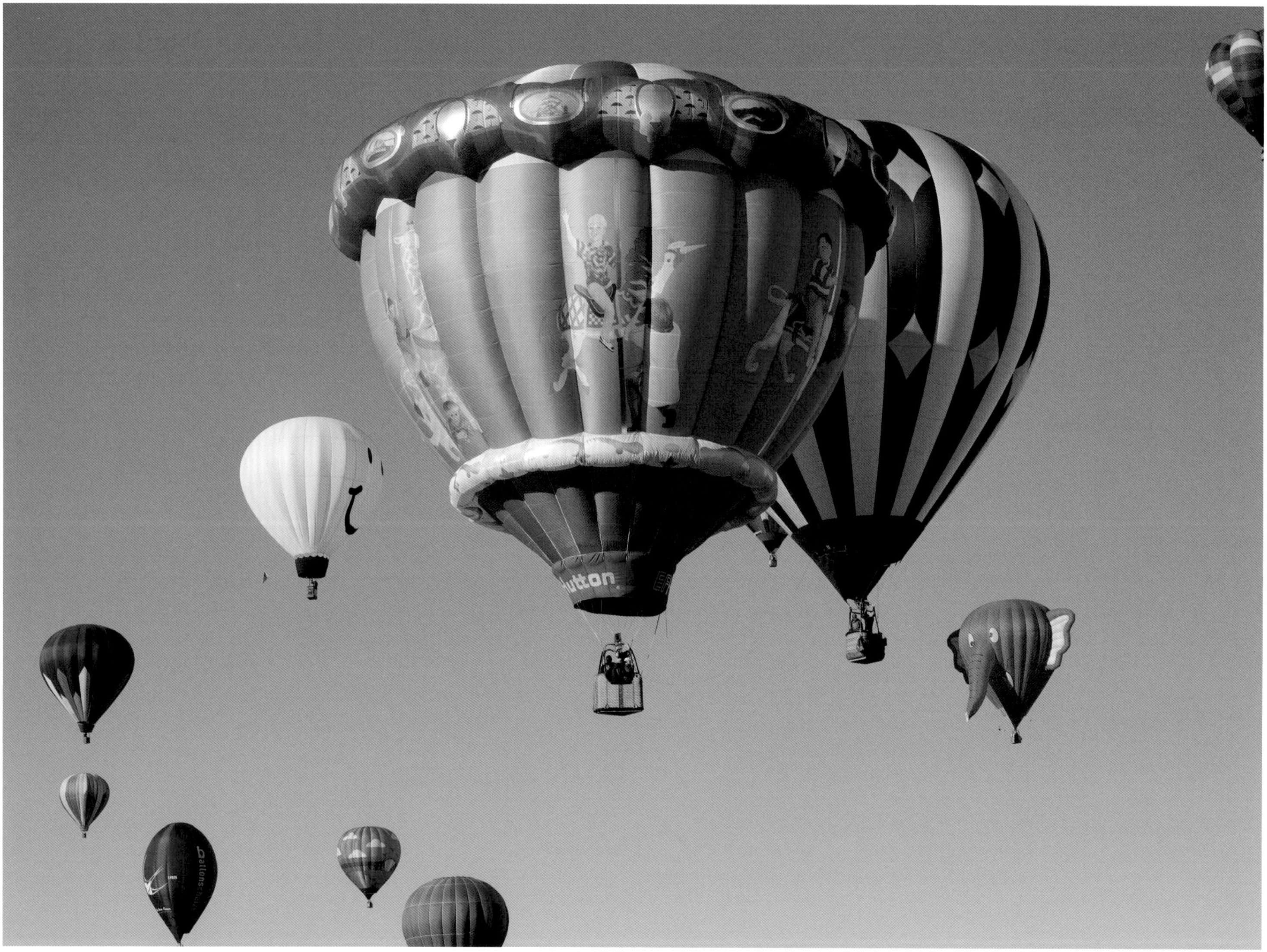

"Carousel" from New York enjoys the carnival atmosphere at Fiesta.

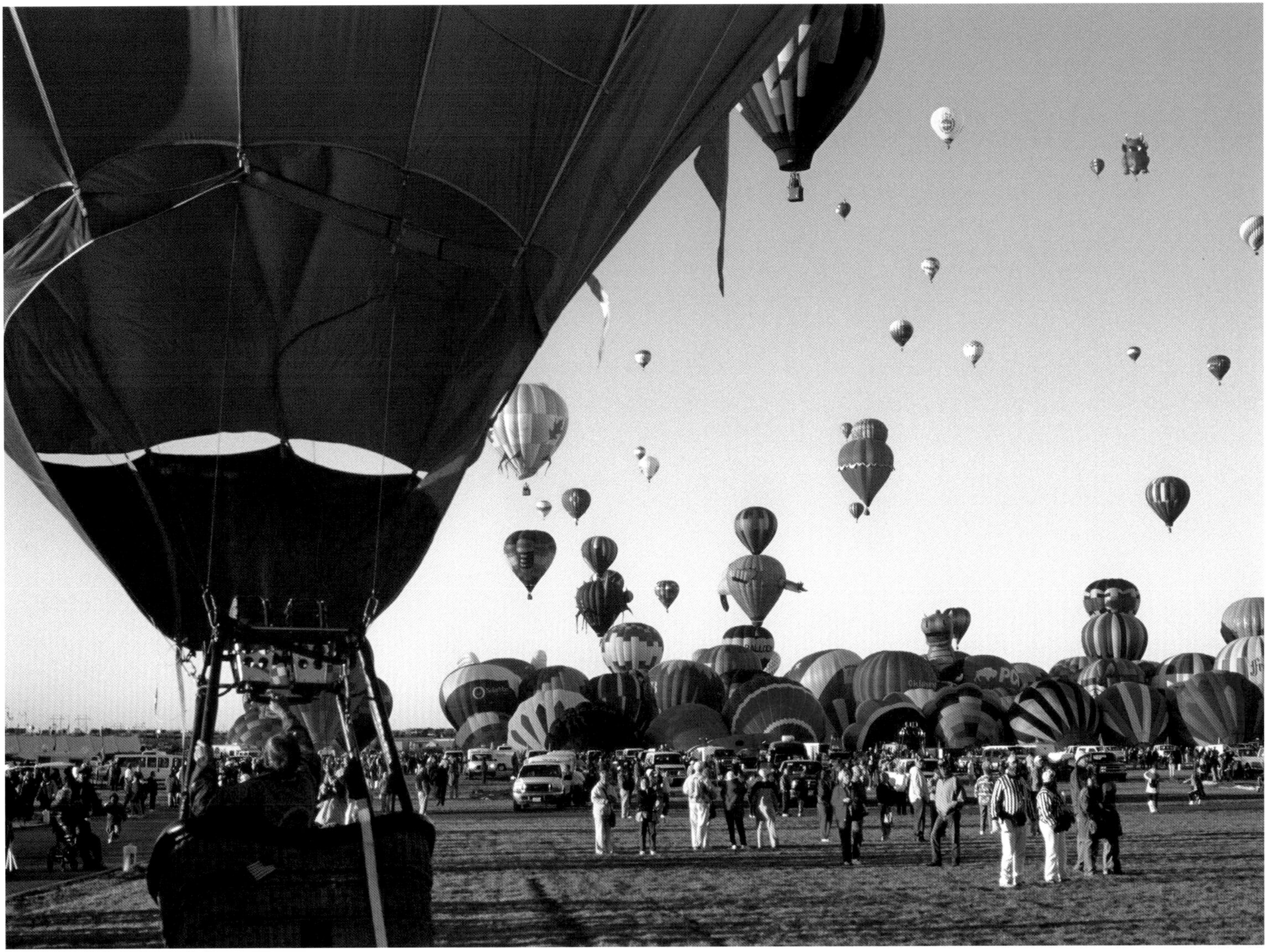

Pilots await as zebras clear a safe area for them to launch.

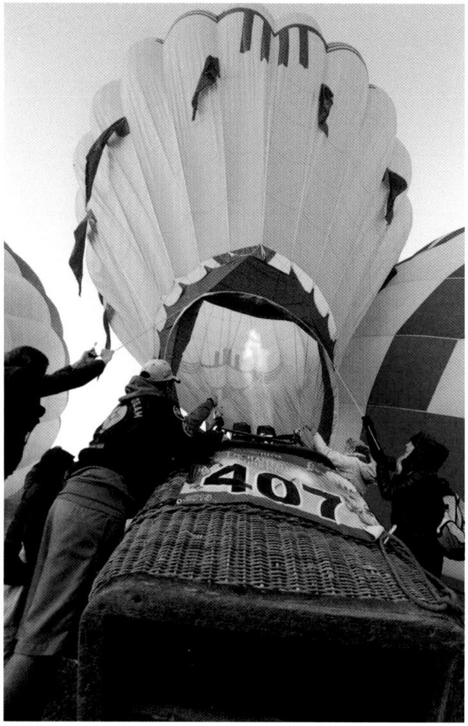

Its air heated, a balloon lifts upright into launch position as crew and volunteers prepare to hold it down.

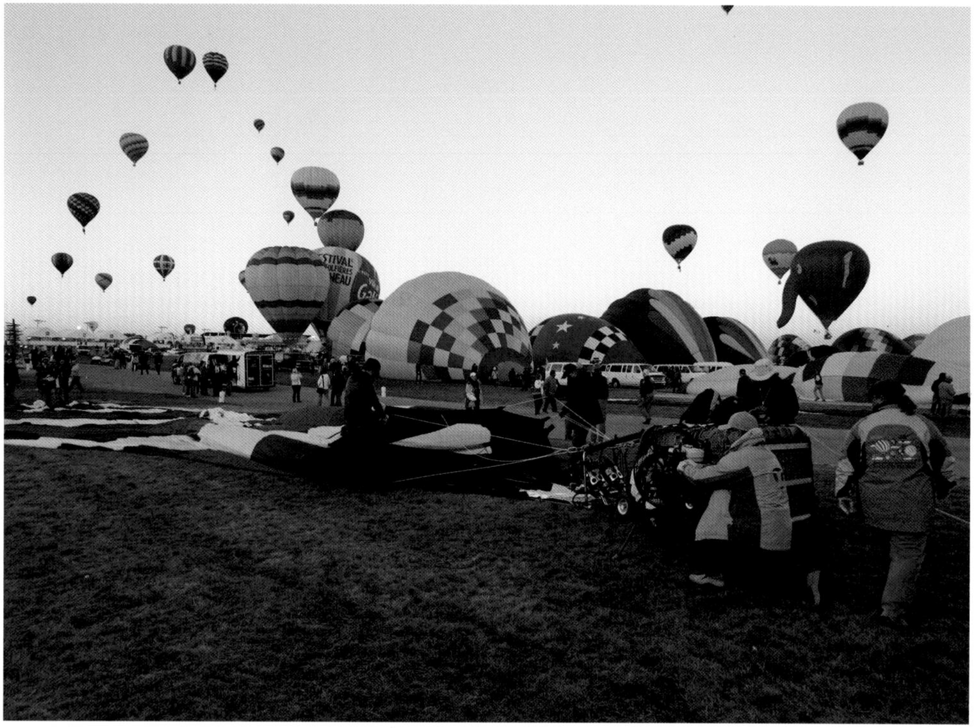

A crew member readies a fan to inflate an envelope during a mass ascension.

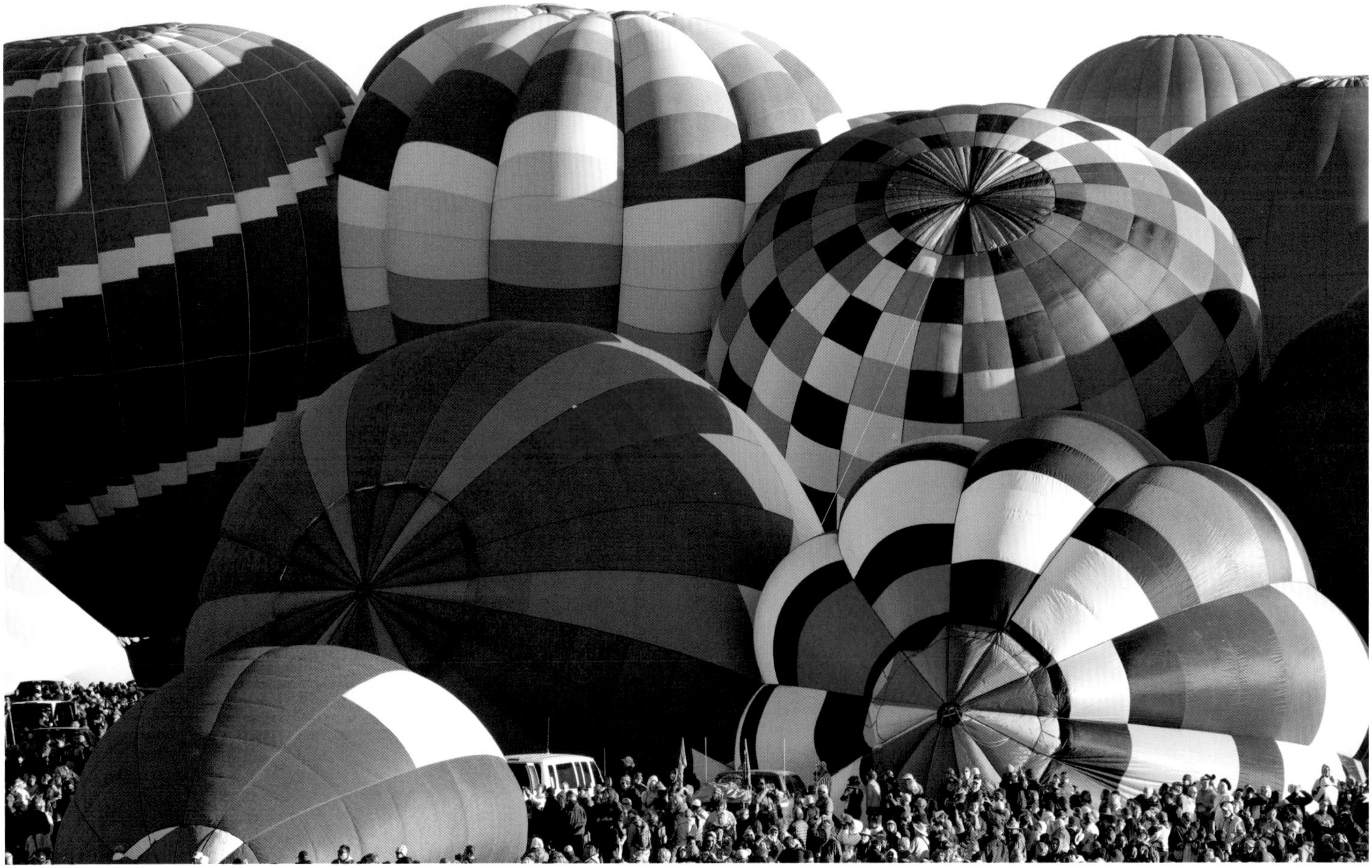

Balloons billow upright, readying to launch.

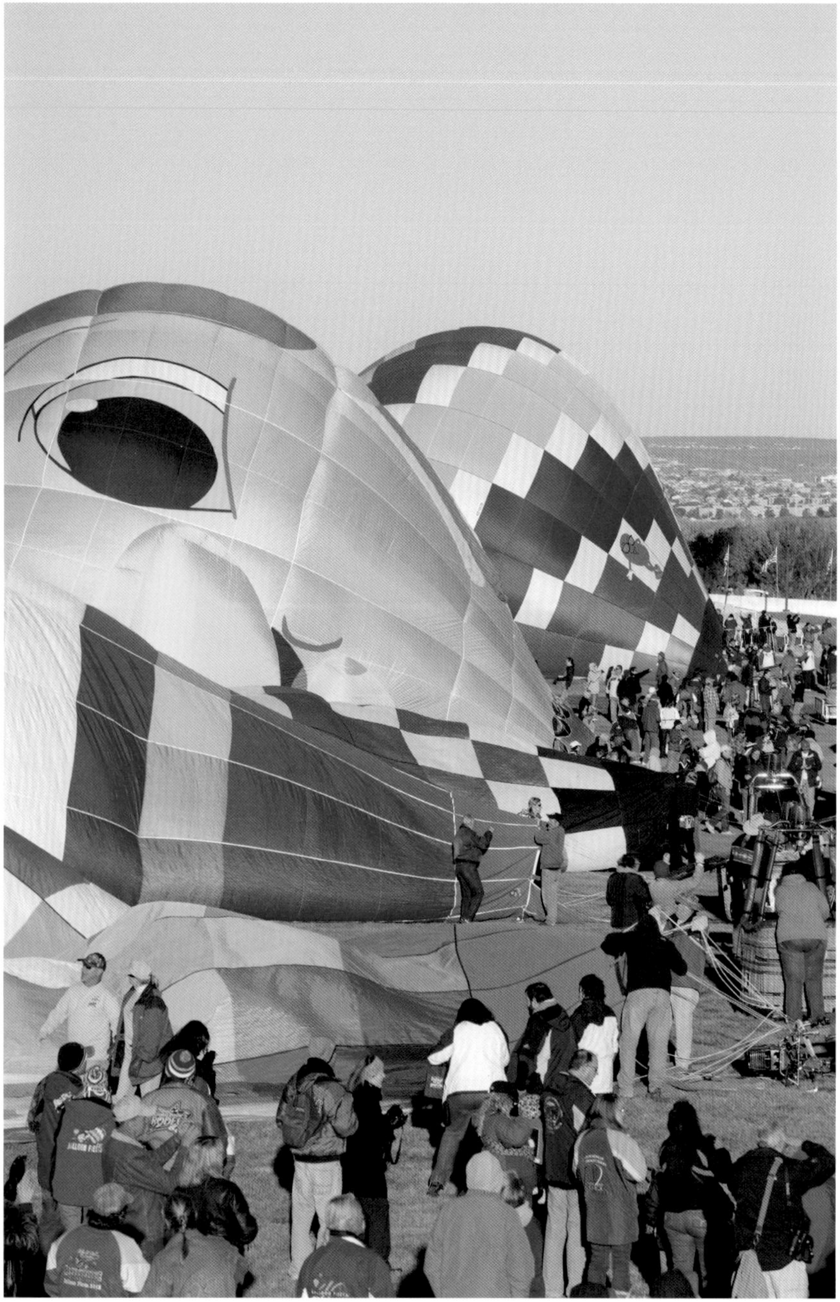

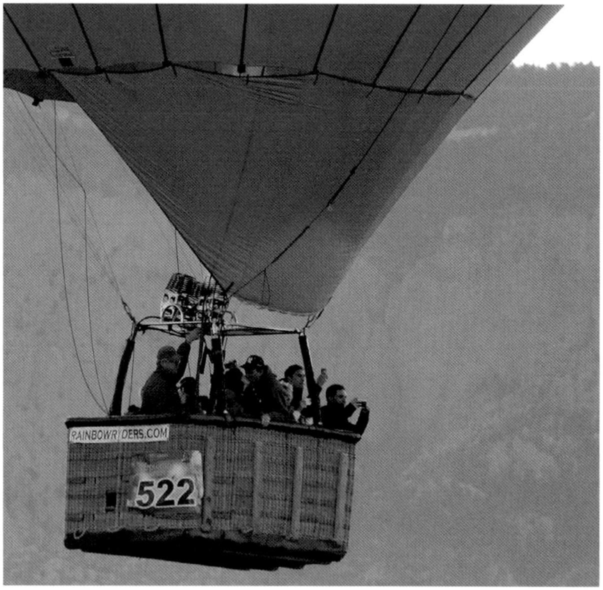

Two romantics steal a kiss during lift off.

A balloon has its eye on the sky
as it's prepared for take off.

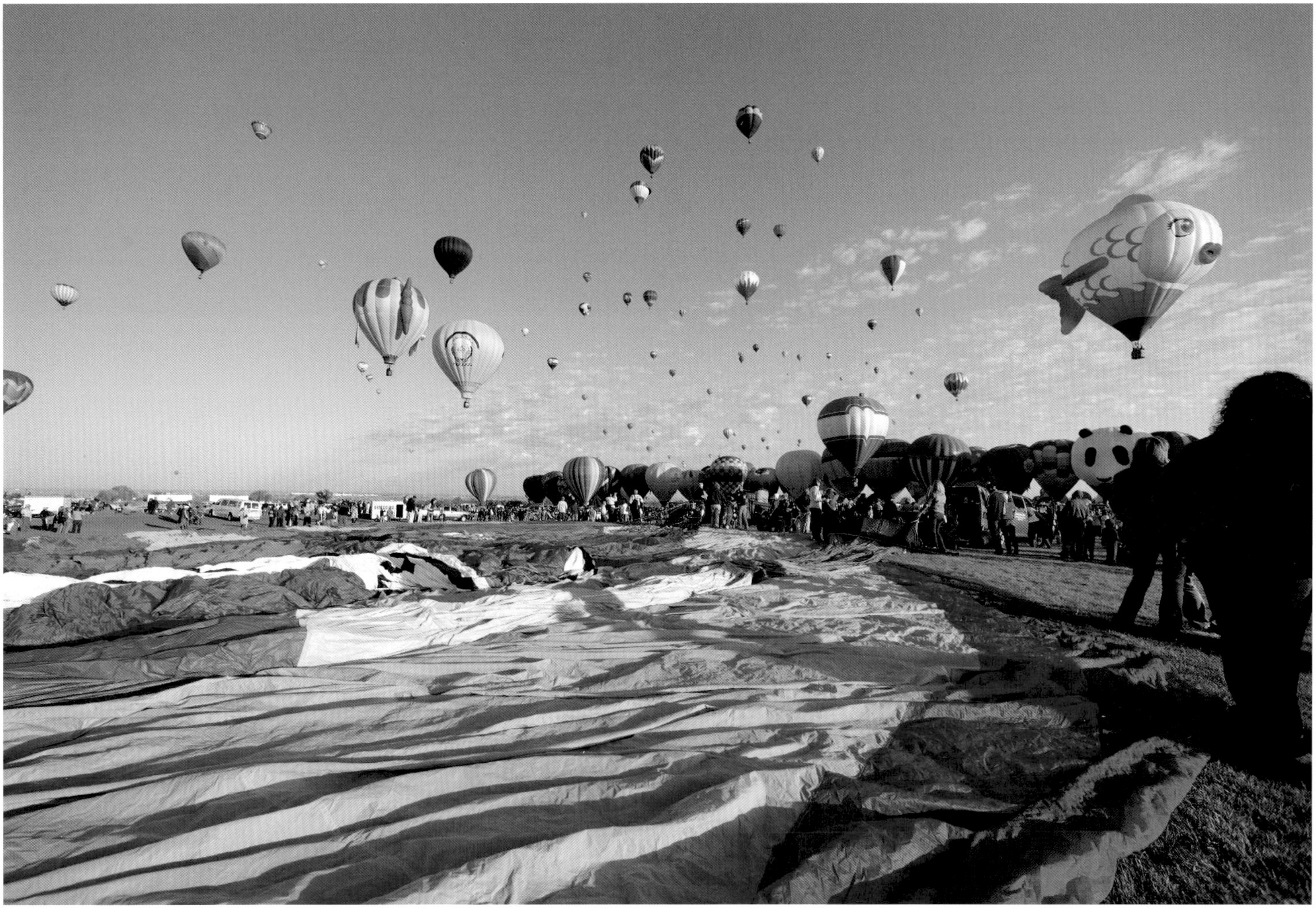

From Nevada, "Sushi" the fish swims above a sea of color.

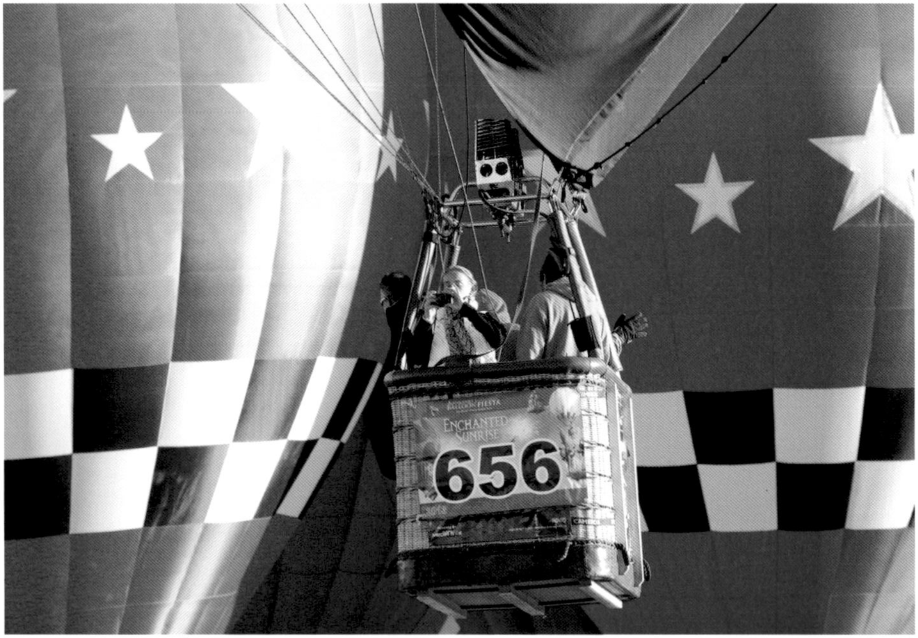

A balloon sails into the stars.

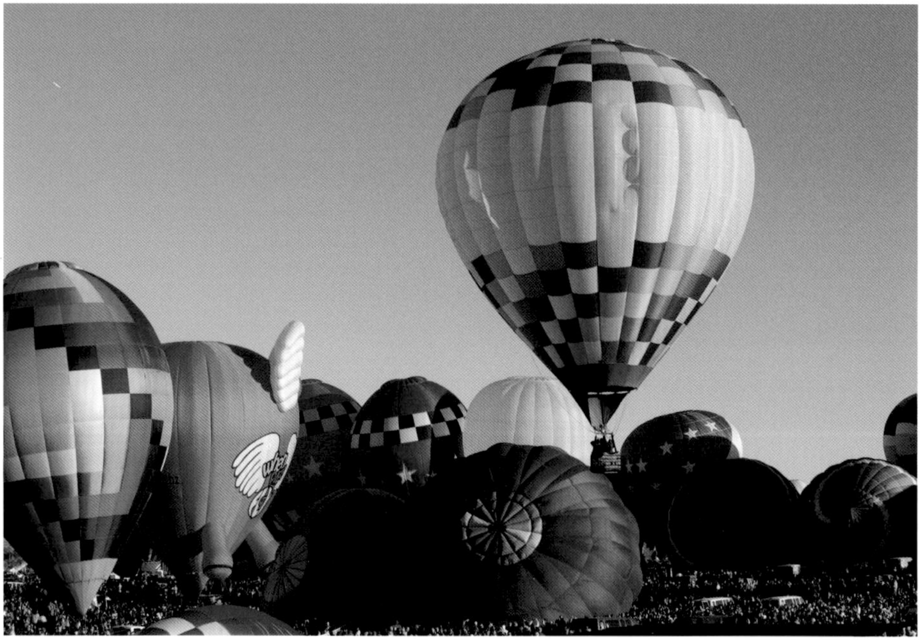

While founder Sid Cutter made his first balloon flight over Albuquerque in 1971, the event wasn't called Balloon Fiesta until 1975.

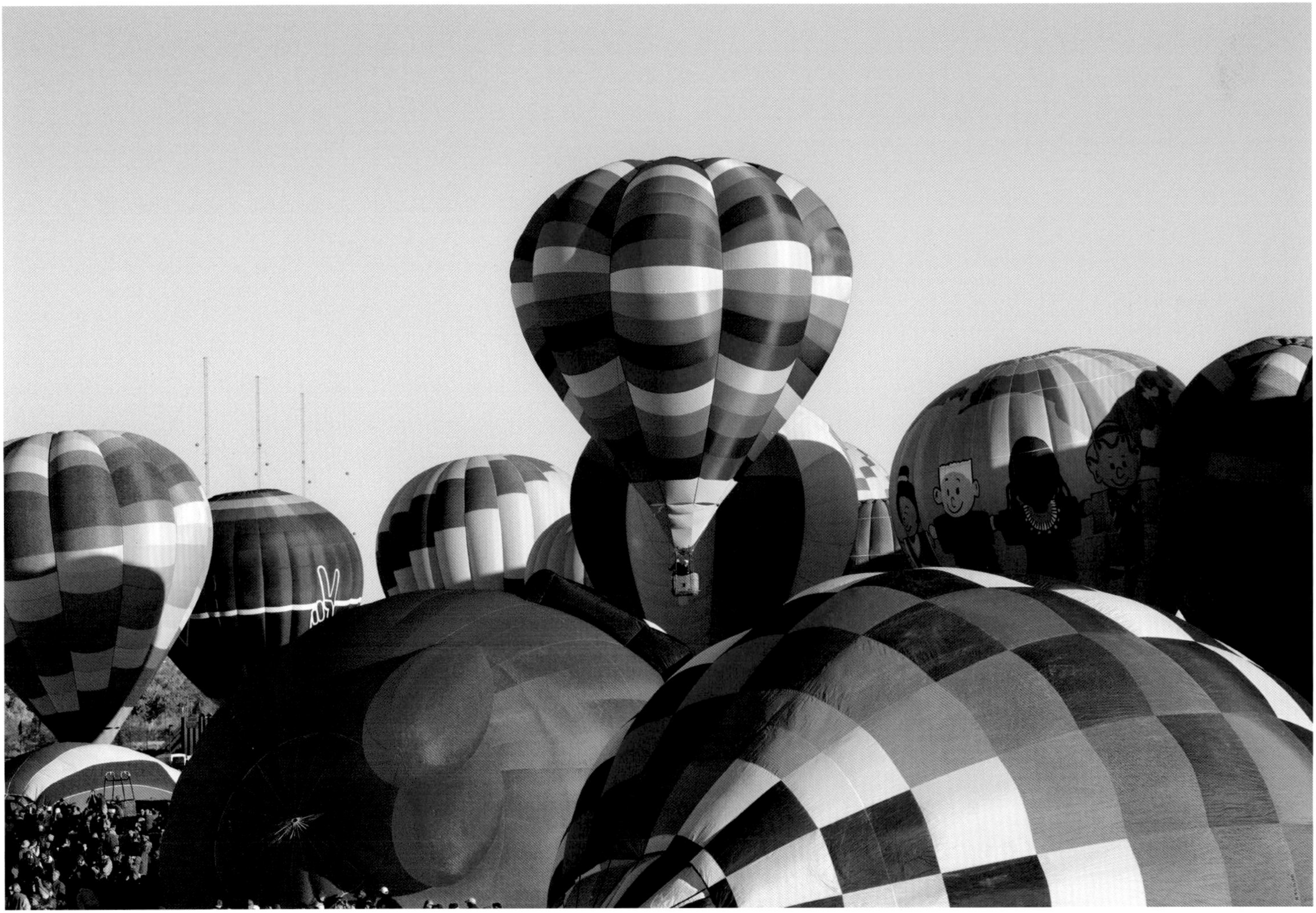

Today, more than 100,000 people on average attend Fiesta each day.

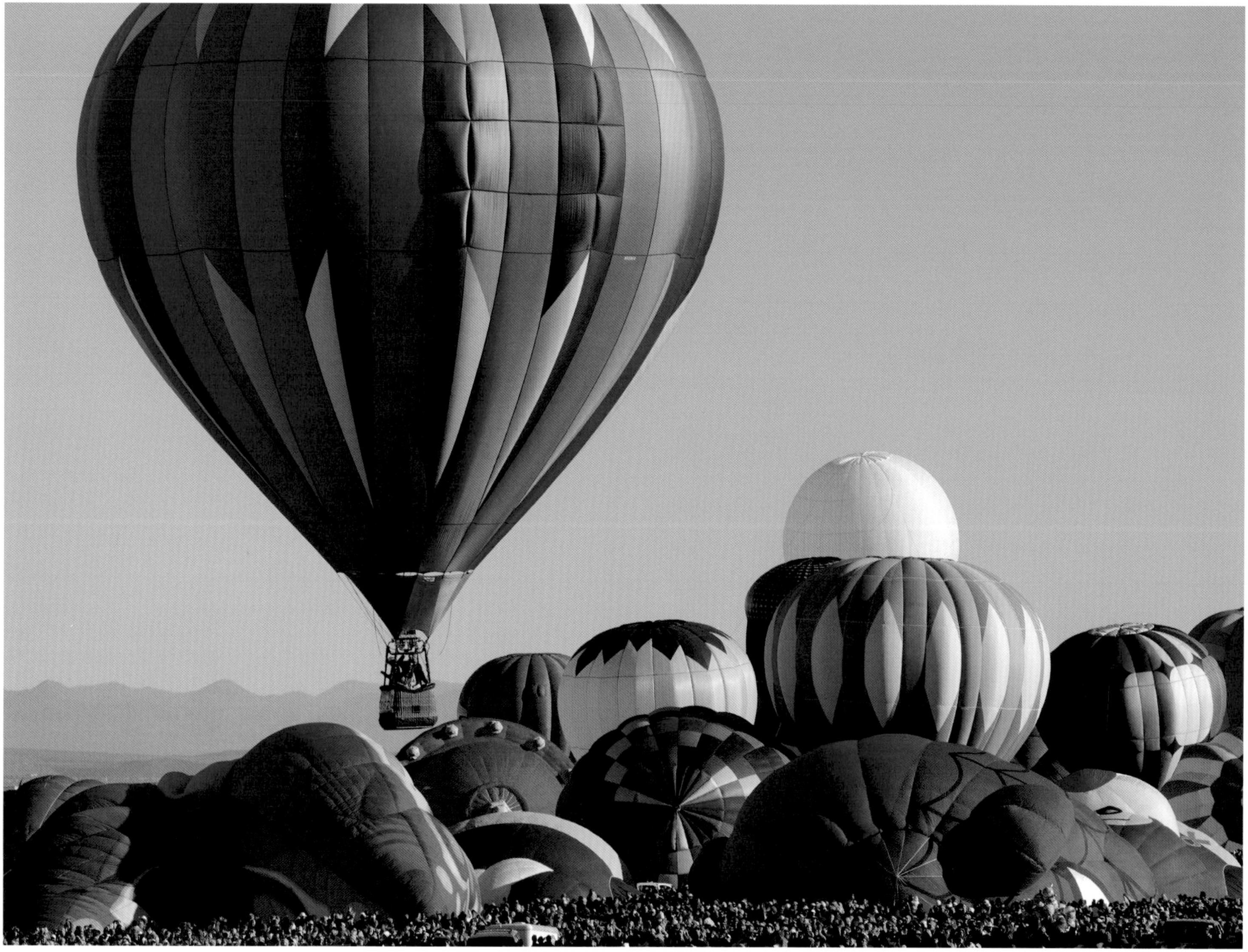

In 2001, the Fiesta capped the number of balloons to 750 for safety reasons. The year prior, more than 1,000 balloons were registered.

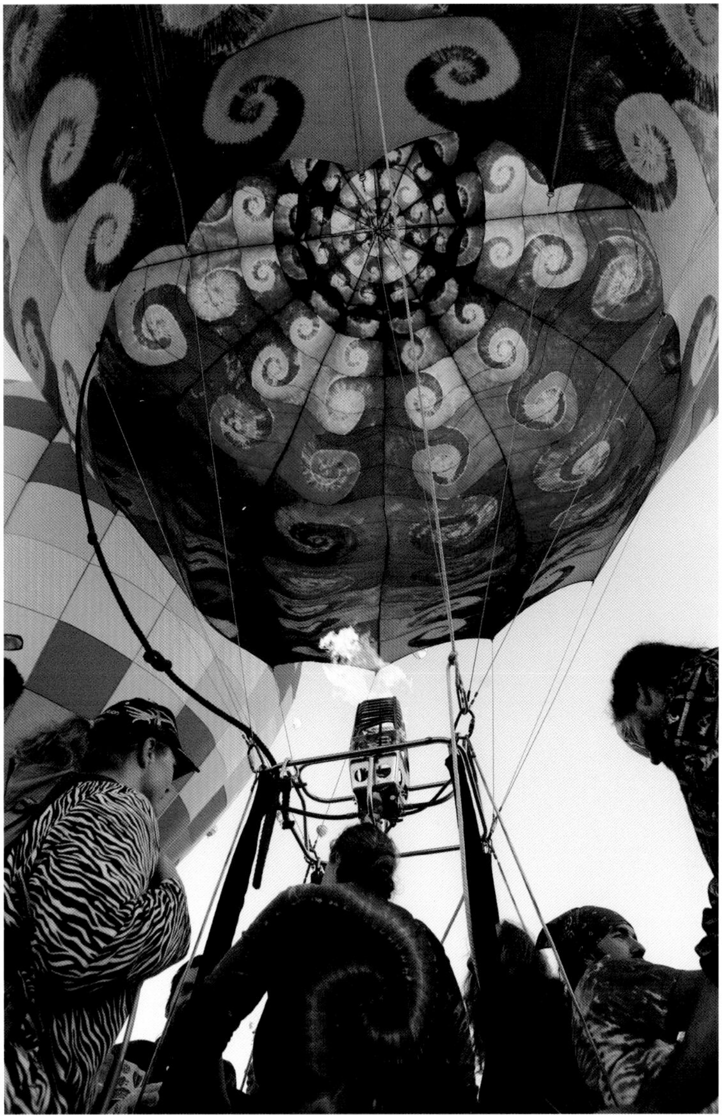

A zebra consults with the Sky Dyes! crew before their launch.

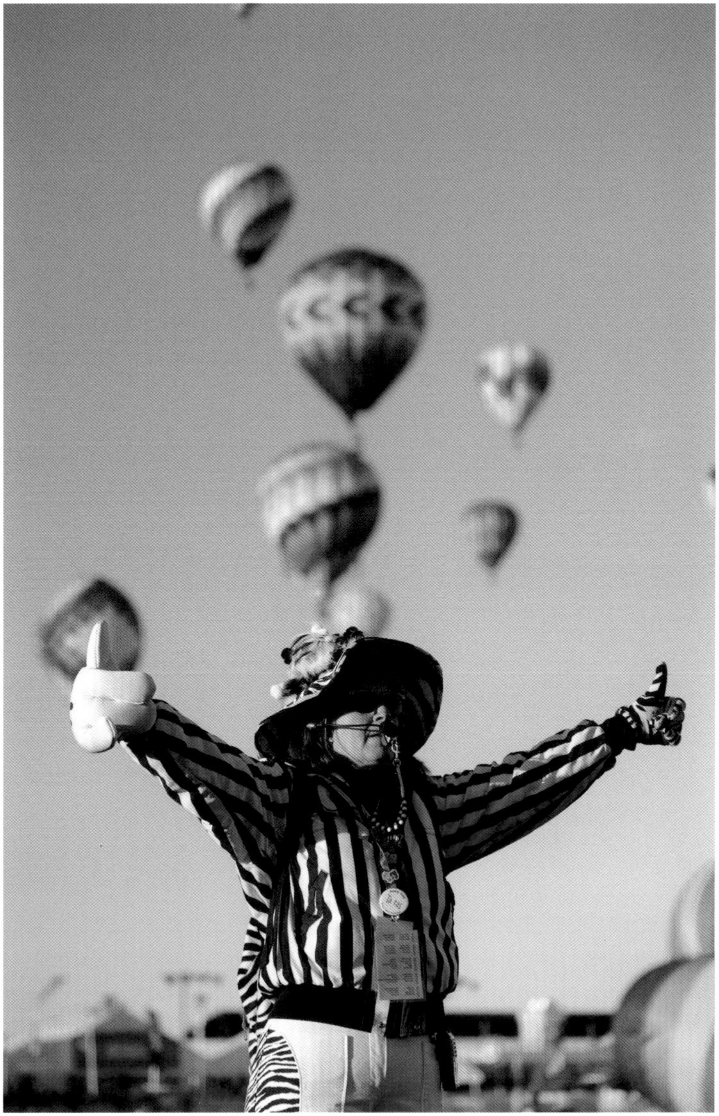

A zebra gives the clear-to-launch signal.

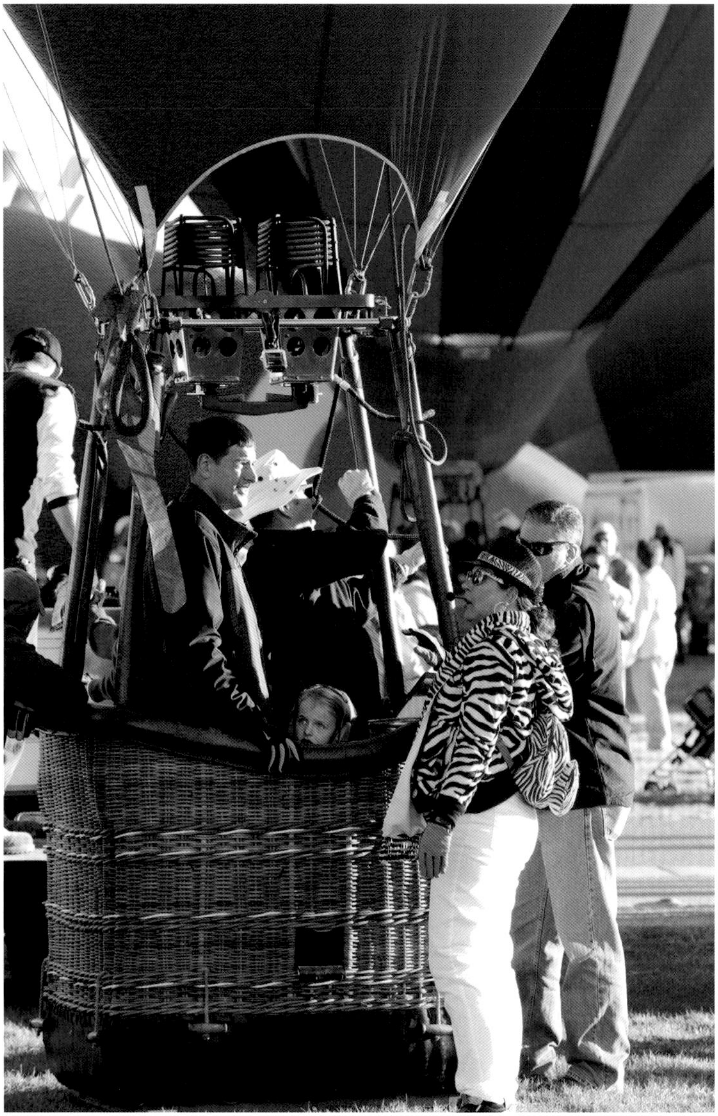

A pilot and zebra discuss launch direction before take off.

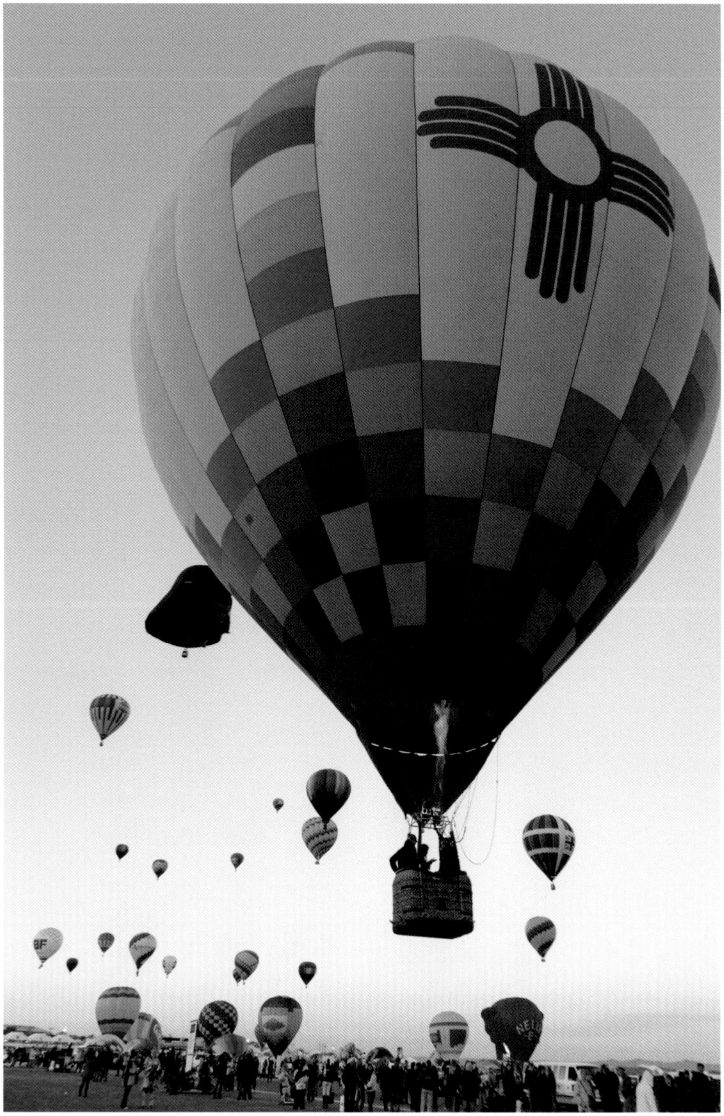

A perfect flying morning.

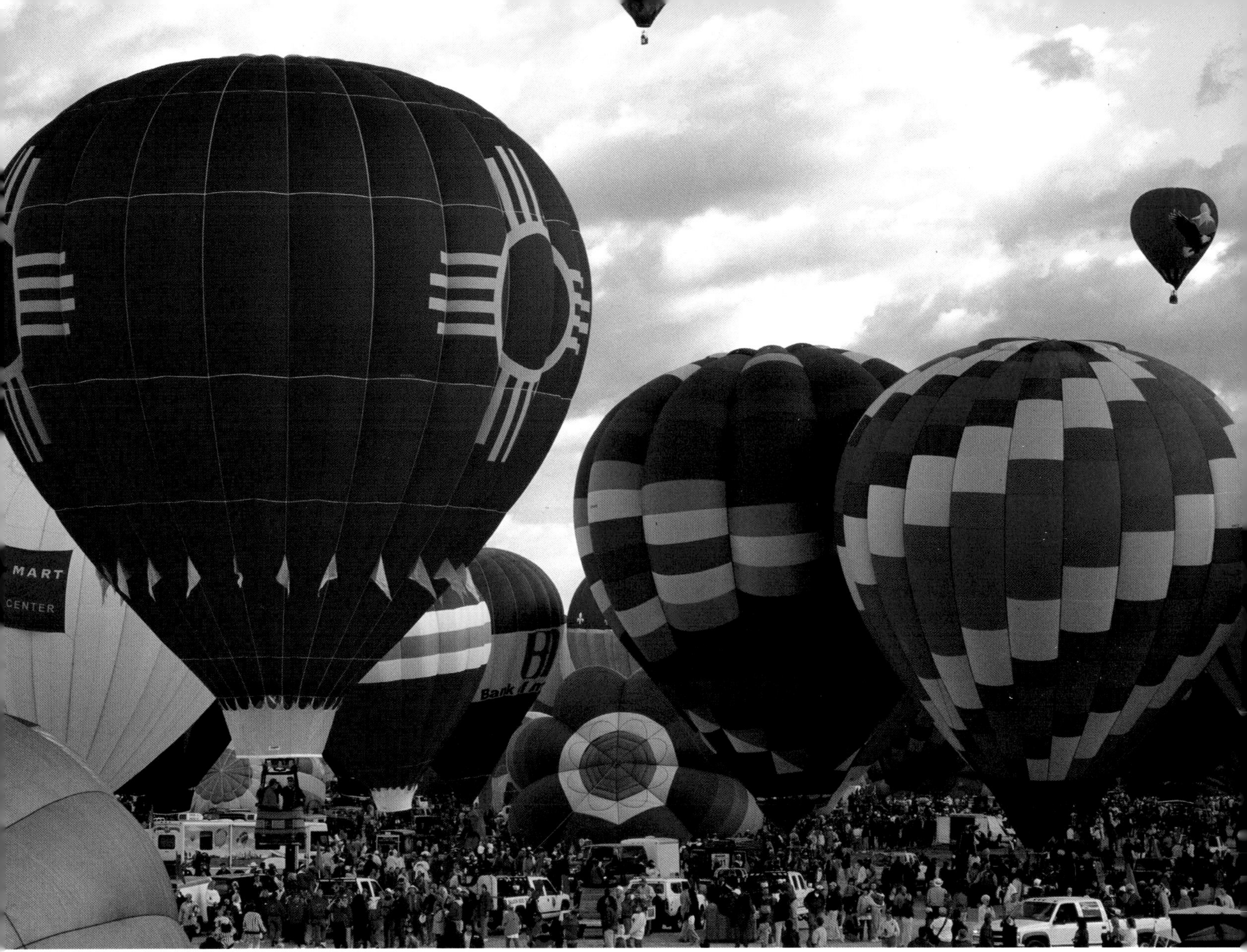

Despite a few clouds, the Fiesta is given the green light this day. The day's flying events are cancelled when winds are eleven miles per hour or greater.

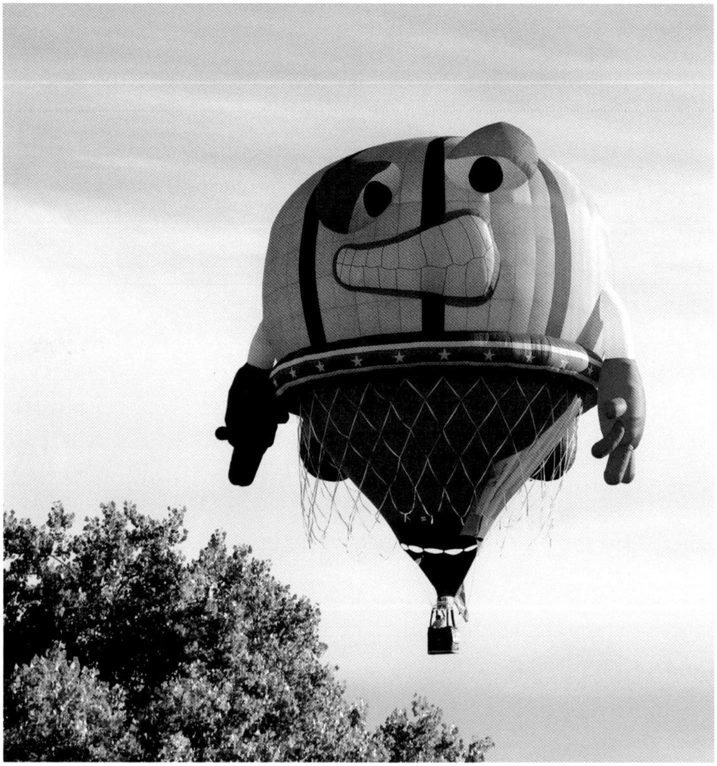

"Basketboll" from Brazil looks for a landing spot in Corrales, a small farming village across the Río Grande from Balloon Fiesta Park.

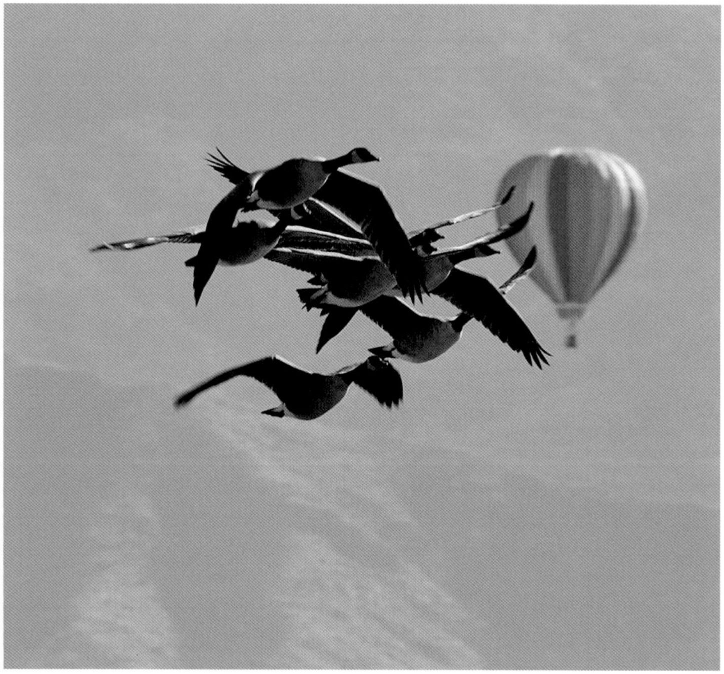

A flock of Canada geese against the Sandía Mountains seem unconcerned with the balloons that share the sky.

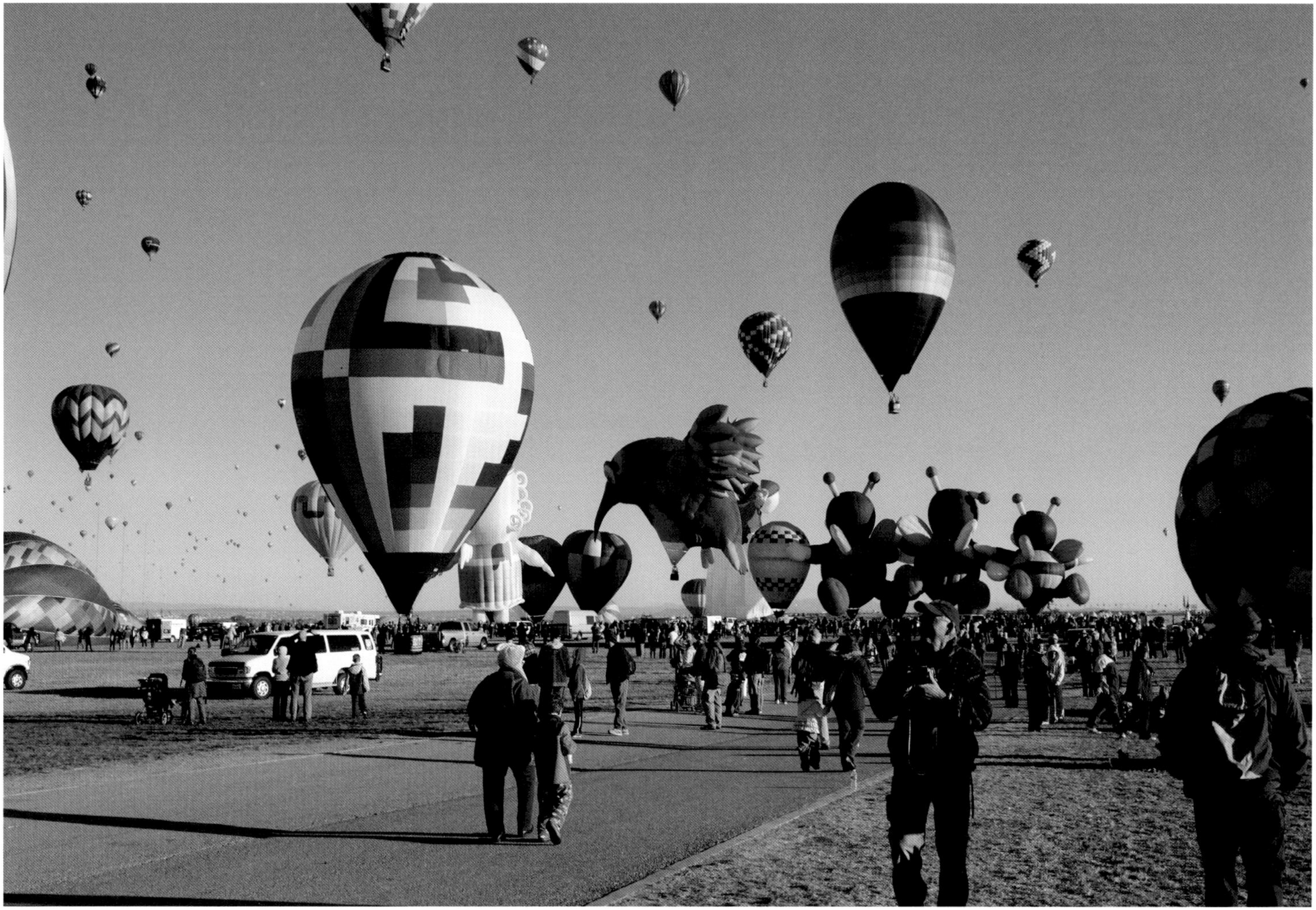

All eyes are upward in Albuquerque the first full week of October.

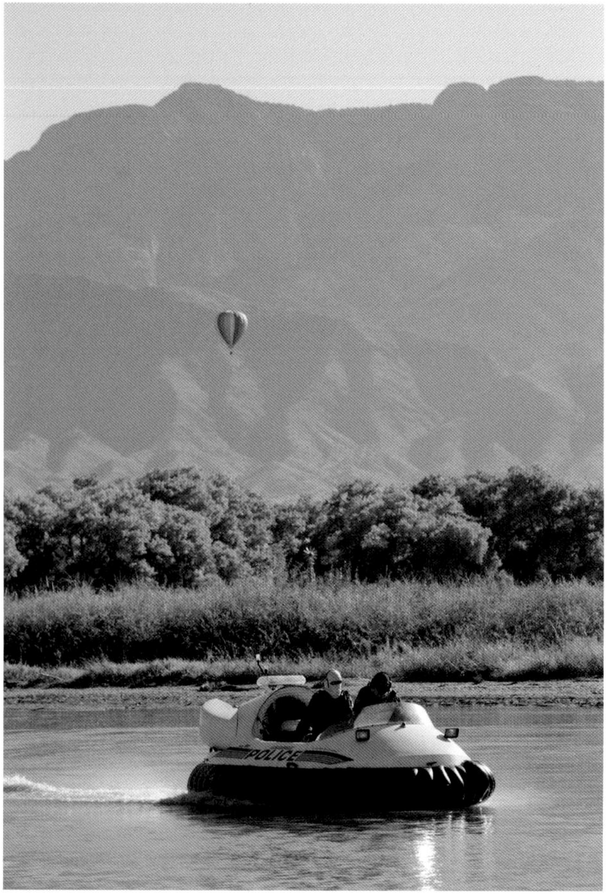

The Albuquerque Police Department patrols the Río Grande with hovercraft for balloonists who need help.

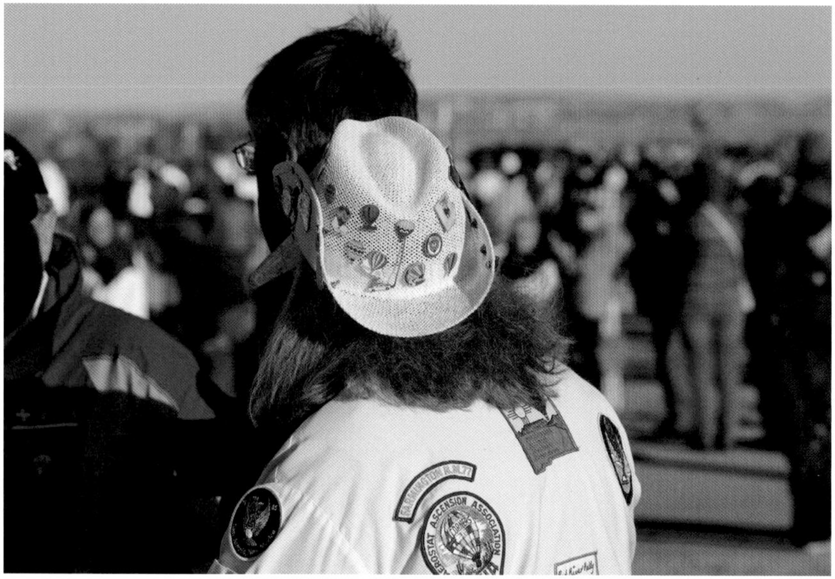

Balloon pins have become treasured souvenirs. Depicting specific balloons and events, they are collected and traded throughout the week.

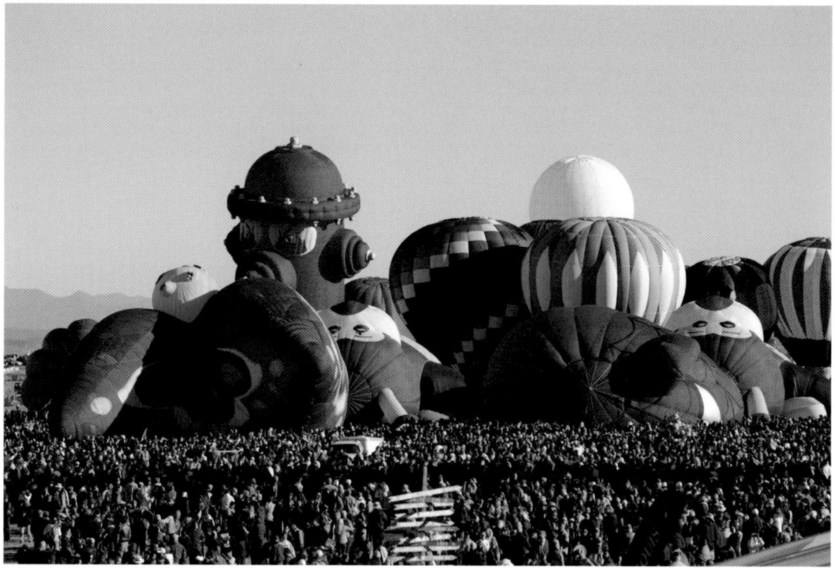

"Squirt" the fire hydrant from Brazil takes shape during a mass ascension.

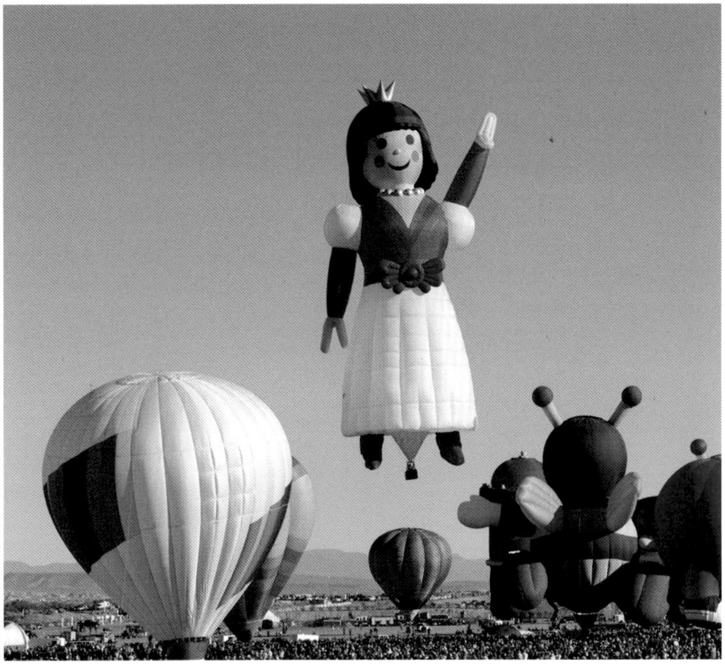

"Snow White" from the United Kingdom waves to the crowd upon lift off.

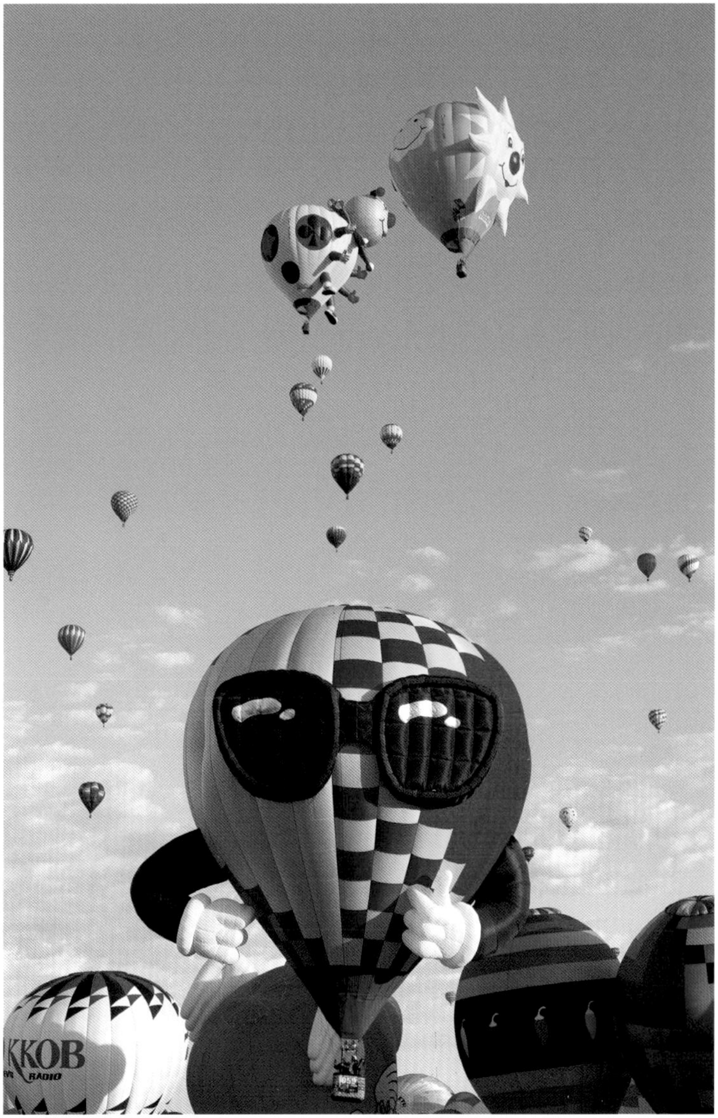

Sporting shades in the New Mexico sun, "Lindy" from Illinois took his first flight in 2010 and is based on a T-shirt design worn at the 2008 Balloon Fiesta.

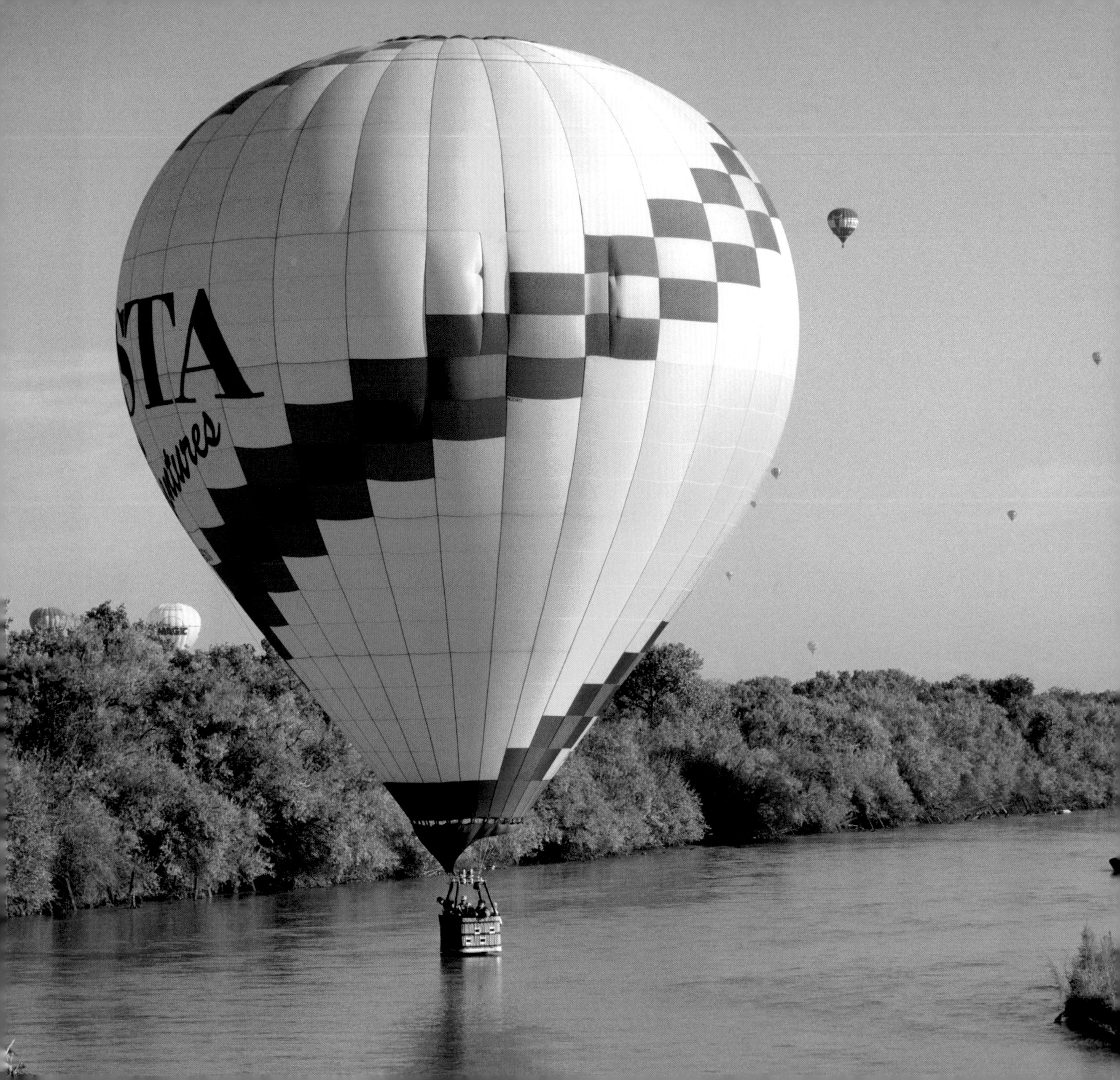
STA
ntures
MAGIC

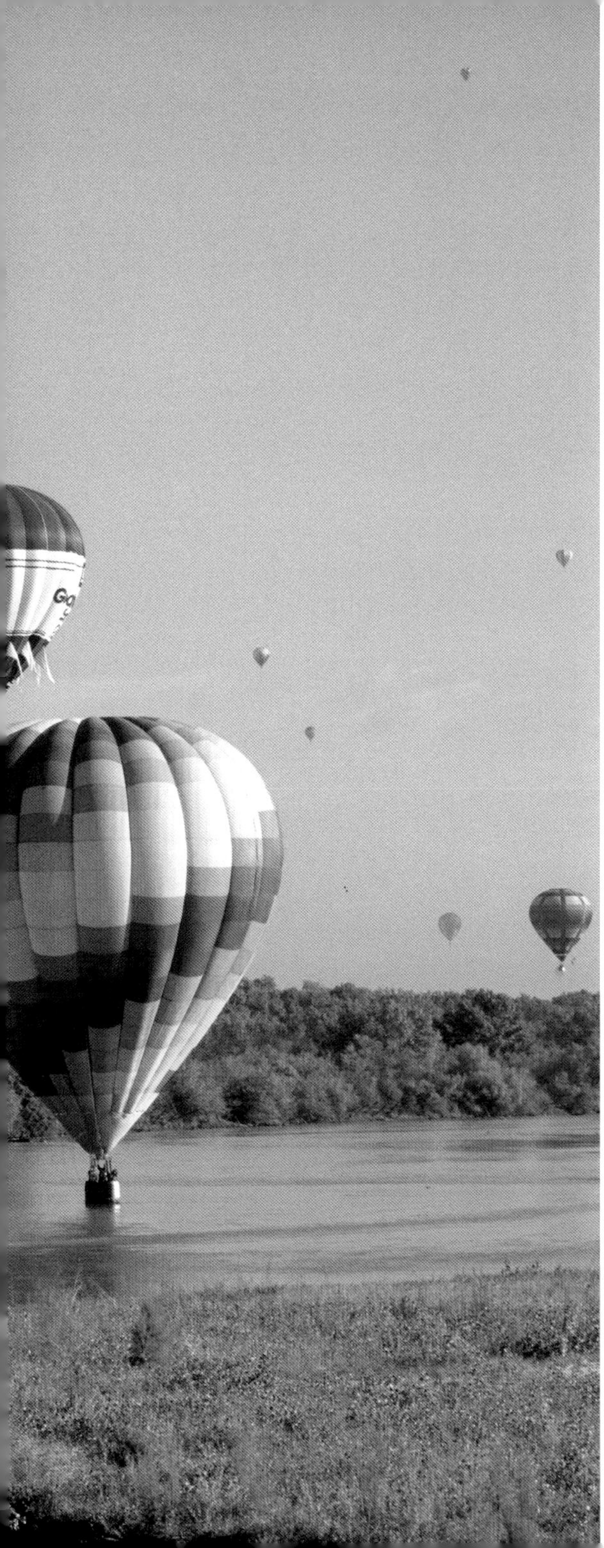

Balloons skim the shallow water of the cottonwood-lined Río Grande.

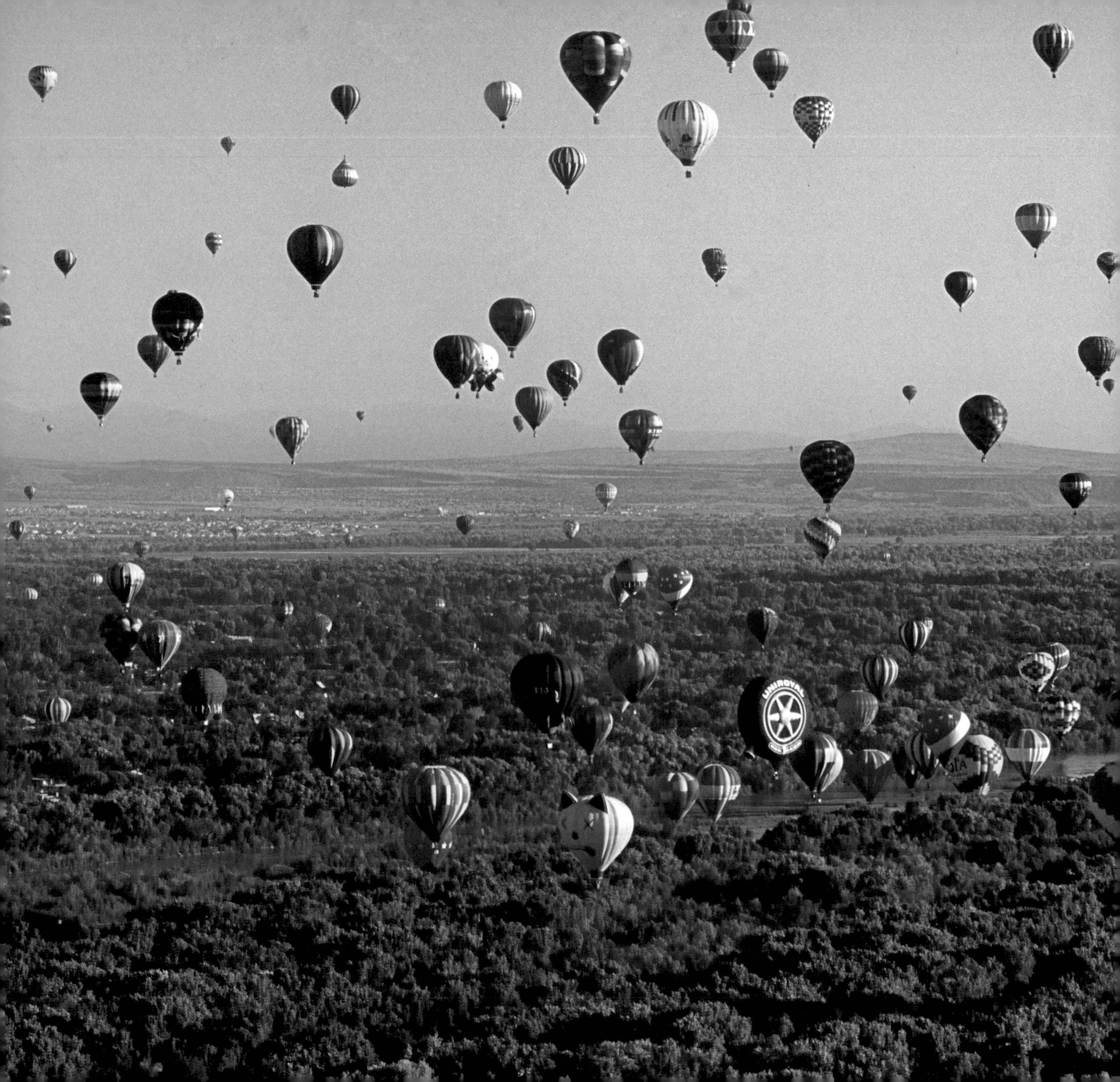
UNIROYAL

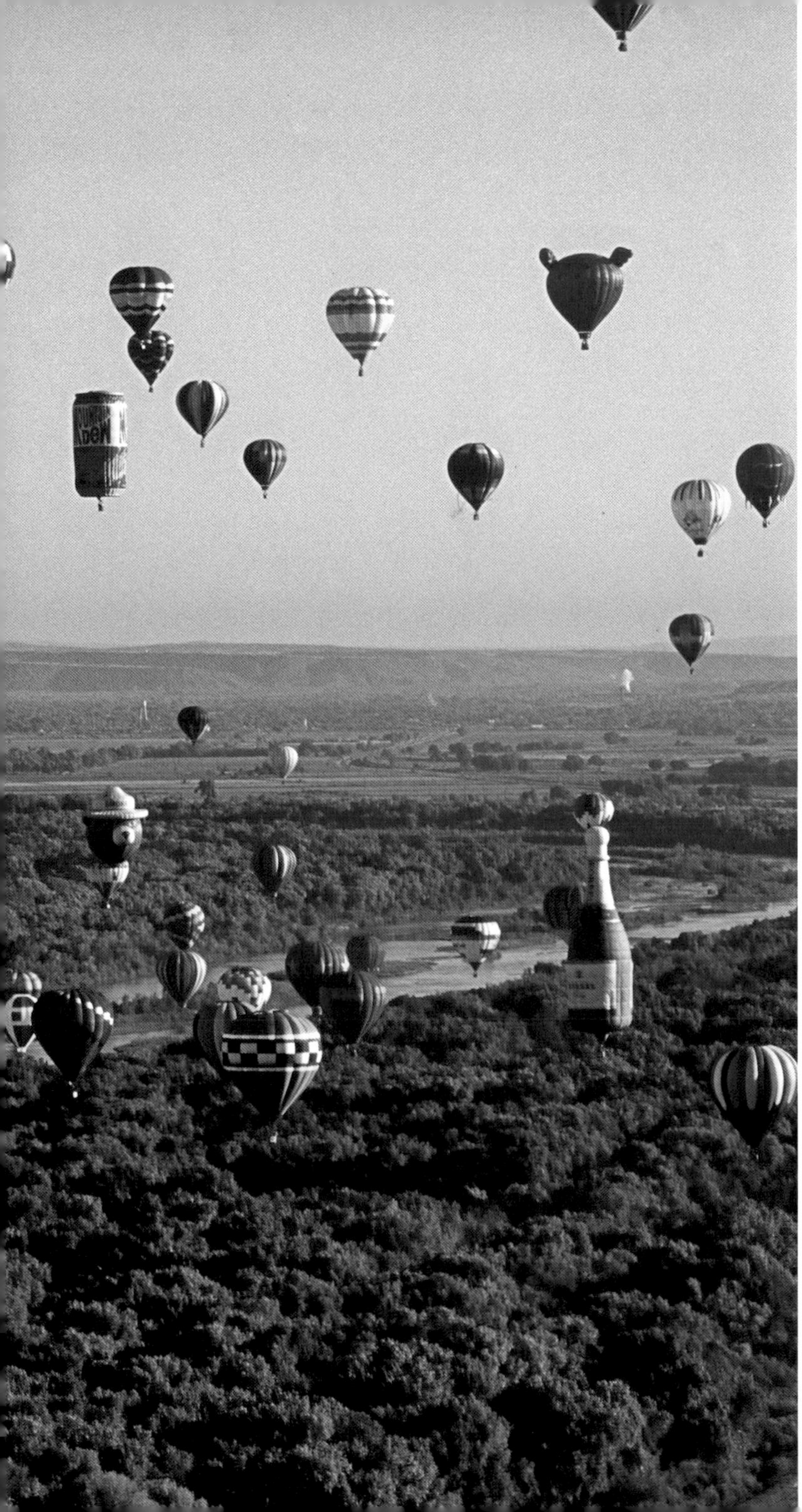

The Río Grande *bosque* (Spanish for "woods") is the largest continuous cottonwood forest in the world.

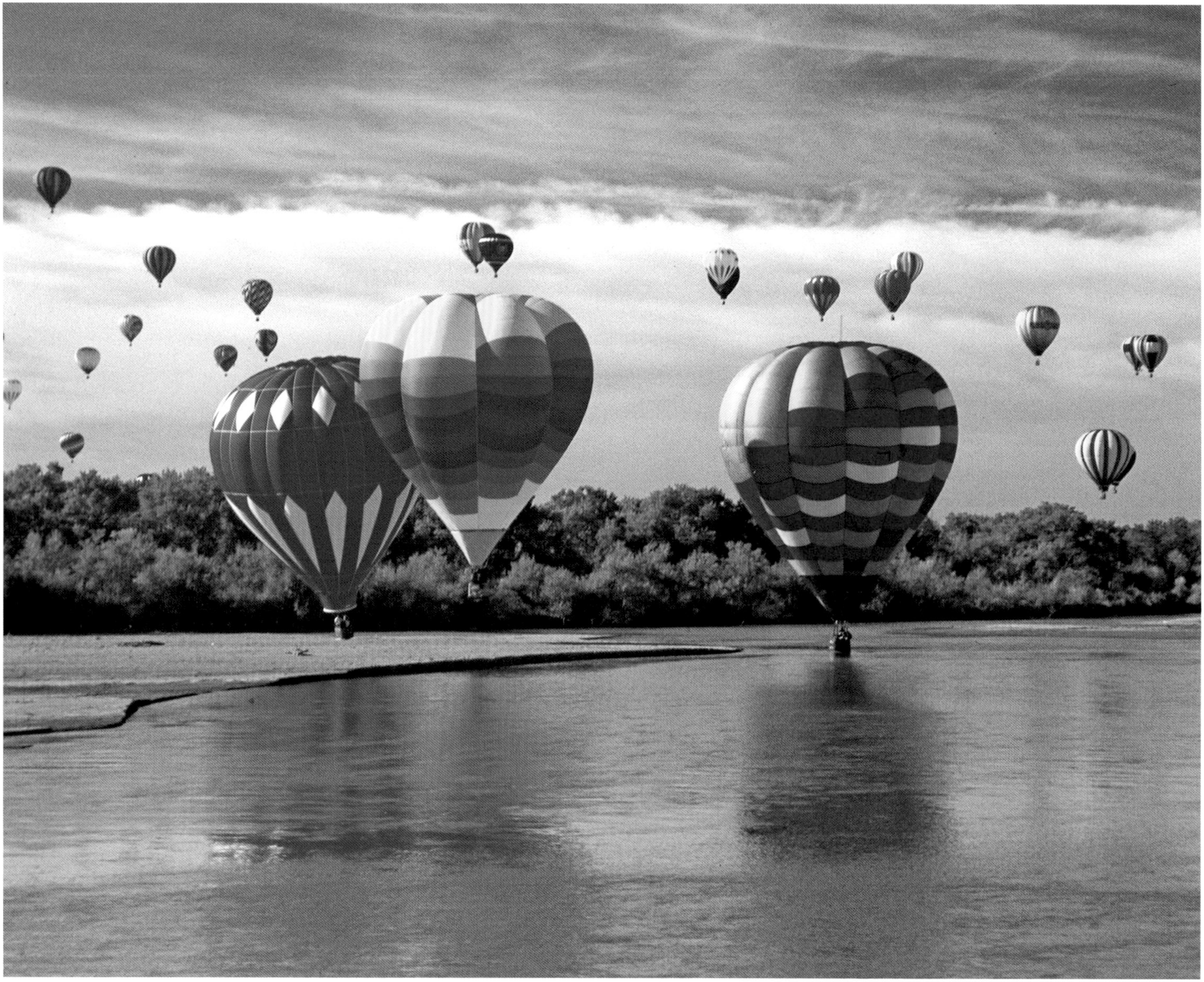

Balloons float above the Río Grande.

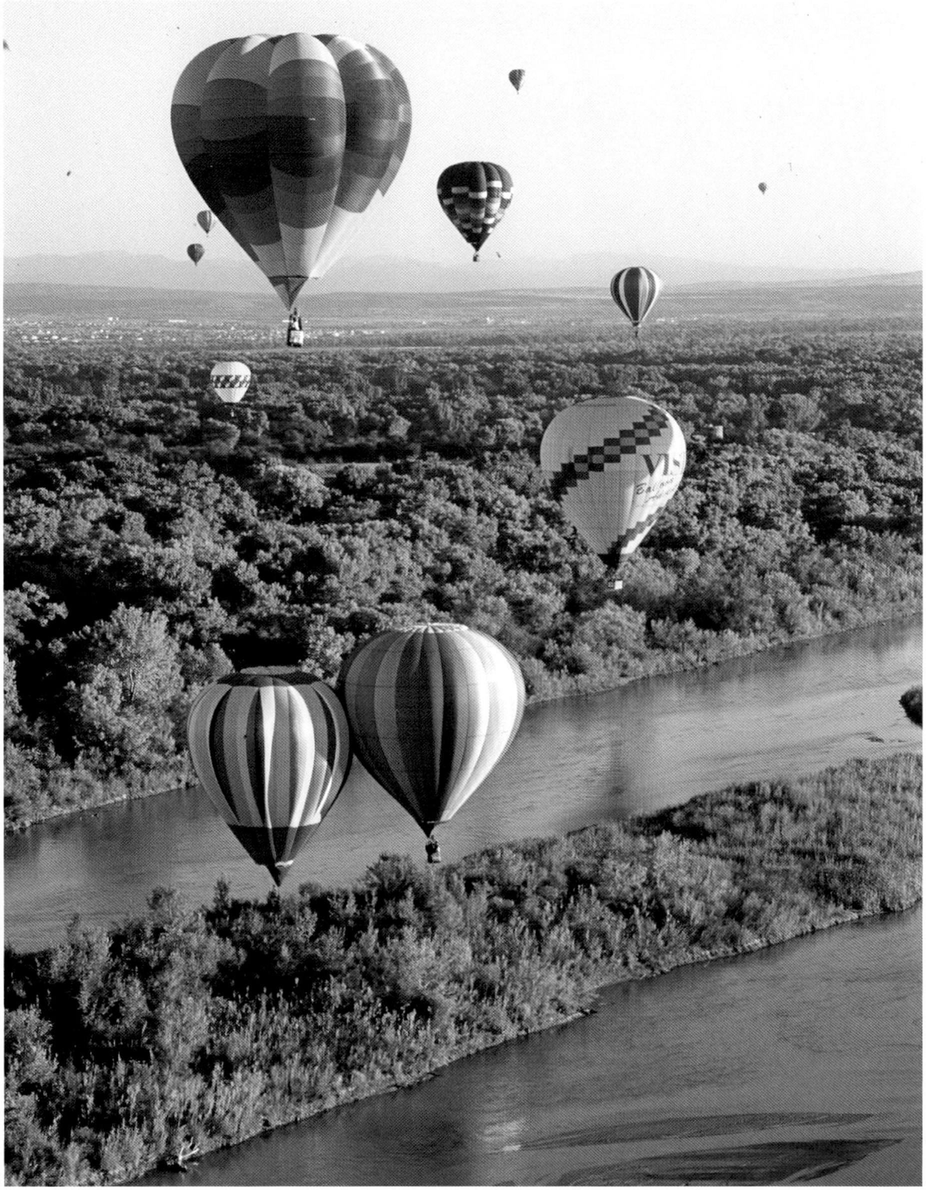

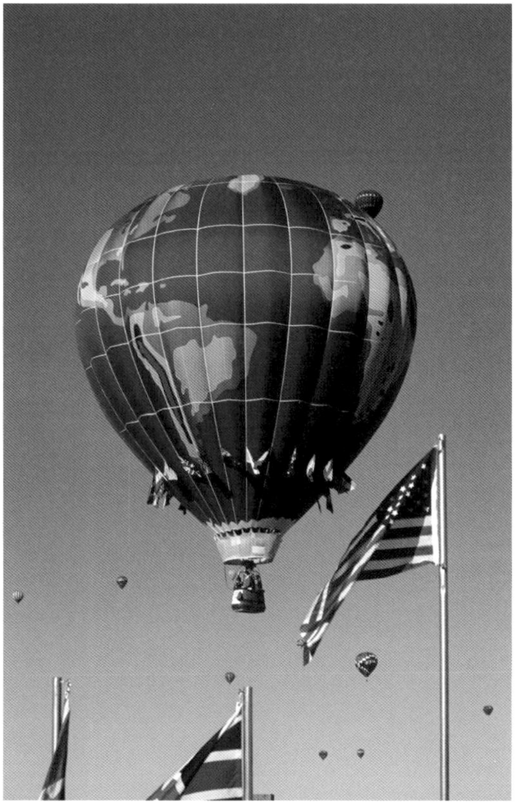

The World Balloon during the Flight of Nations.

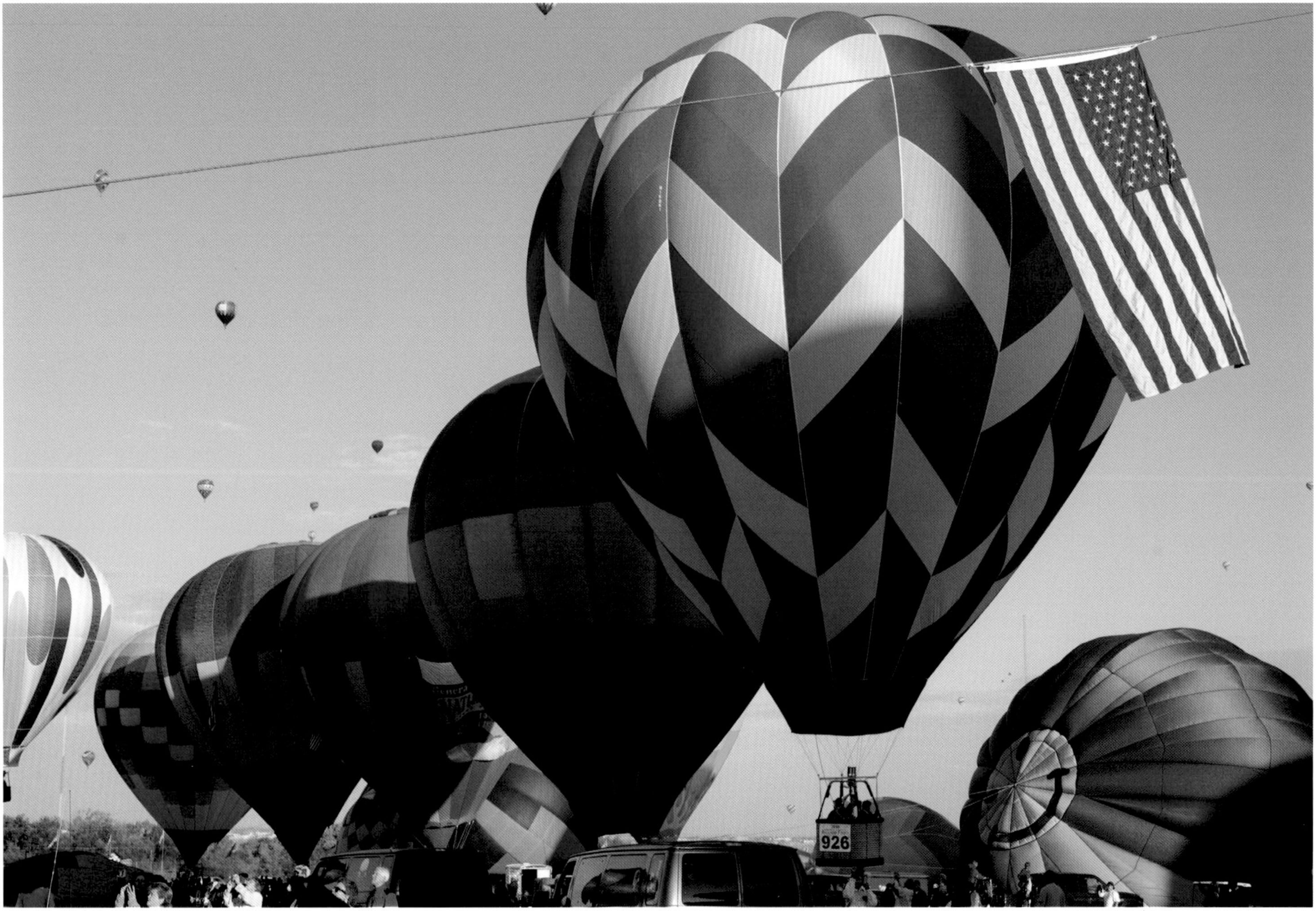

A line of balloons prepares for lift off.

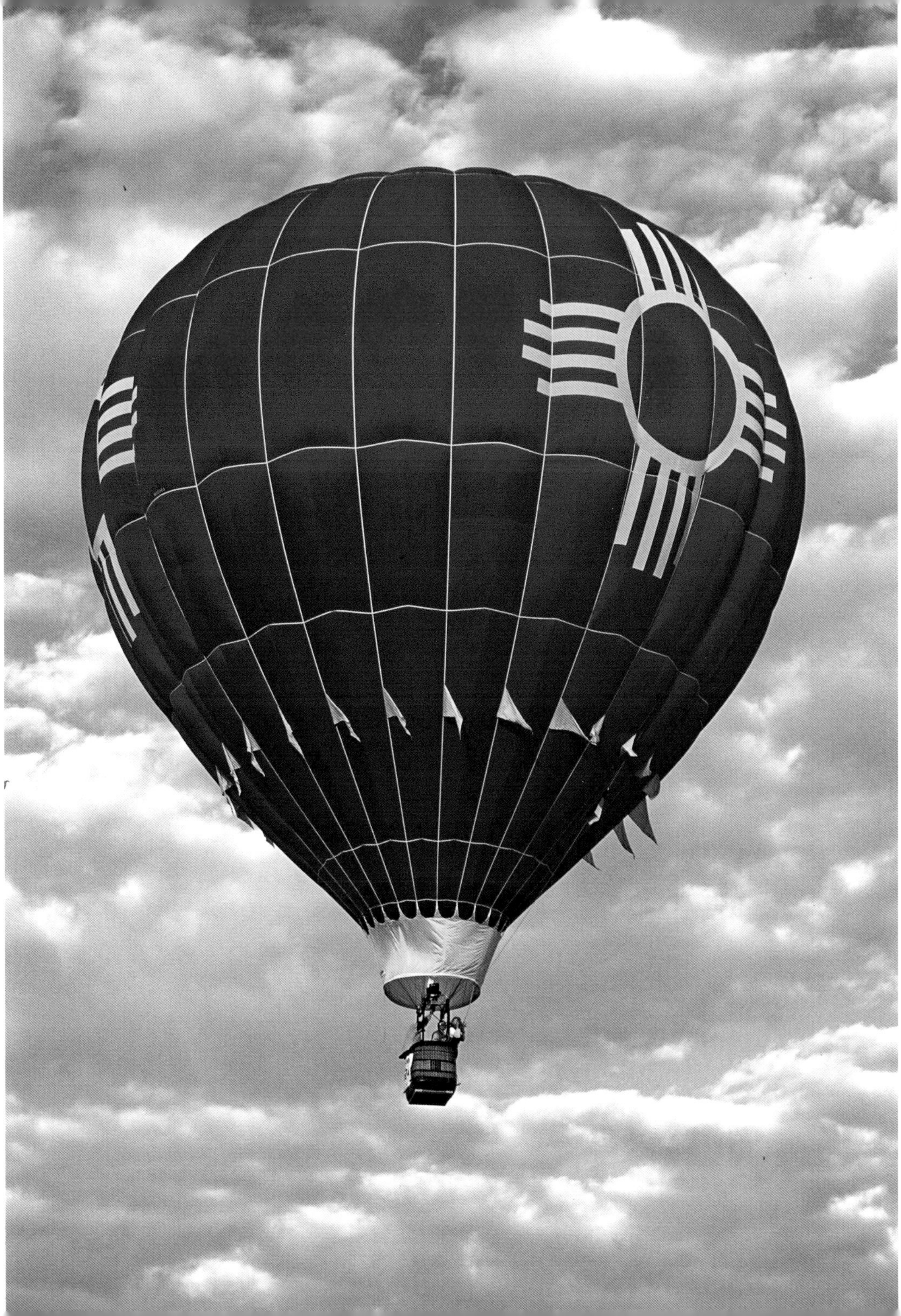

New Mexico's state symbol, the Zia, comes from Zia Pueblo and has multiple meanings, including representing the seasons and stages of life.

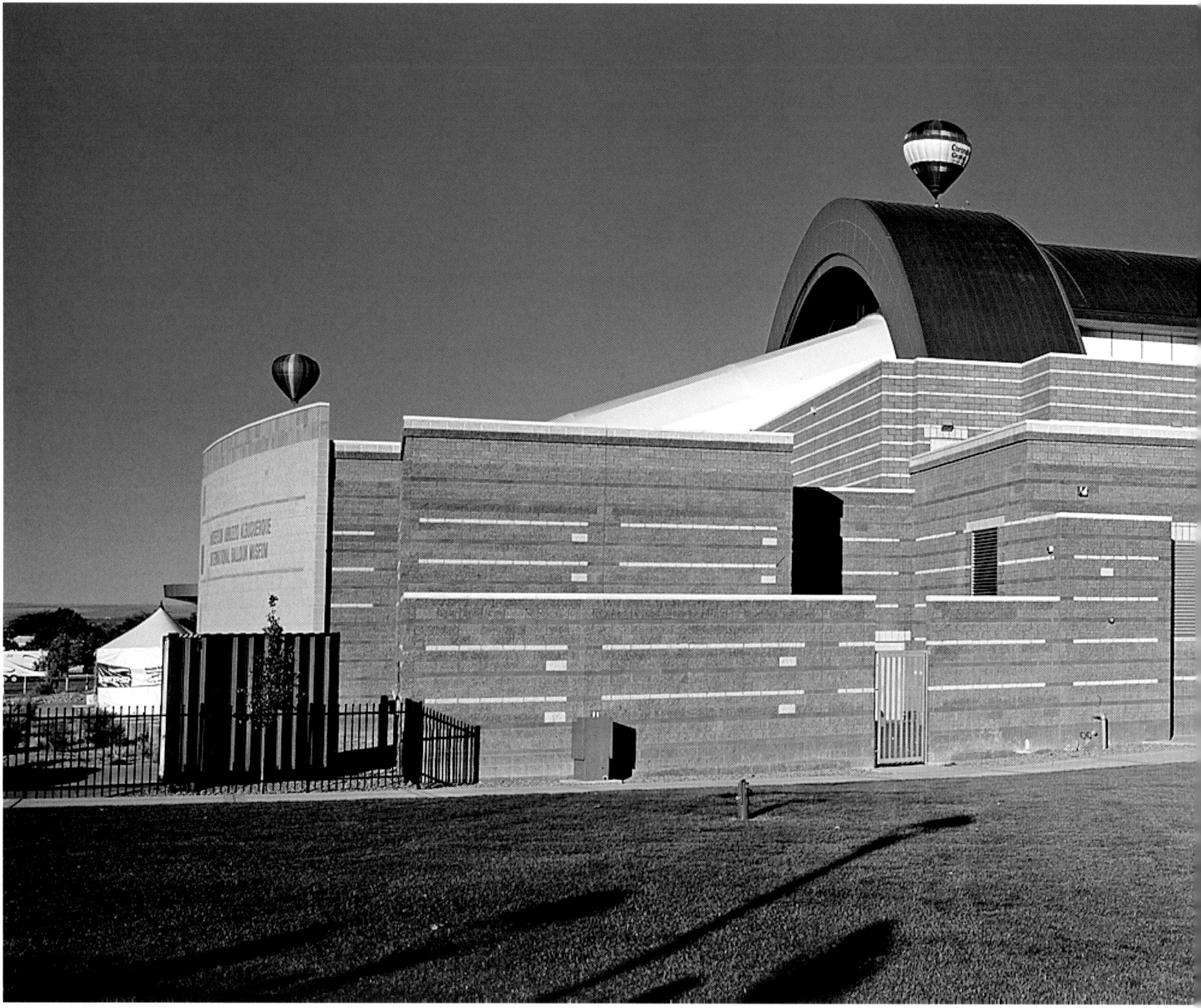

The Anderson-Abruzzo International Balloon Museum at the field's south end explores the history of ballooning and its impact on human events and exploration. It is named for Albuquerqueans Ben Abruzzo and Maxie Anderson, who along with Larry Newman in 1978 piloted the hot-air balloon Double Eagle II across the Atlantic Ocean from Presque, Maine, to Miserey, France, making them the first people to fly a balloon across the Atlantic.

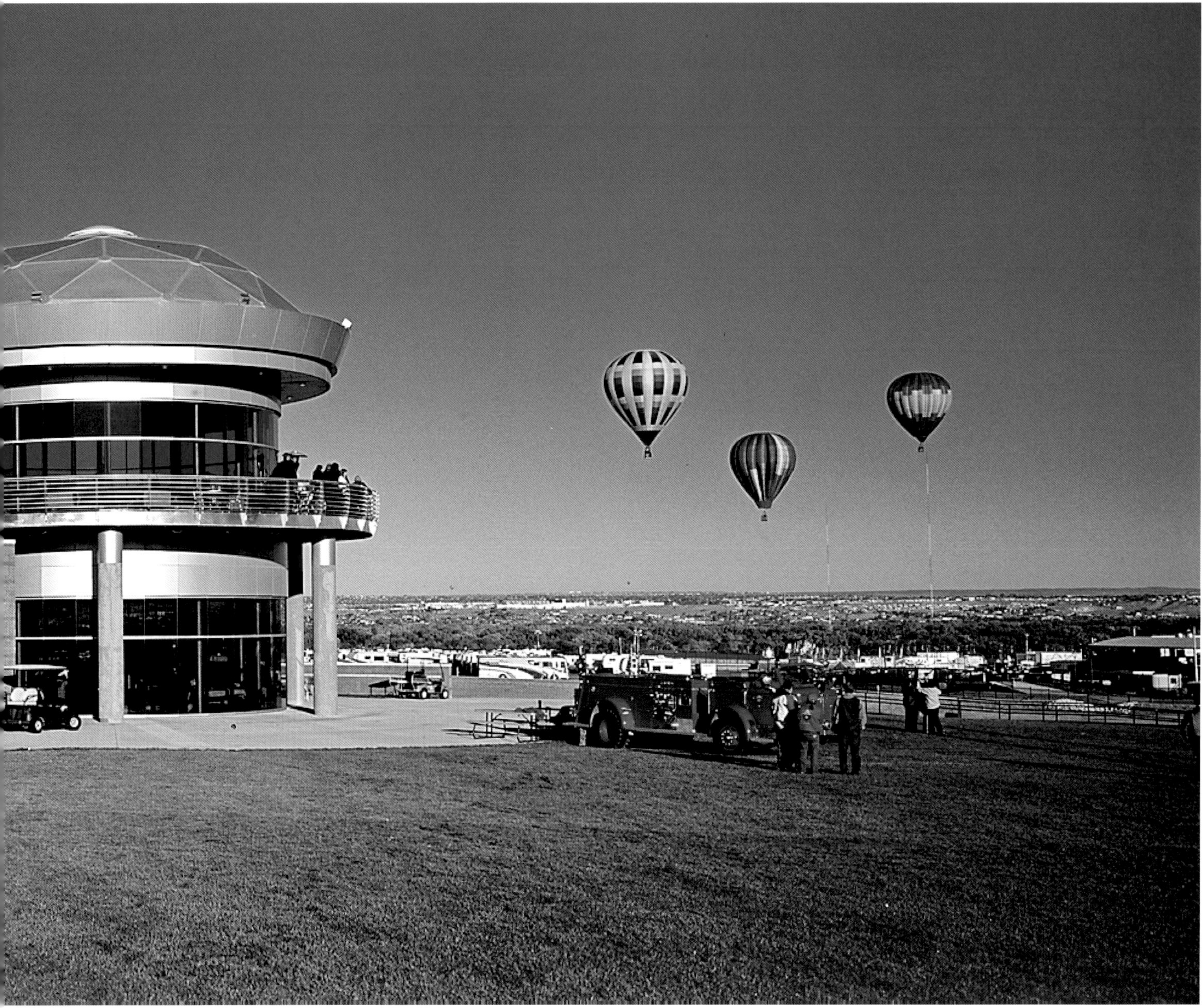

They were honored with Congressional Gold Medals in 1979. Abruzzo went on to pilot Double Eagle V, a gas balloon, across the Pacific Ocean in 1981. Anderson, with his son, Kristian, made the first nonstop flight across North America in 1980, and in January 1981 circumnavigated the world in 48 hours, leaving from Egypt and landing in India, a distance of 2,682 miles.

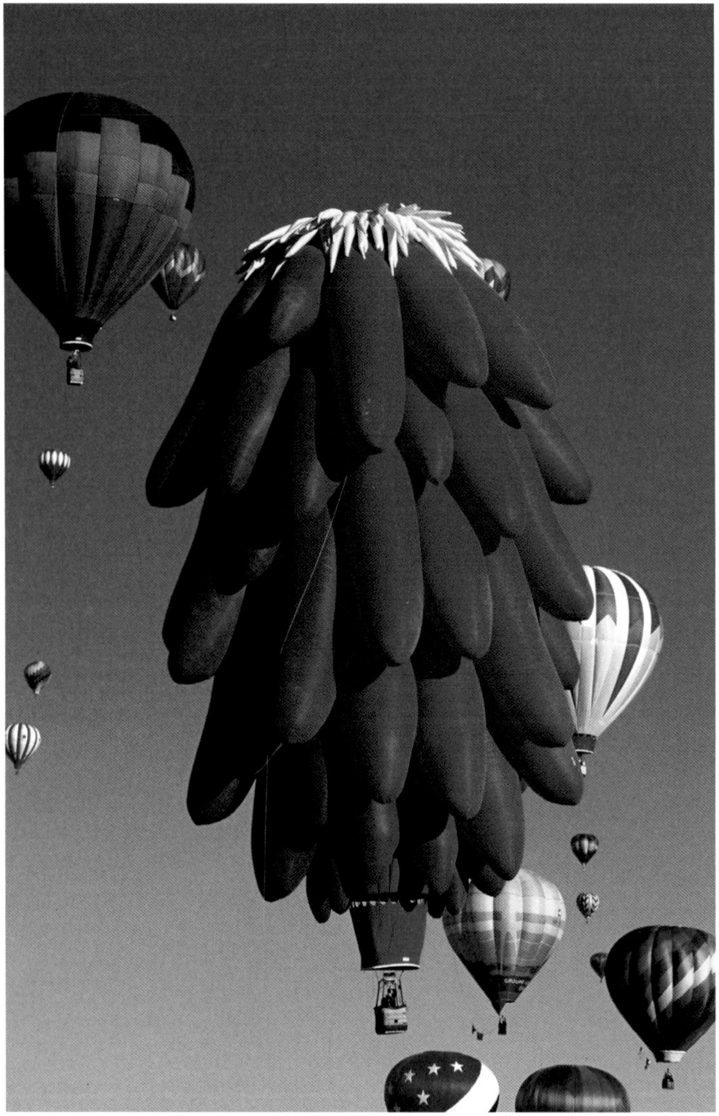

"La Ristra" of the Flying Chili Peppers Balloon Company in Socorro, New Mexico, represents a *ristra*—a string of red chile peppers tied together in order to dry. *Ristras* are common decorations in New Mexico.

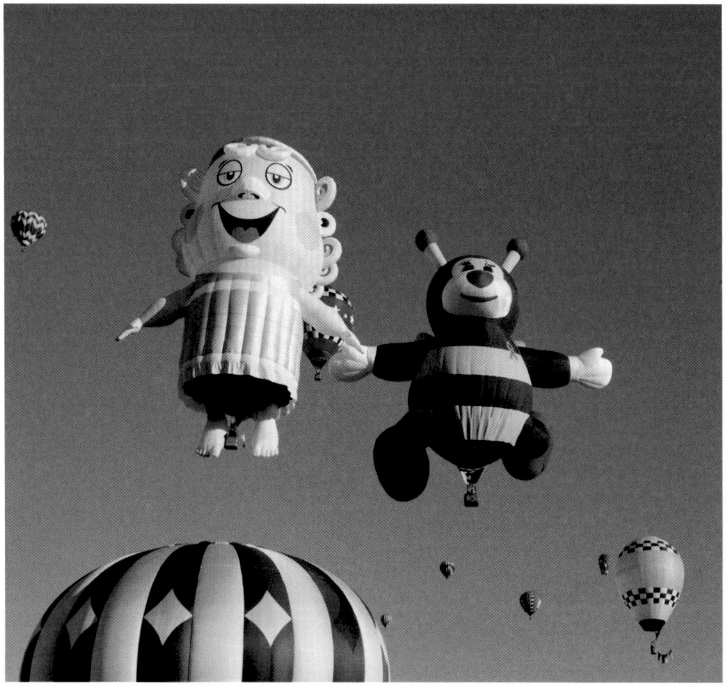

"Little Angel" ascends to heaven with "Little Bee Lilly."

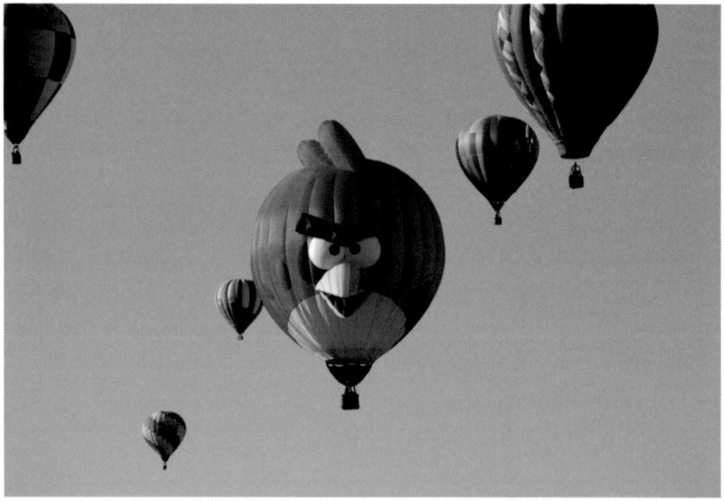

"Angry Bird" from Albuquerque looks for flying pigs to attack.

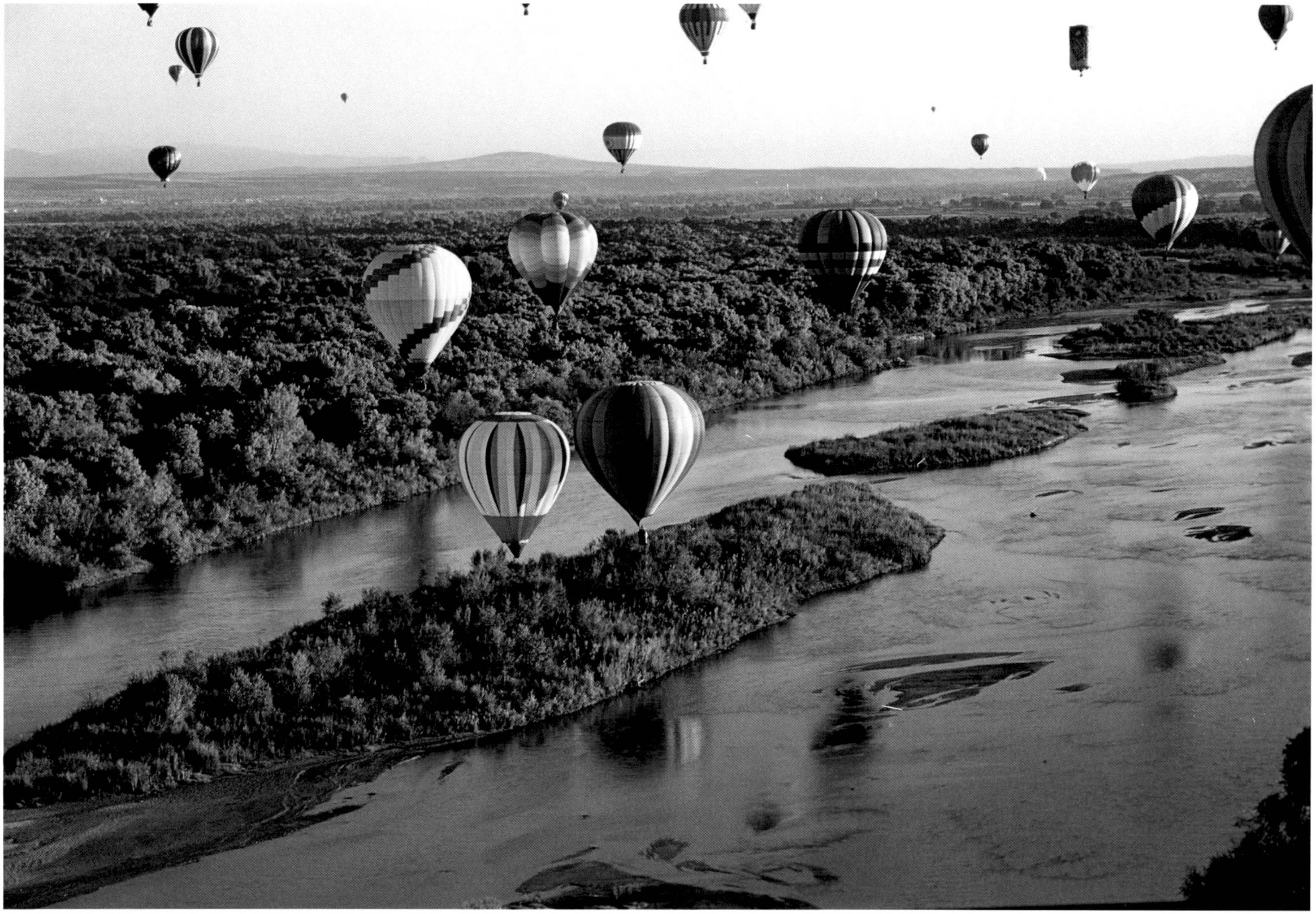
Skilled pilots carefully skim the surface of the Río Grande.

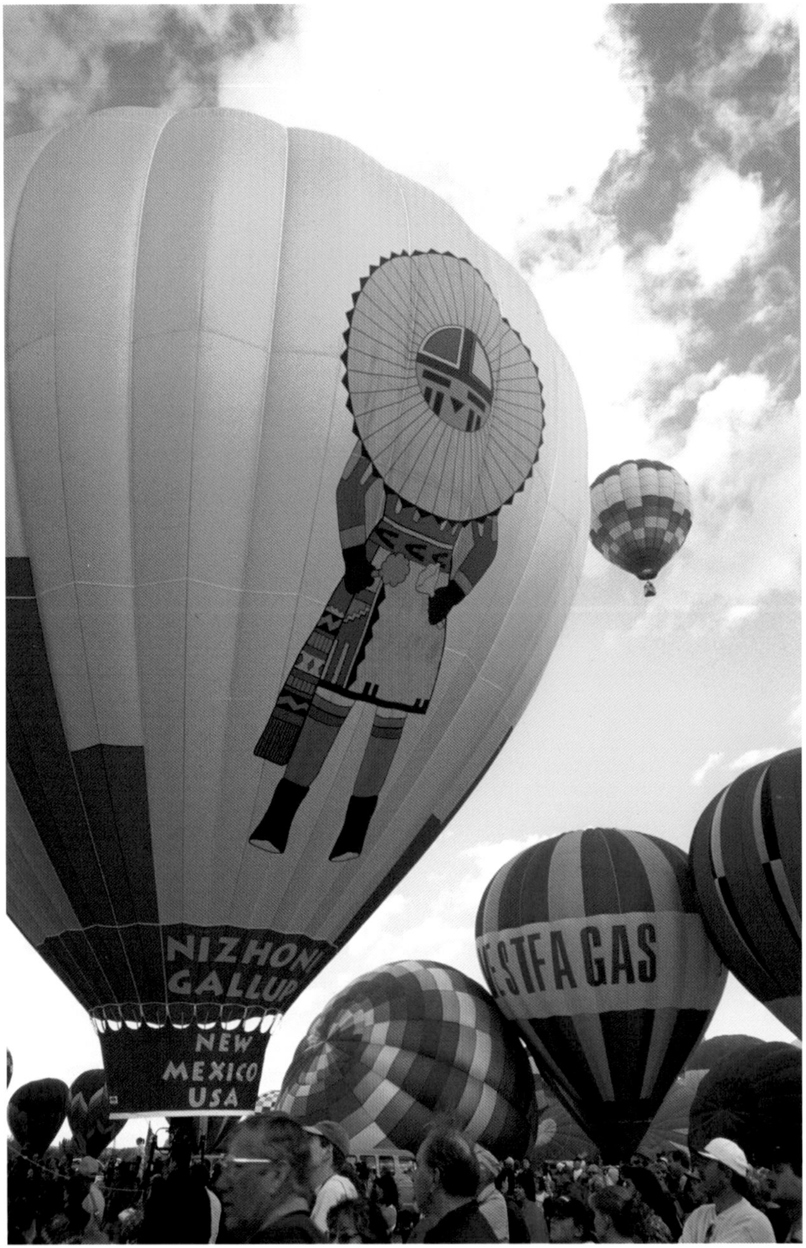

A balloon from Gallup, New Mexico, features a Navajo YeiBiChi dancer.

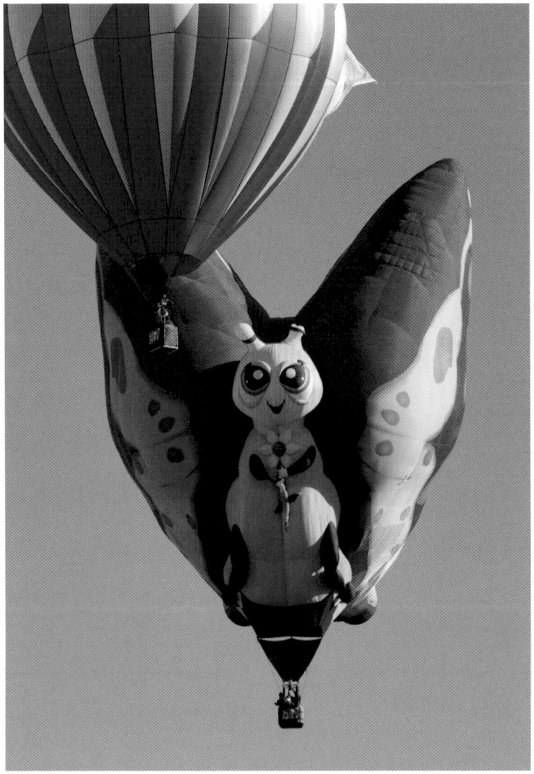

"Butterfly" from Arizona looks right at home against New Mexico's blue sky.

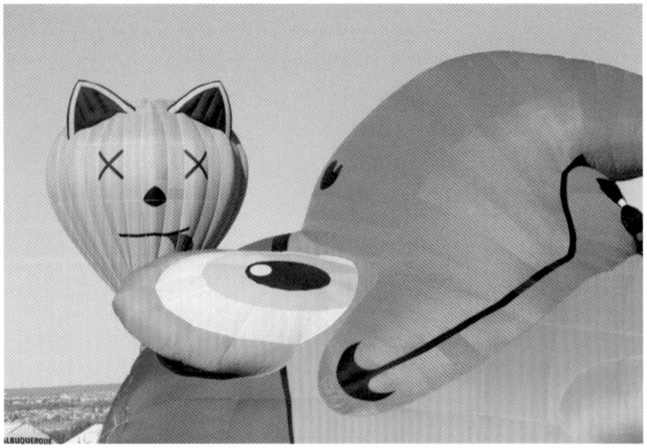

"1 Down 8 2 Go" thinks better than to mess with an inflating "Peg leg Pete."

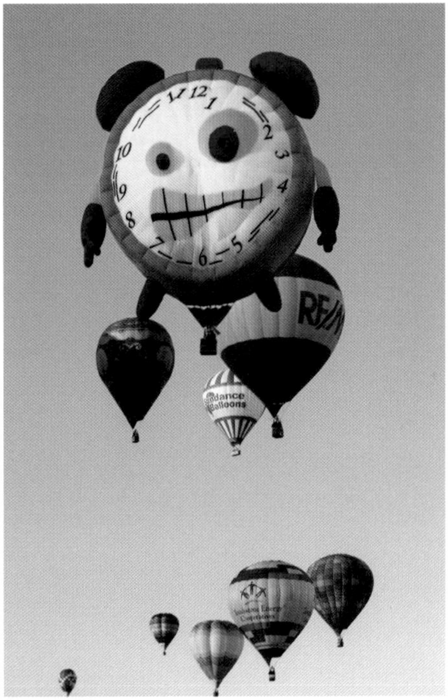

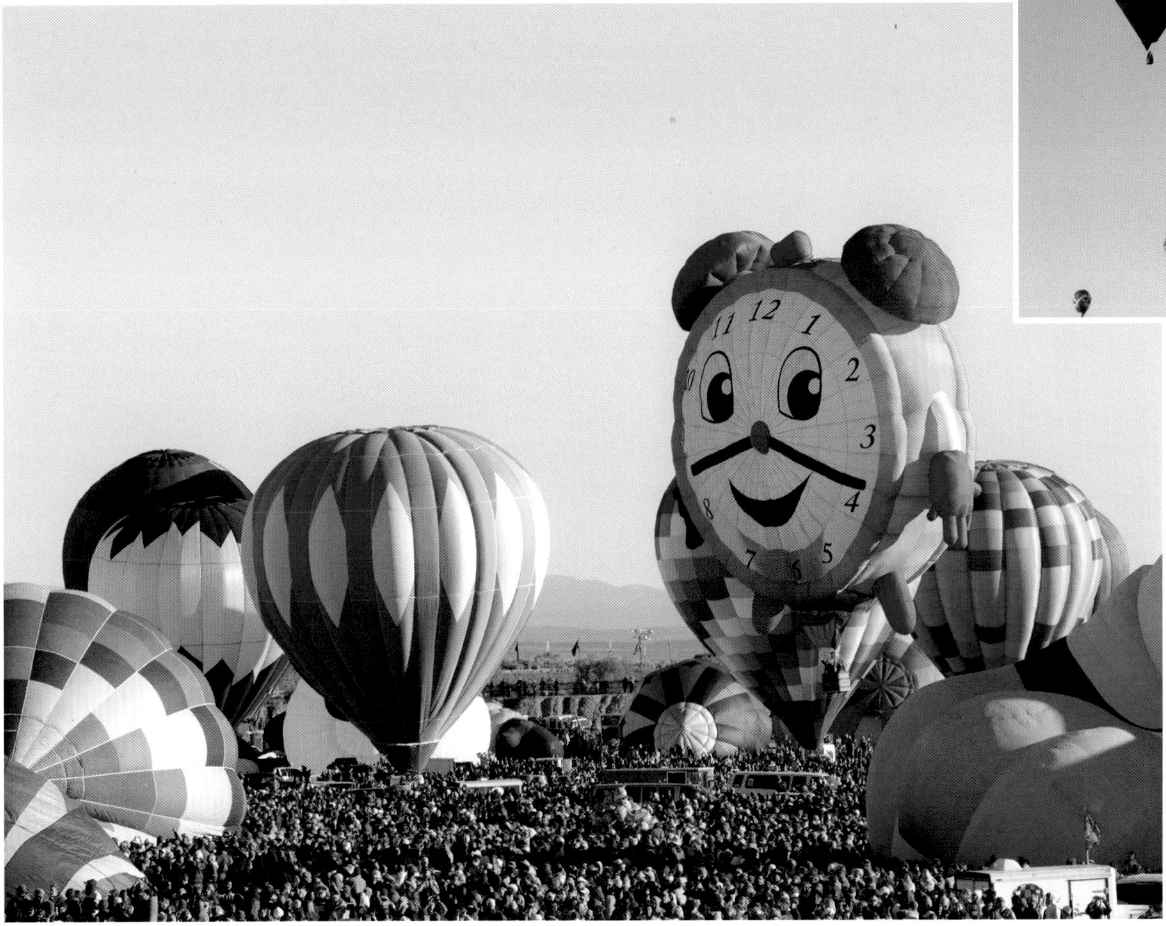

"Tic Toc" from Brazil demonstrates that time does fly.

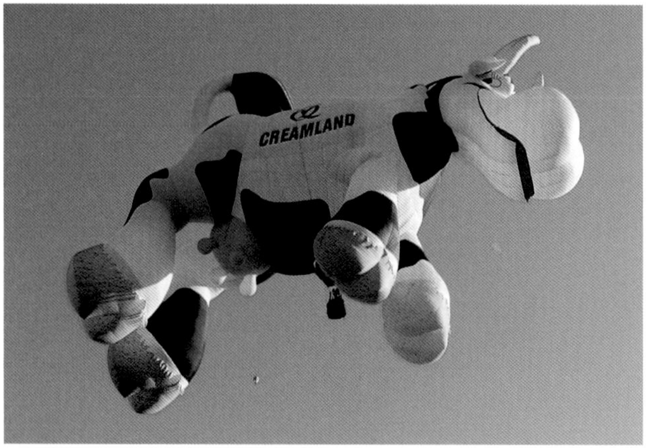

Airabelle is one of Albuquerque's favorite special shapes and advertises for Albuquerque-based Creamland Dairy. Flying conditions have to be great in order for the balloon to take off, given her size and vulnerability to the slightest breeze.

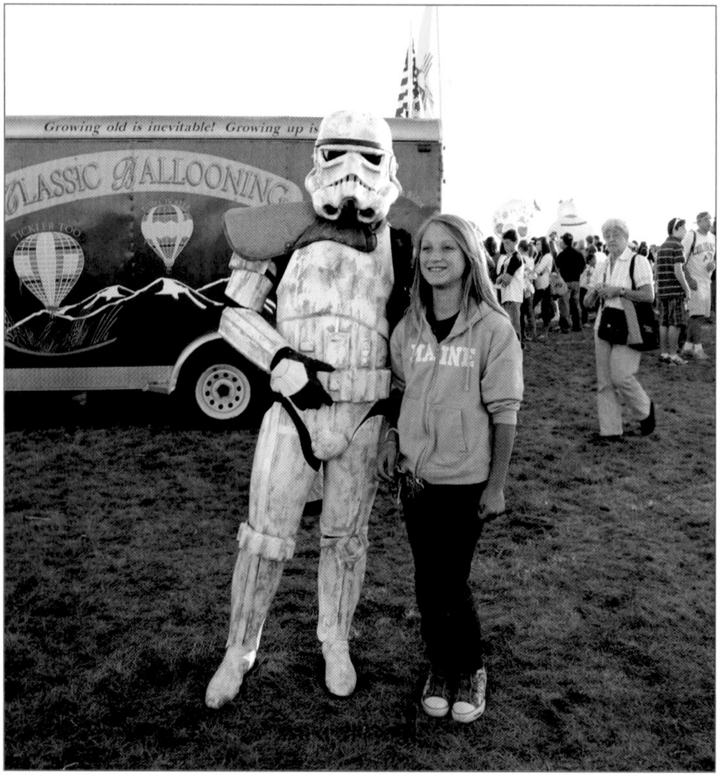

A Stormtrooper from the movie *Star Wars* poses with spectators at the popular "Darth Vader" special shape balloon from Belgium.

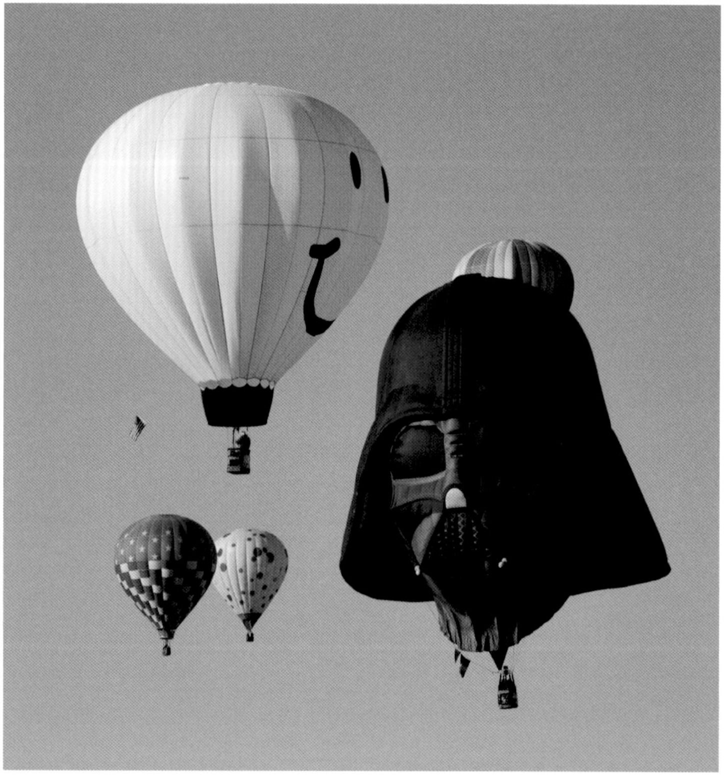

"Darth Vader" seems to be having a nice day of flying.

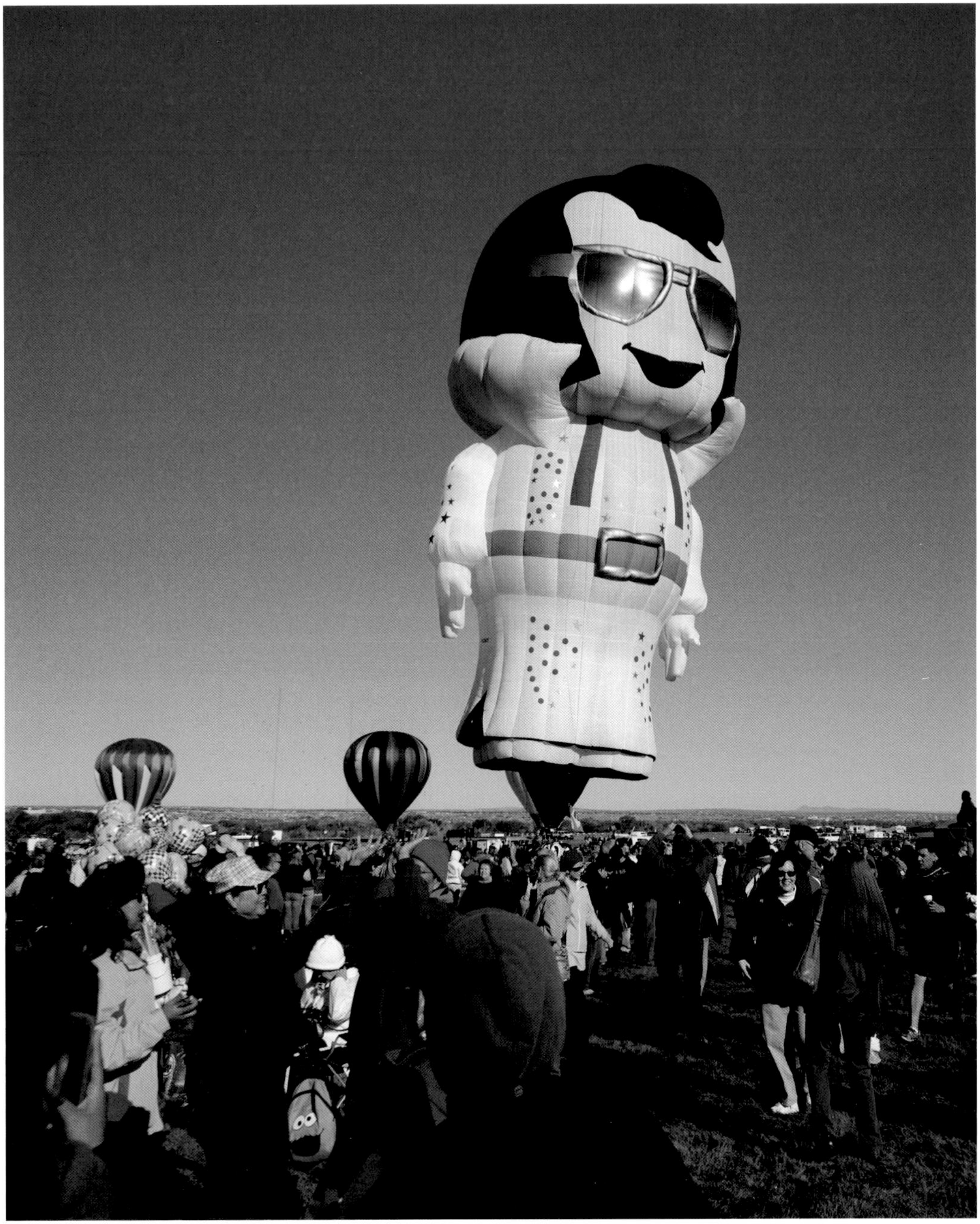

"Aaron" (named for Elvis Aaron Presley) thanks the crowd for coming out.

A pilot executes a "splash 'n' dash" on the Río Grande.

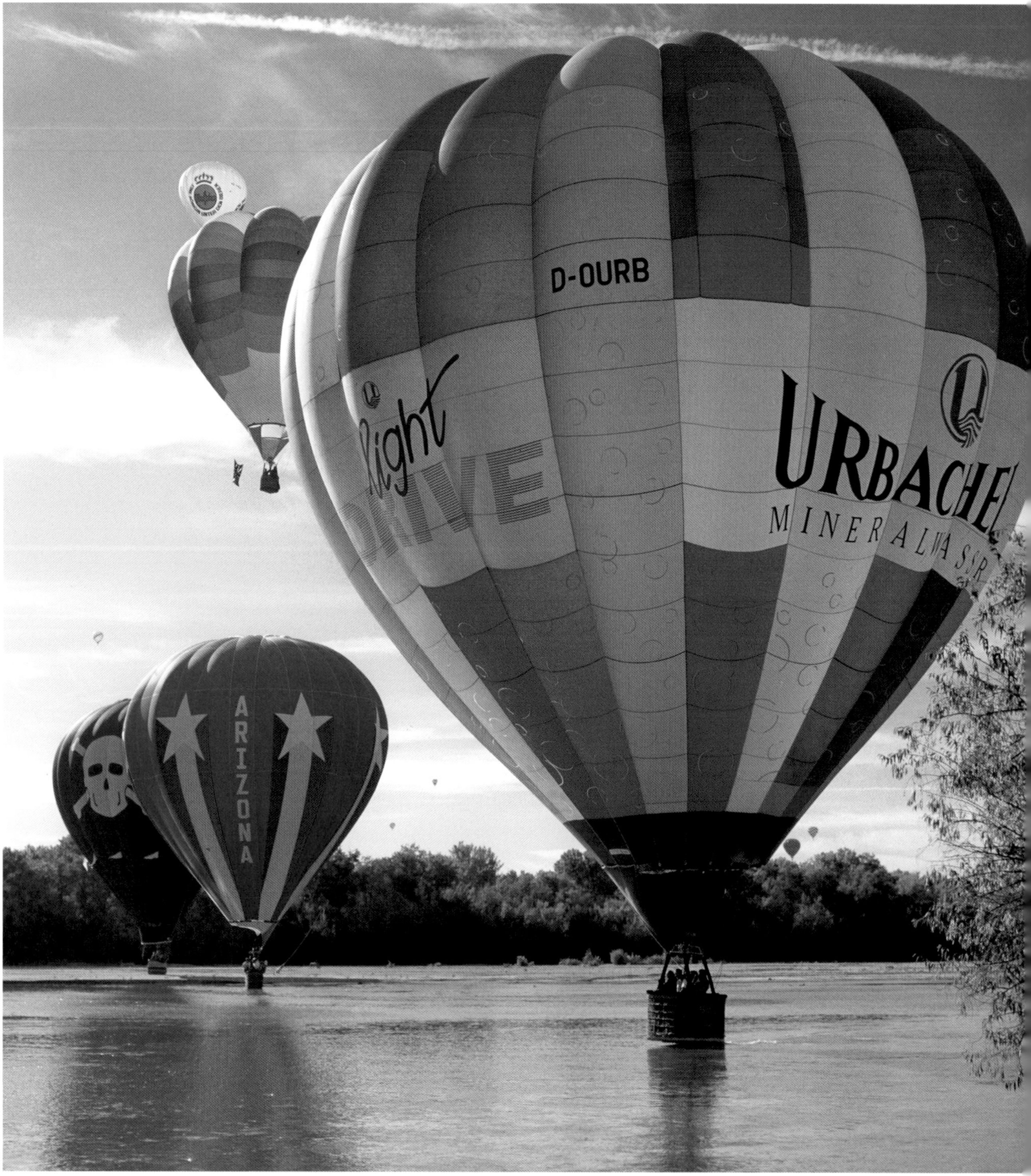

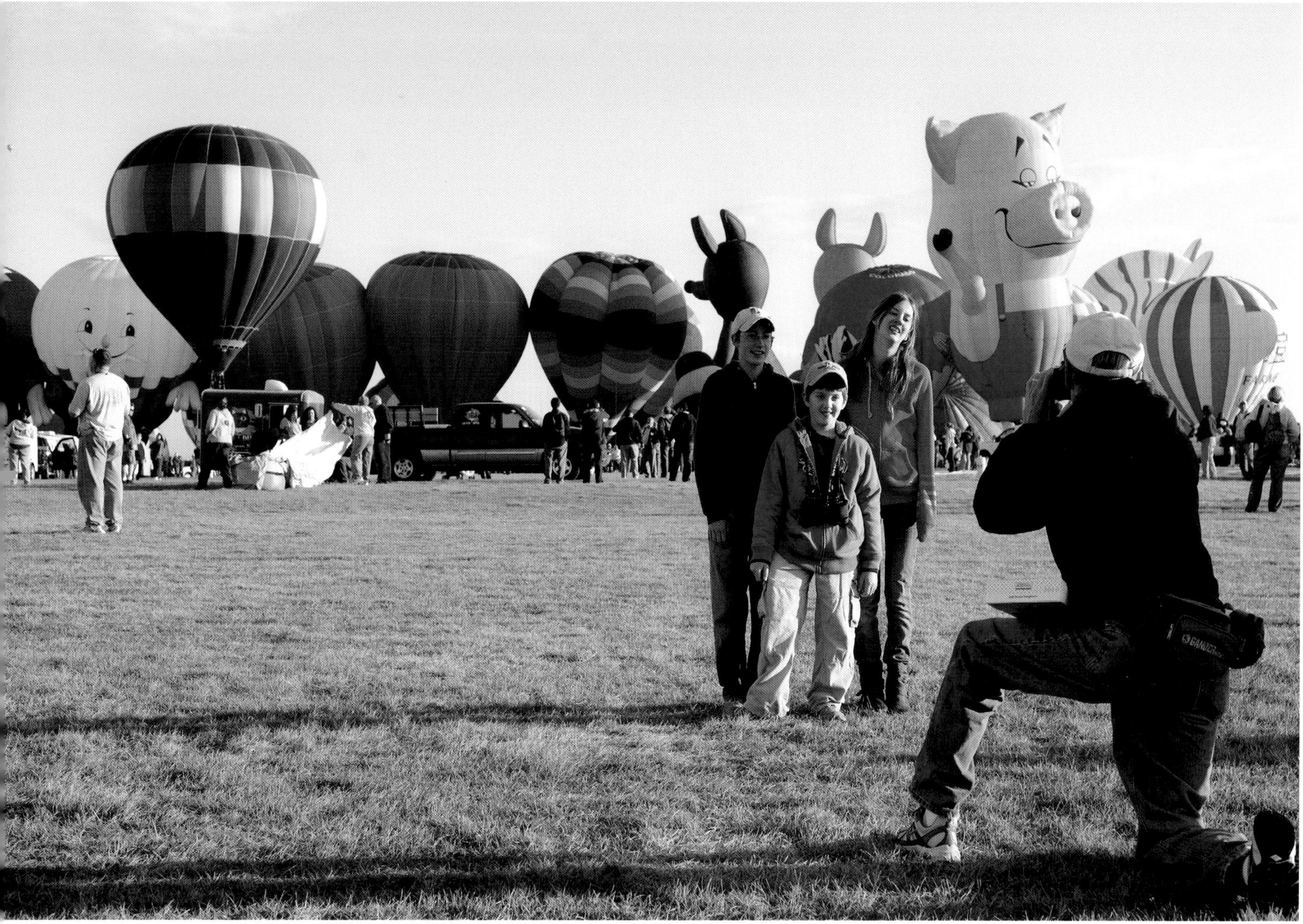

The Fiesta was sponsored by Kodak from 1992 until 2002, and during that time was called the Kodak Albuquerque International Balloon Fiesta.

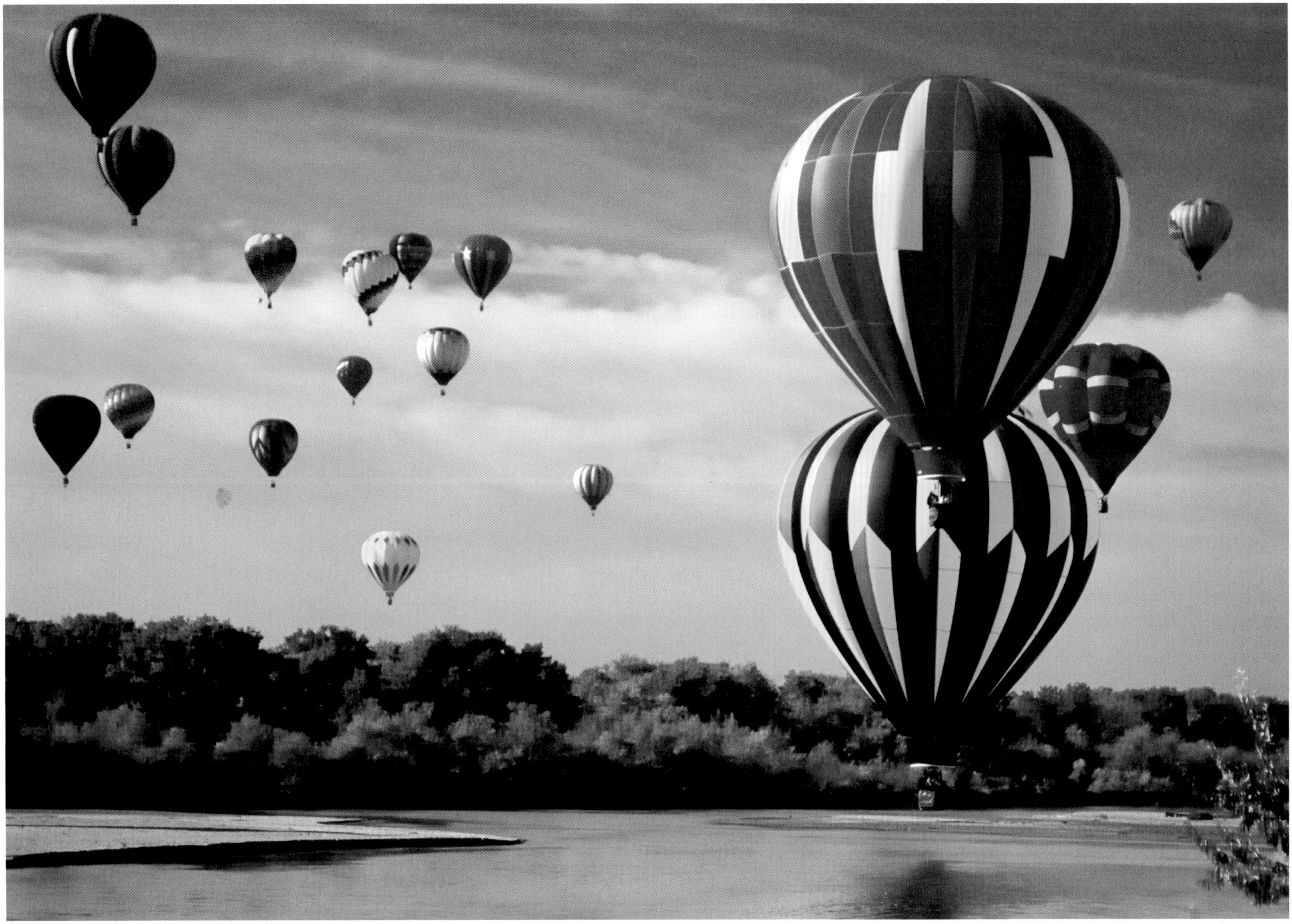

A good day of flying.

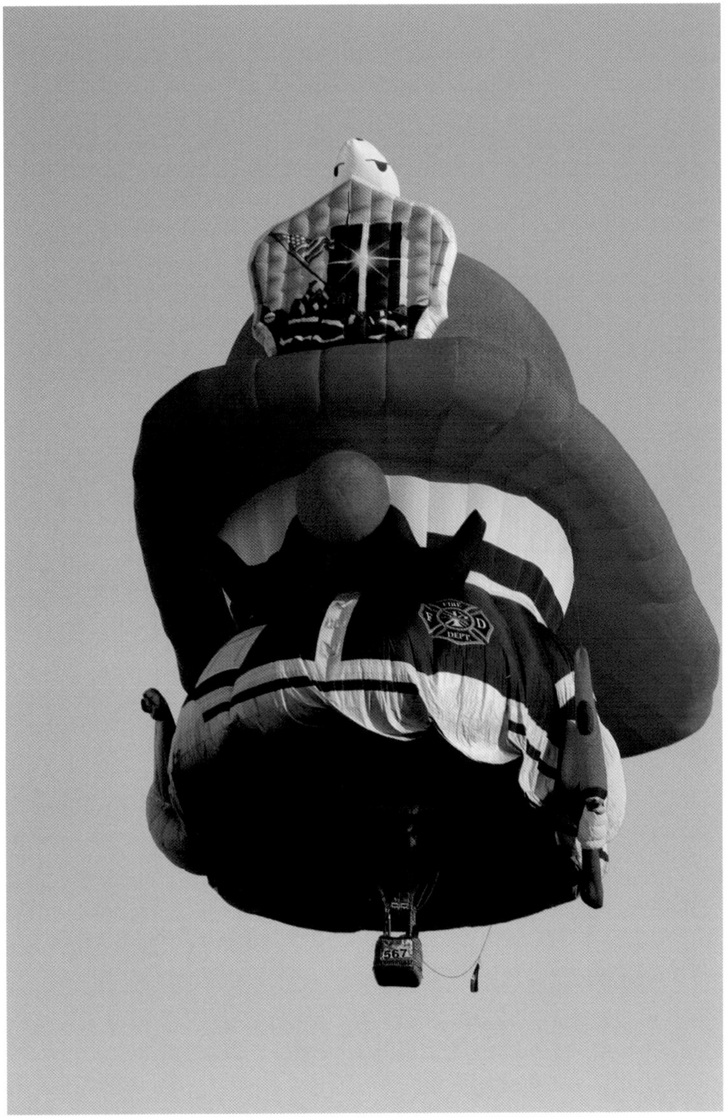

"Little Fireman" from Glens Falls, New York, honors the rescue personnel of September 11.

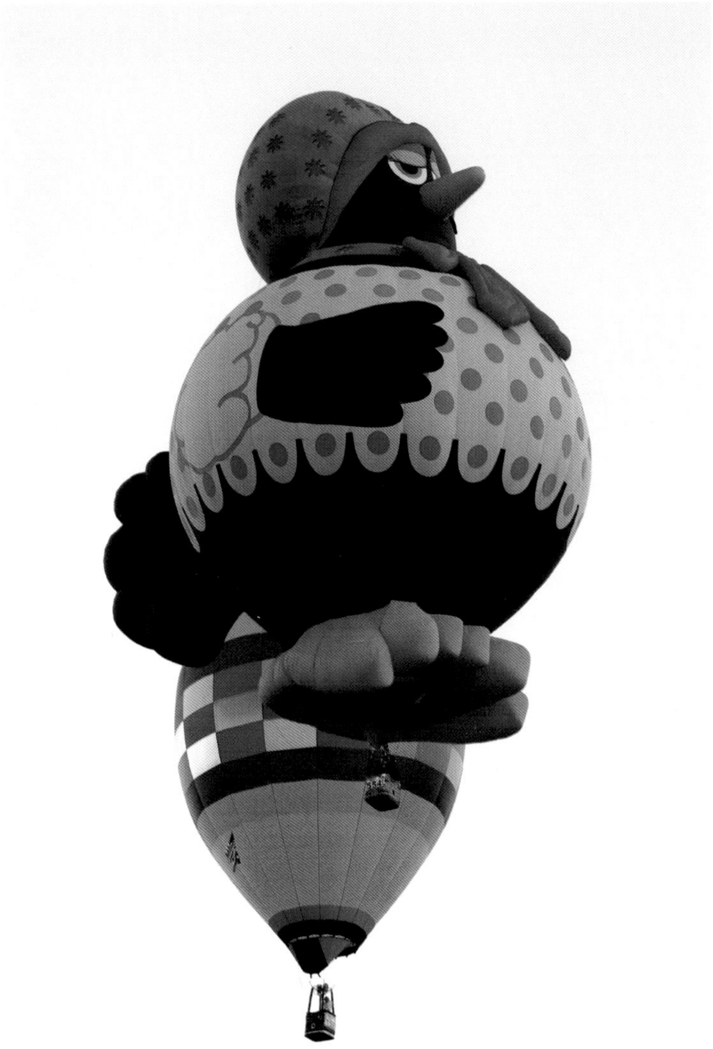

"Farm Chicken" finds some time for flying.

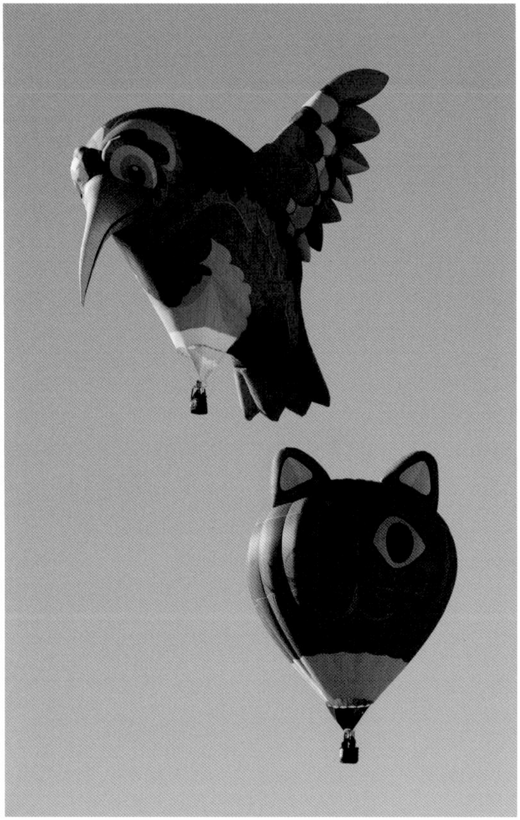

"Hummingbird" keeps its distance from "Cutie Dink" of Corrales, New Mexico.

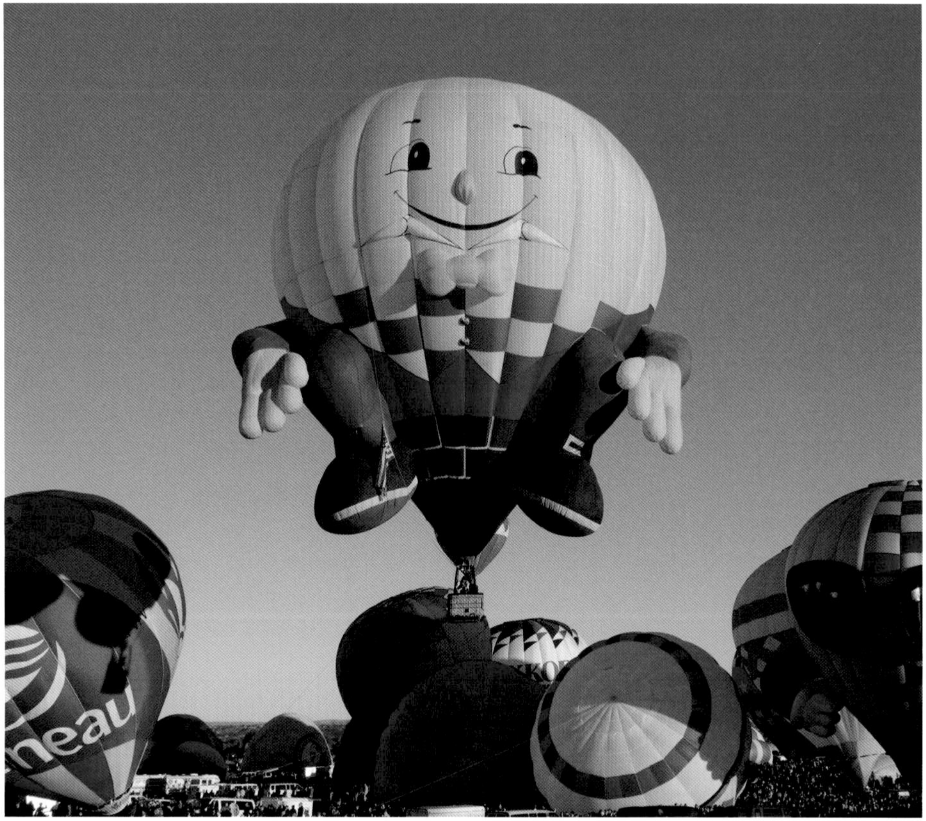

"Humpty Dumpty" of Kentucky doesn't worry about having great falls.

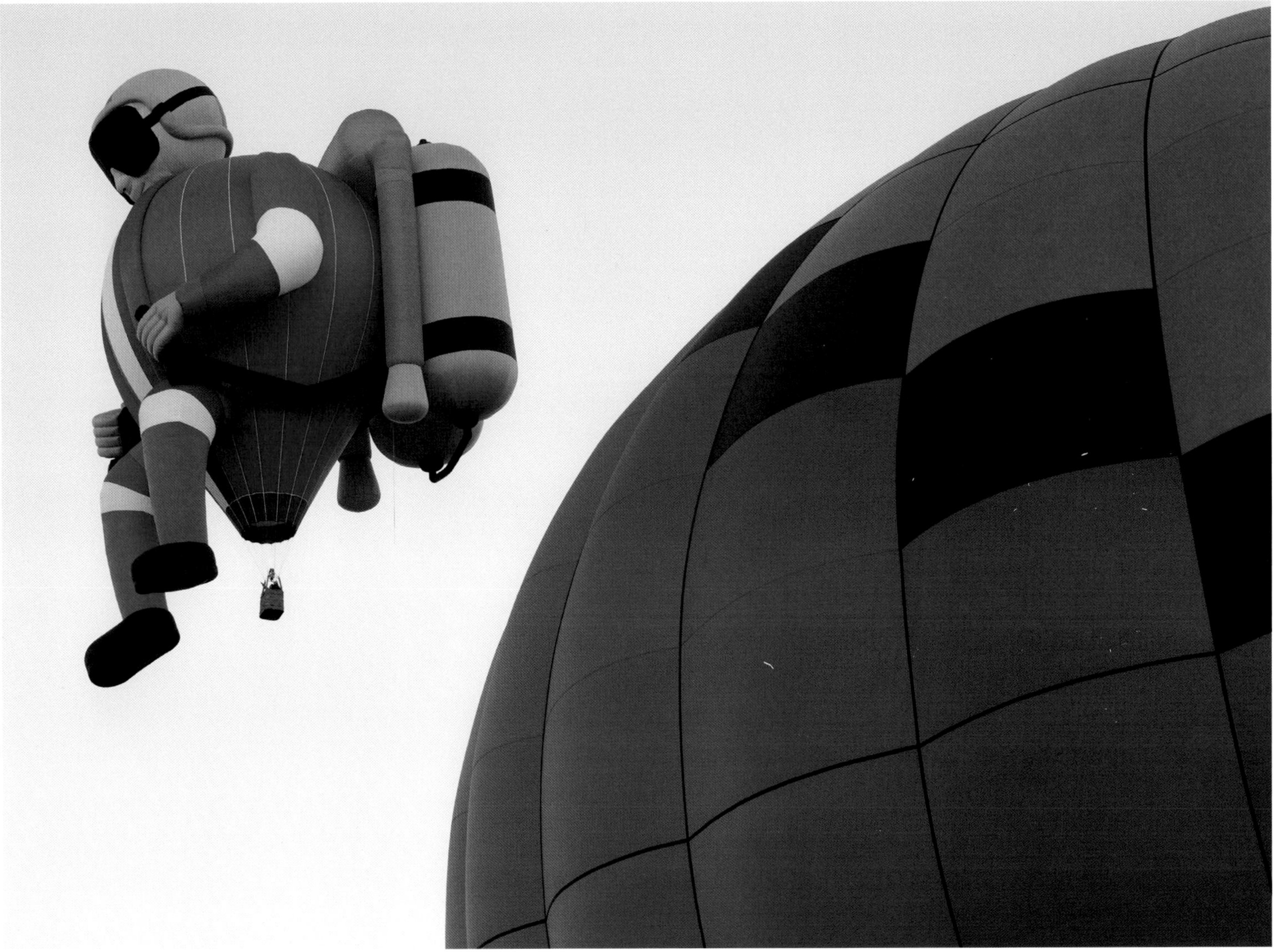

Despite his getup, "Jet Pilot" is mostly hot air.

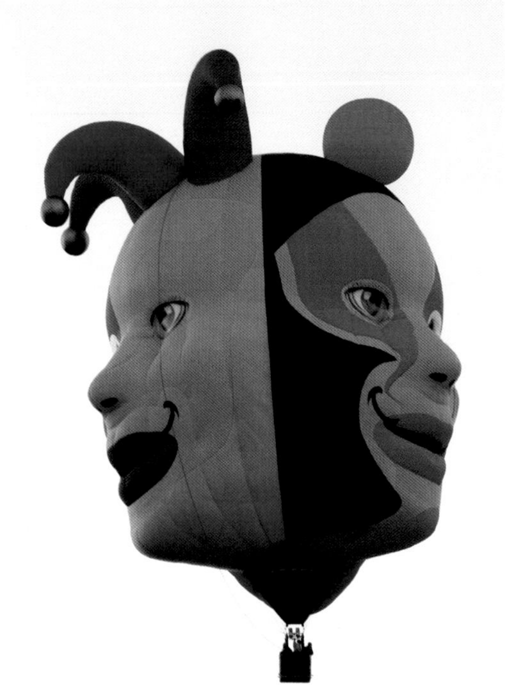

With a third side out of view, no one can say "Triple Clown" is two-faced.

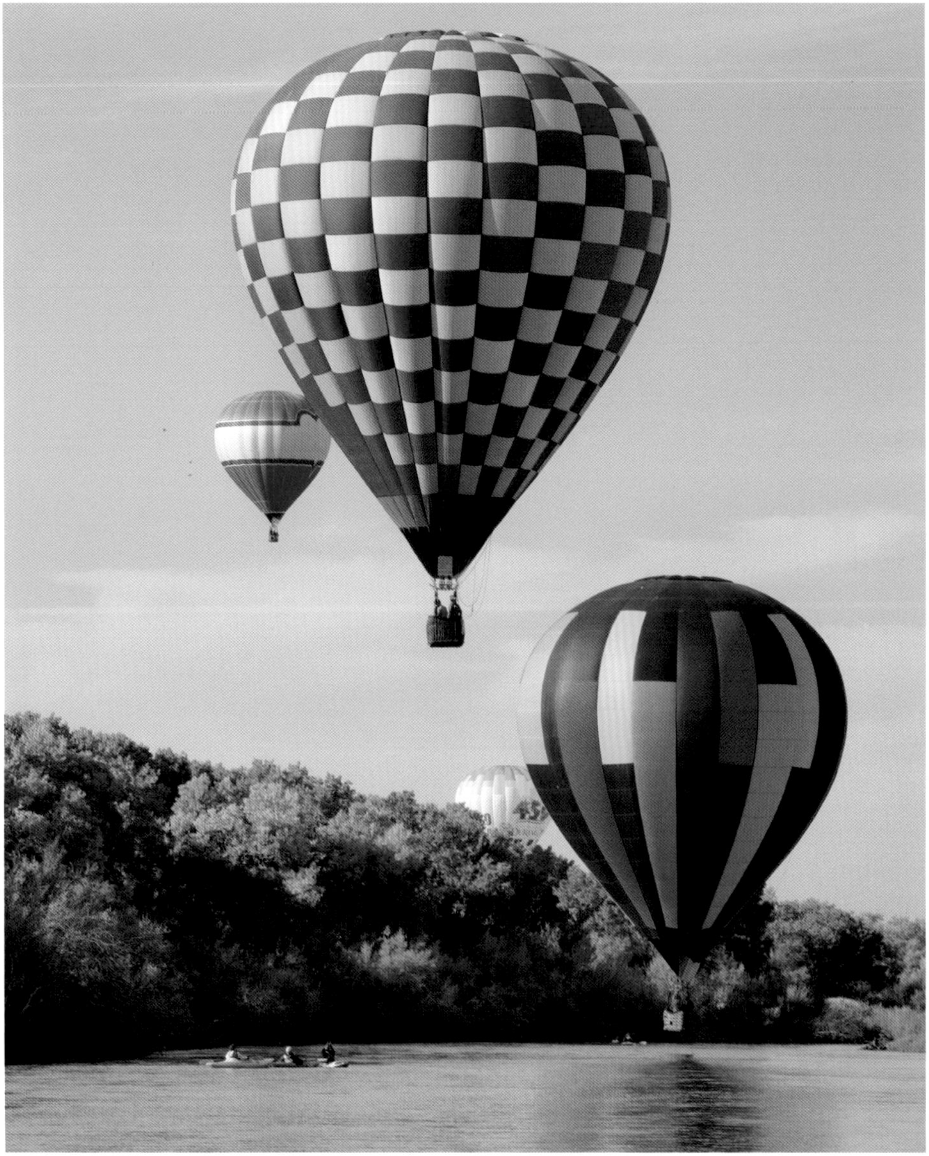

Kayakers greet balloonists on the Río Grande.

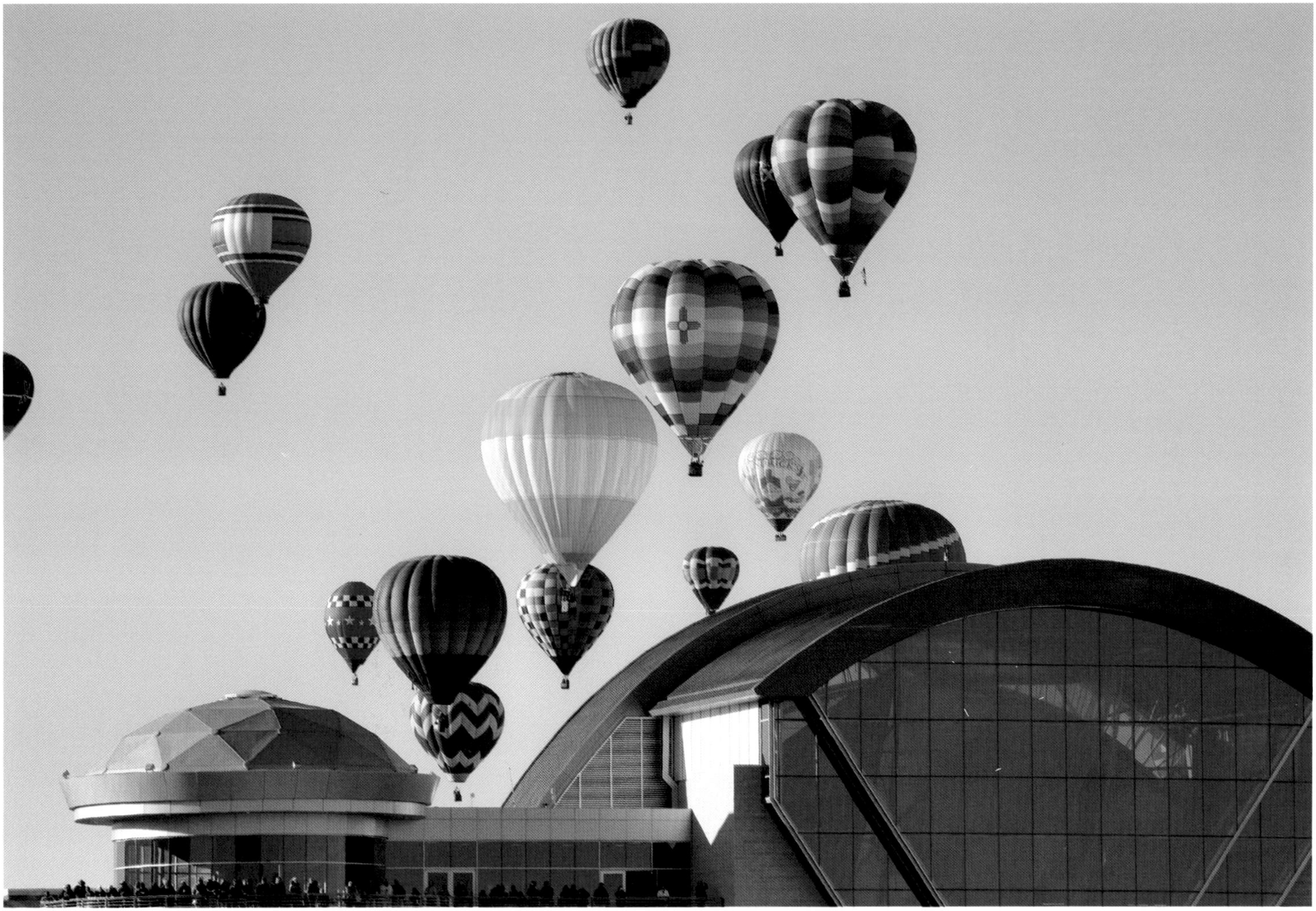

Spectators enjoy Fiesta from the Anderson-Abruzzo International Balloon Museum balcony.

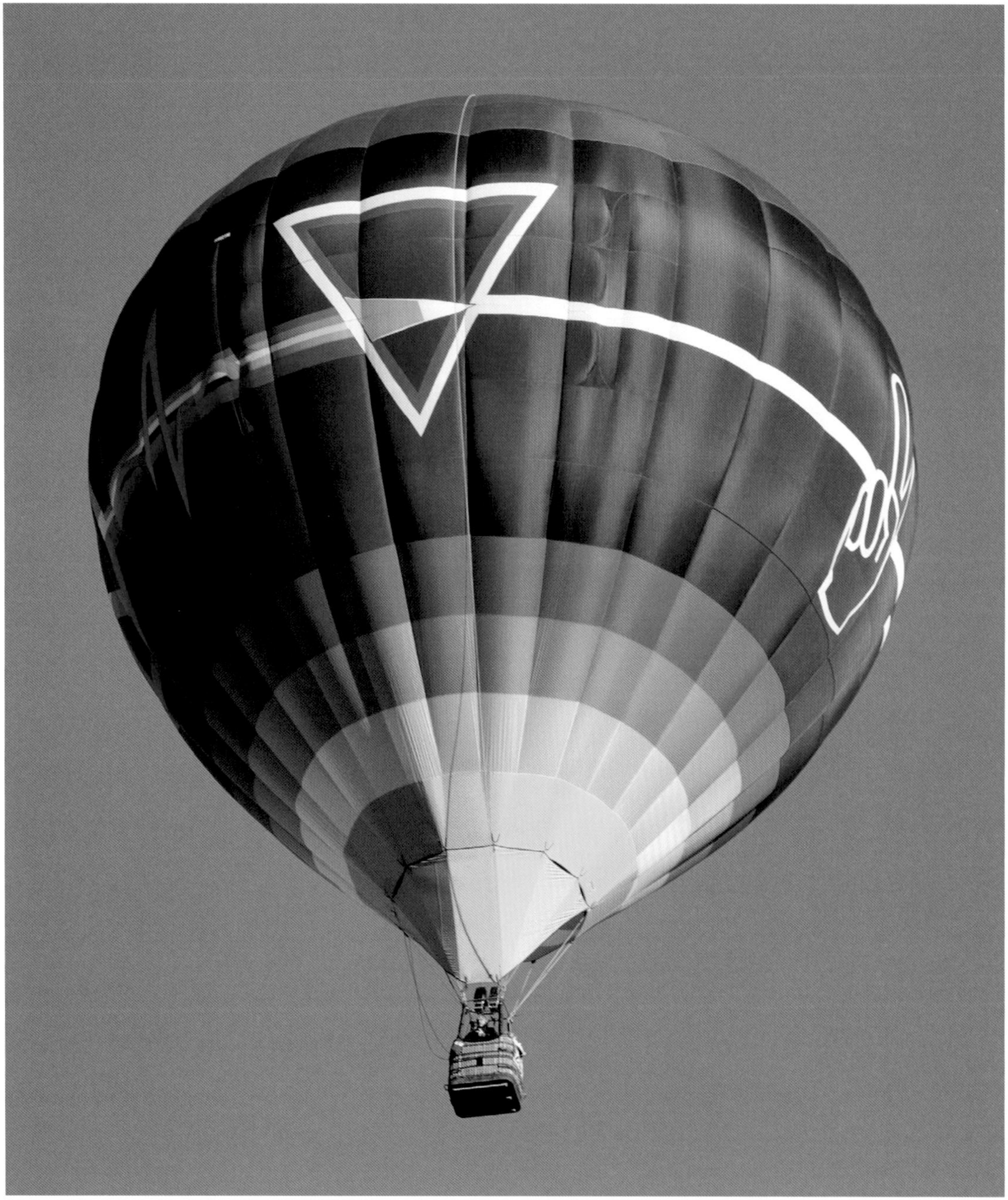

A Pink Floyd-inspired balloon shoots for the dark side of the moon.

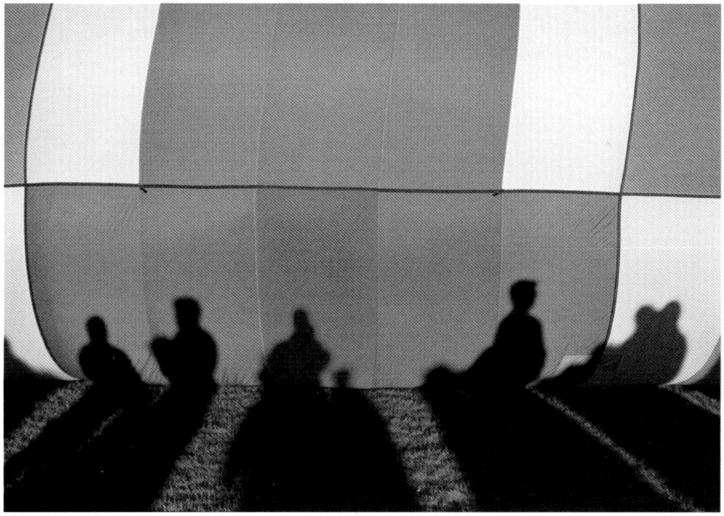

Shadows and light play together.

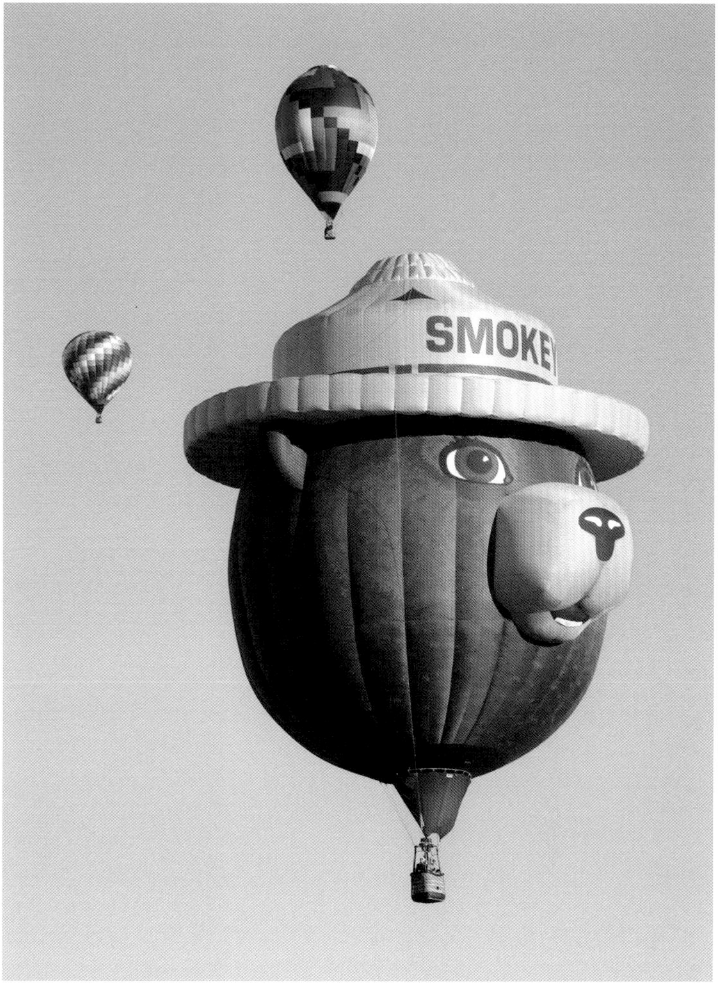

Crowd favorite "Smokey Bear" first flew in 2003 and is sponsored by the Albuquerque-based Friends of the Smokey Bear Balloon, Inc., a nonprofit group that assists agencies in preventing human-caused fires. A first balloon was destroyed in 2004 after it hit a radio tower during Fiesta; a replacement was made nine months later in time for the 2005 Fiesta.

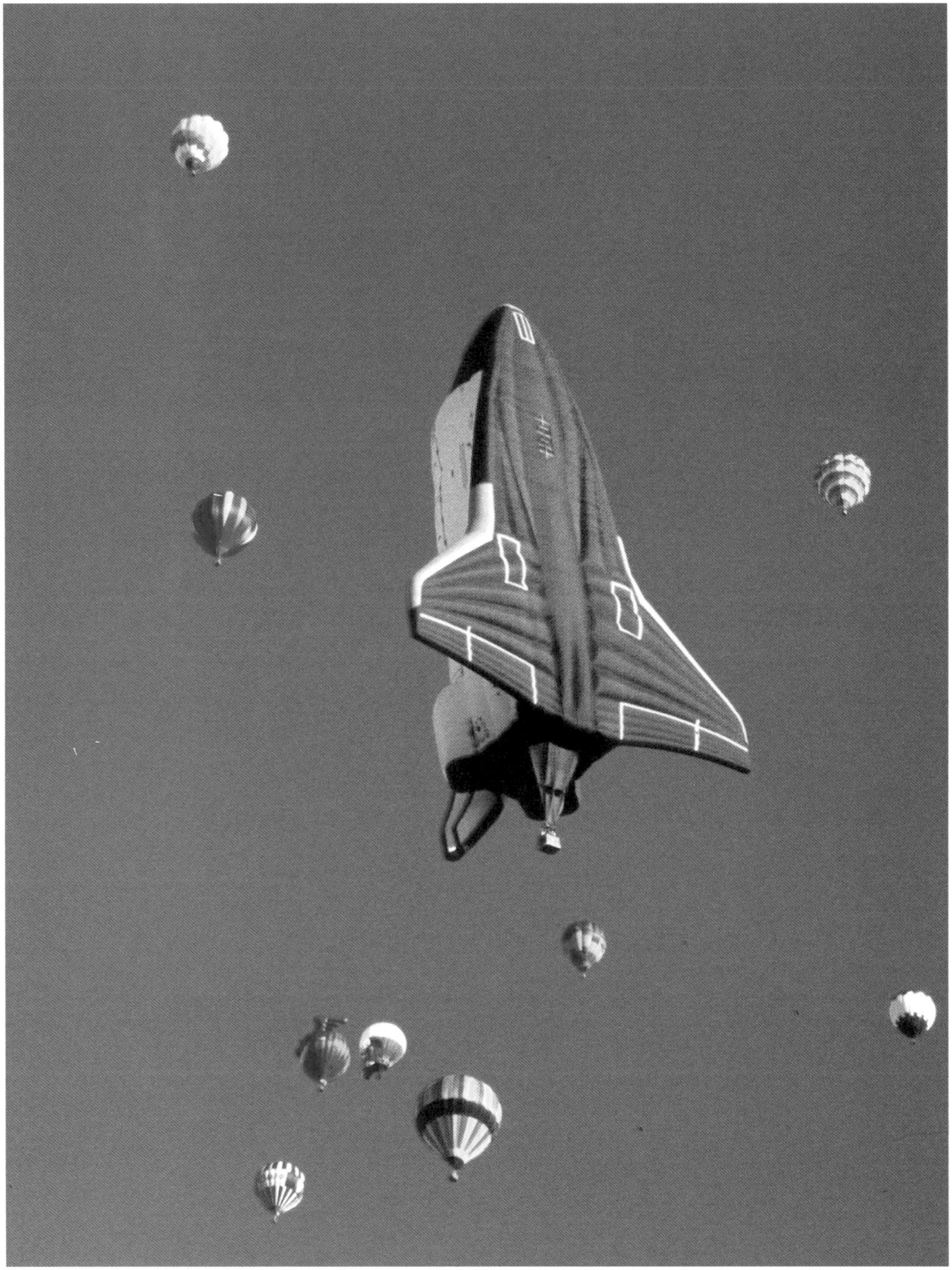

"Patriot" stands 190 feet tall and is forty percent larger than real space shuttles. It is operated by Socorro, New Mexico-based Flying Chili Peppers Balloon Company, LLC.

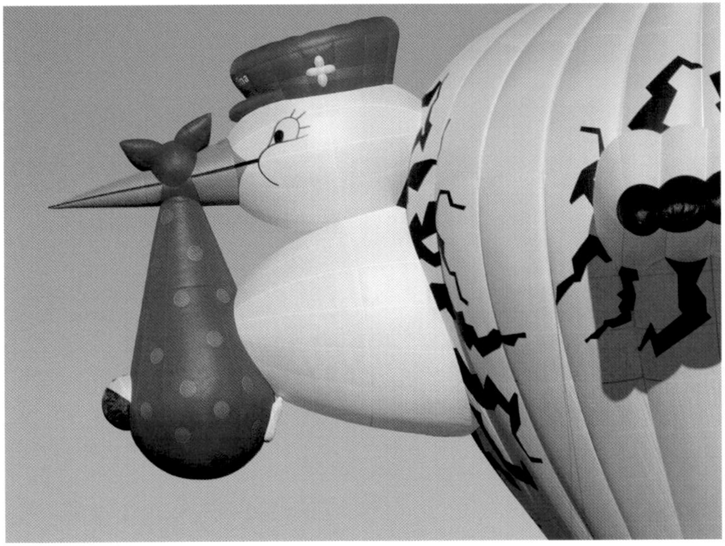

"The Stork" is a big bundle of joy owned by a Corrales, New Mexico, obstetrician.

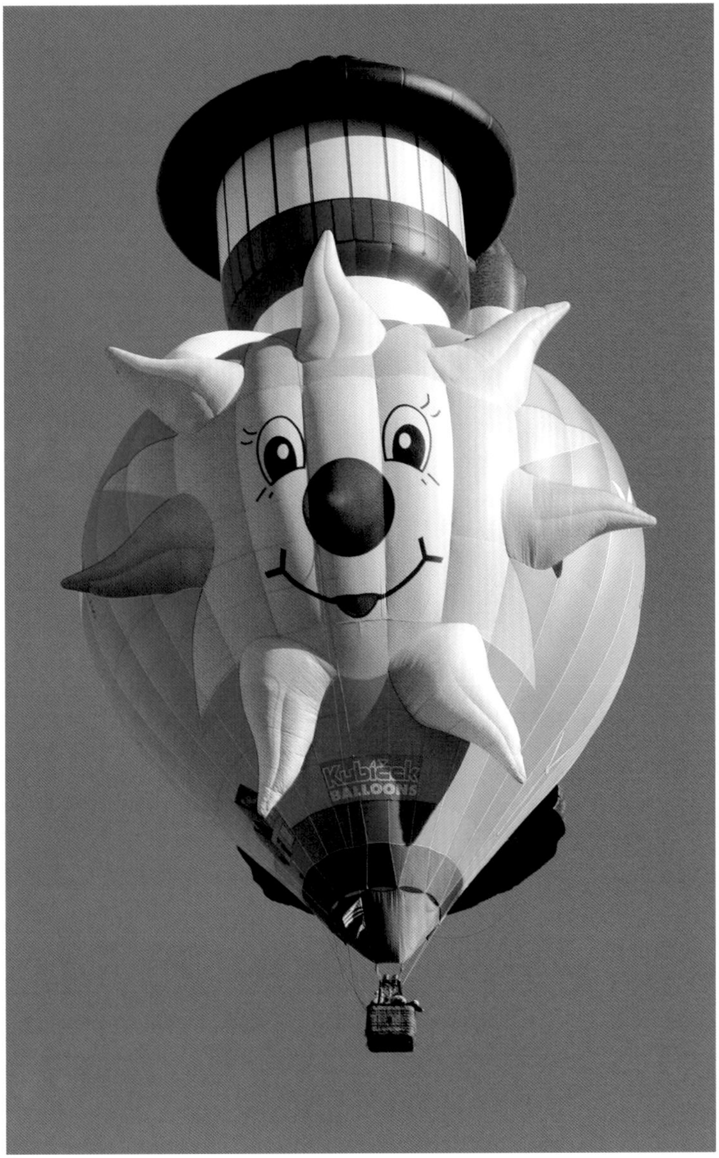

France's "Lady Sun" adds to an already bright New Mexico sky.

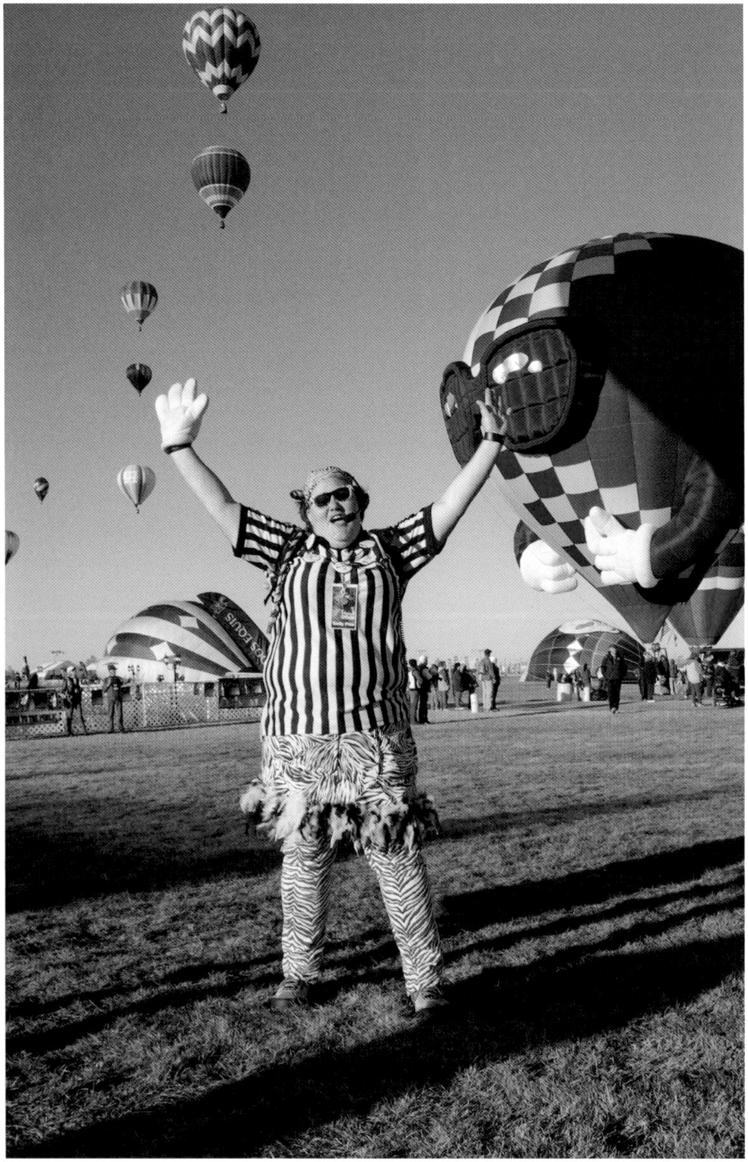

Although the uniform always incorporates stripes, zebras enjoy personalizing their attire. The bold, unique outfits help pilots quickly identify them.

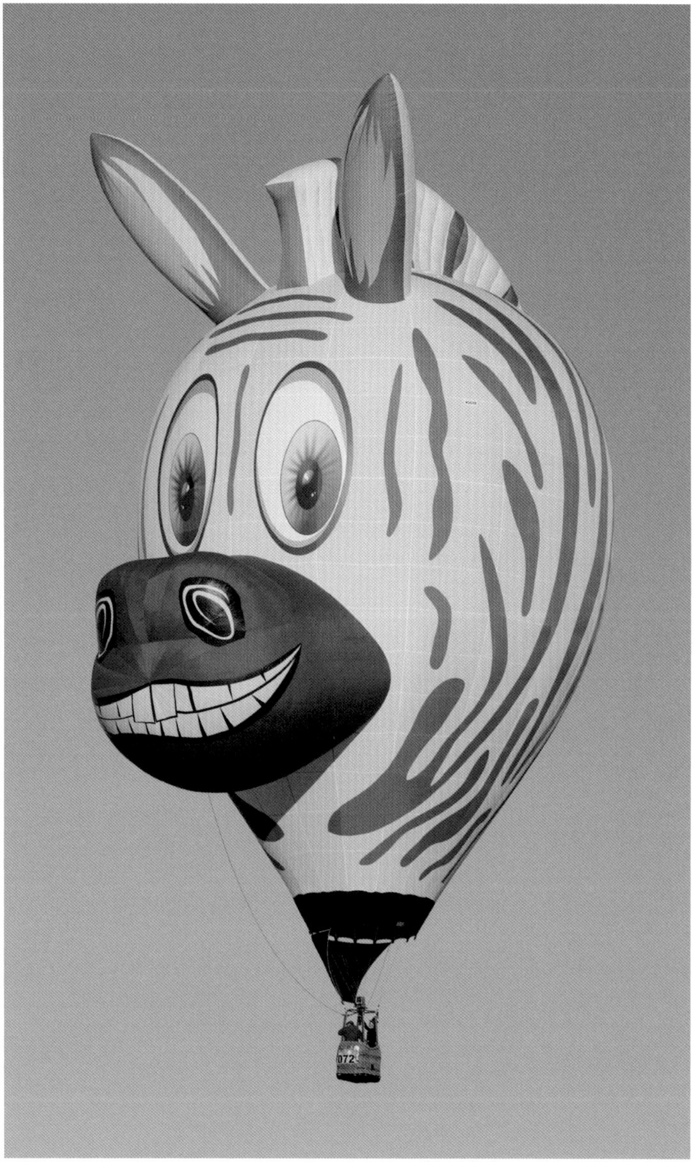

"Mister Z" of Albuquerque is a tribute to the zebras who coordinate safe launches at Fiesta.

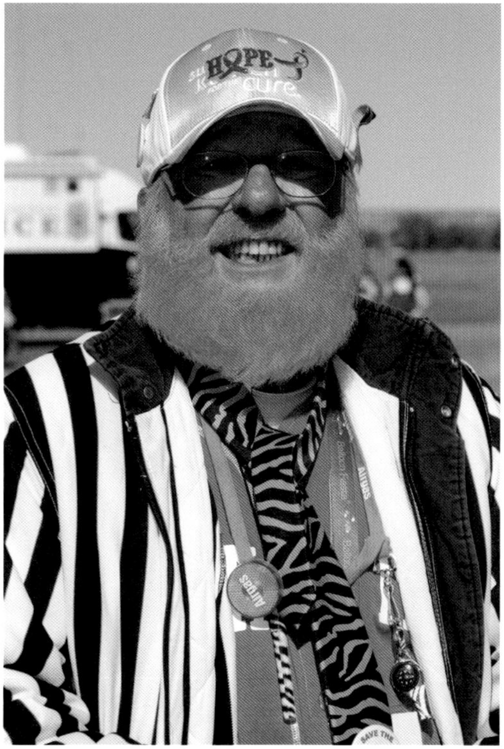

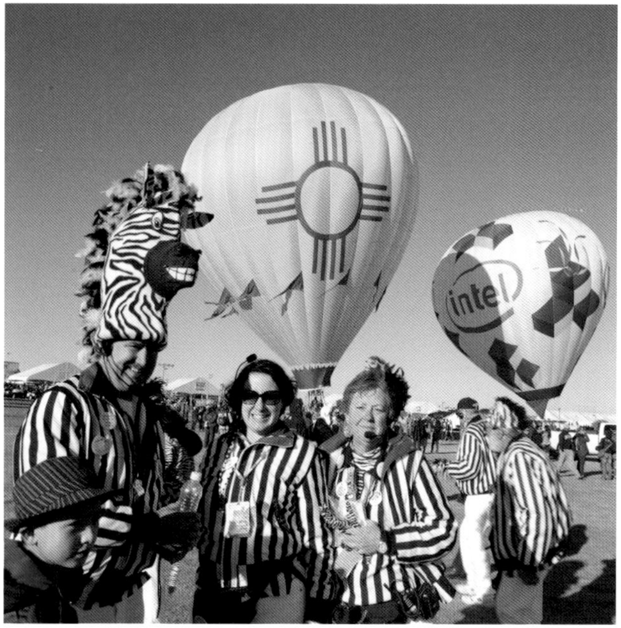

Ensuring that guests and balloon crews stay safe while having a great time, zebras have become the face of Balloon Fiesta.

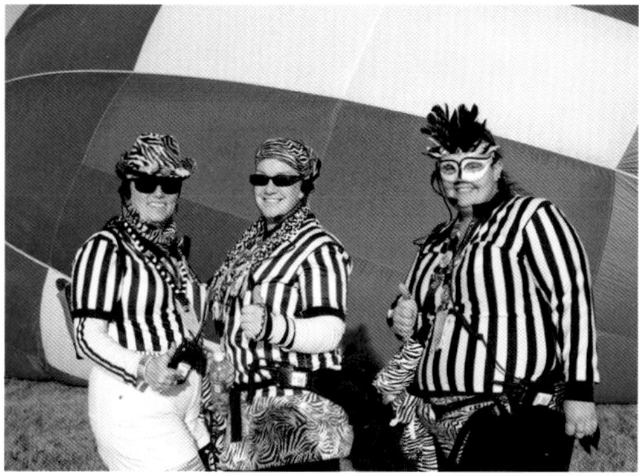

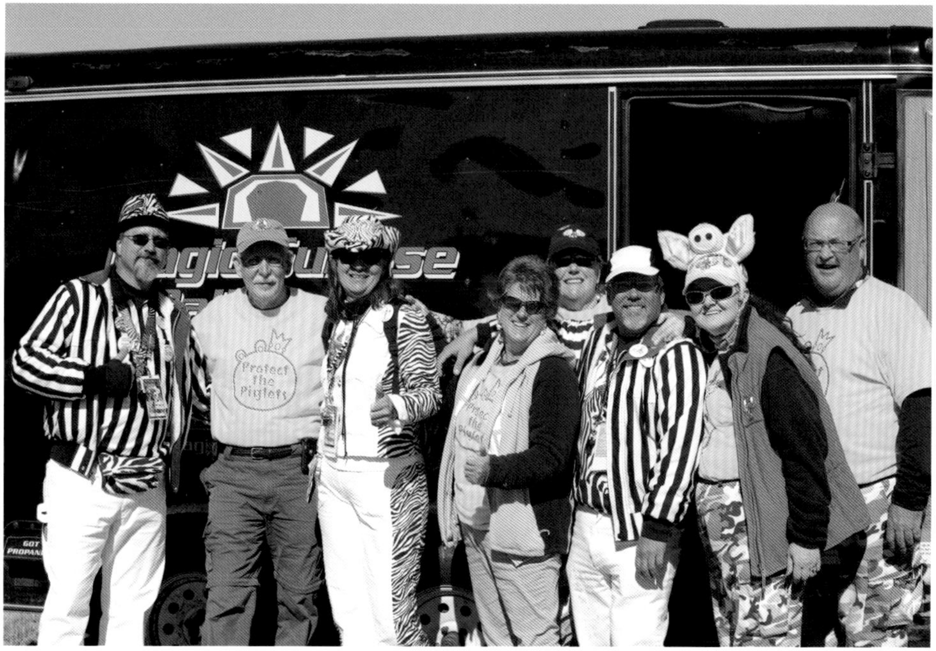

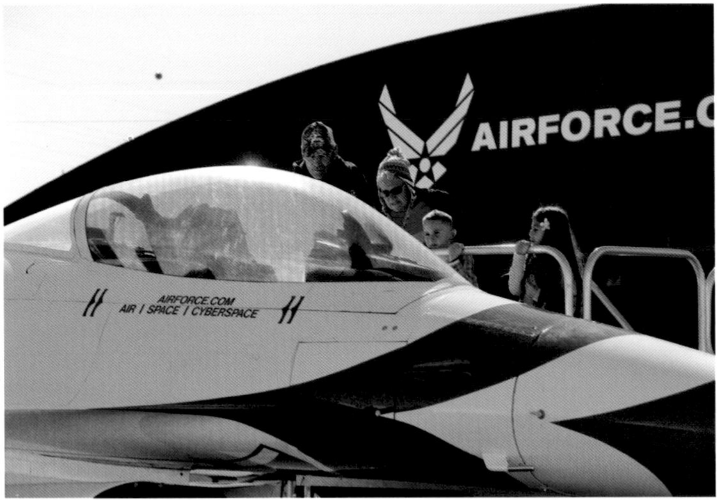

Visitors view an F-16 display at the U.S. Air Force booth on Main Street.

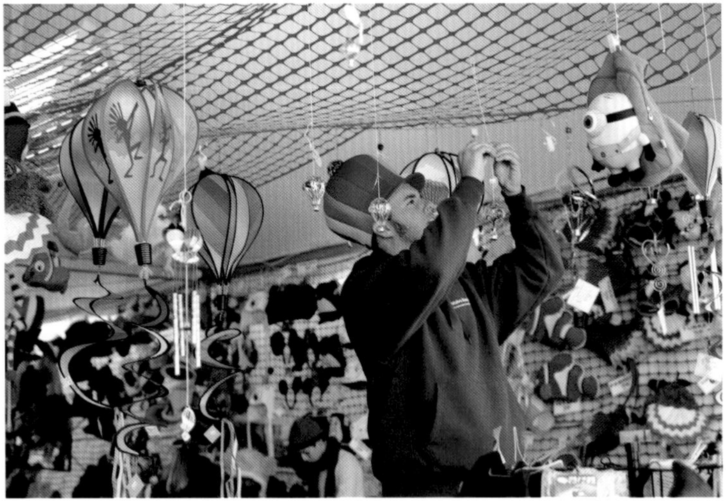

All things balloons may be purchased at any number of booths and food stands along Main Street.

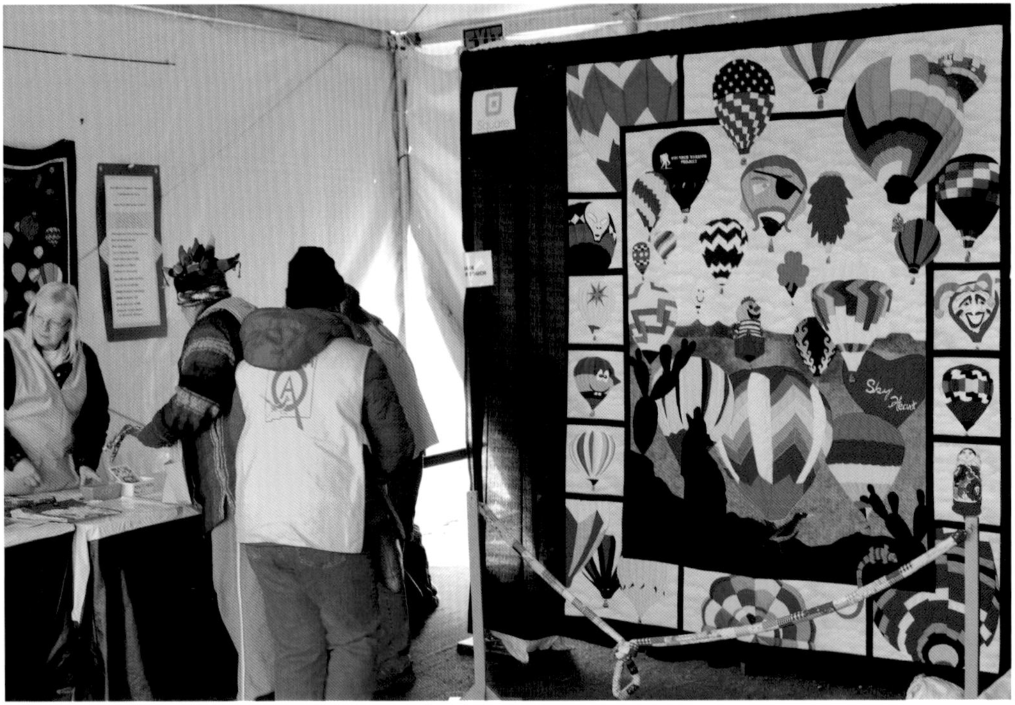

The Official Balloon Fiesta Quilt has become a Fiesta tradition. Proceeds from its raffling benefit the New Mexico Quilter's Association.

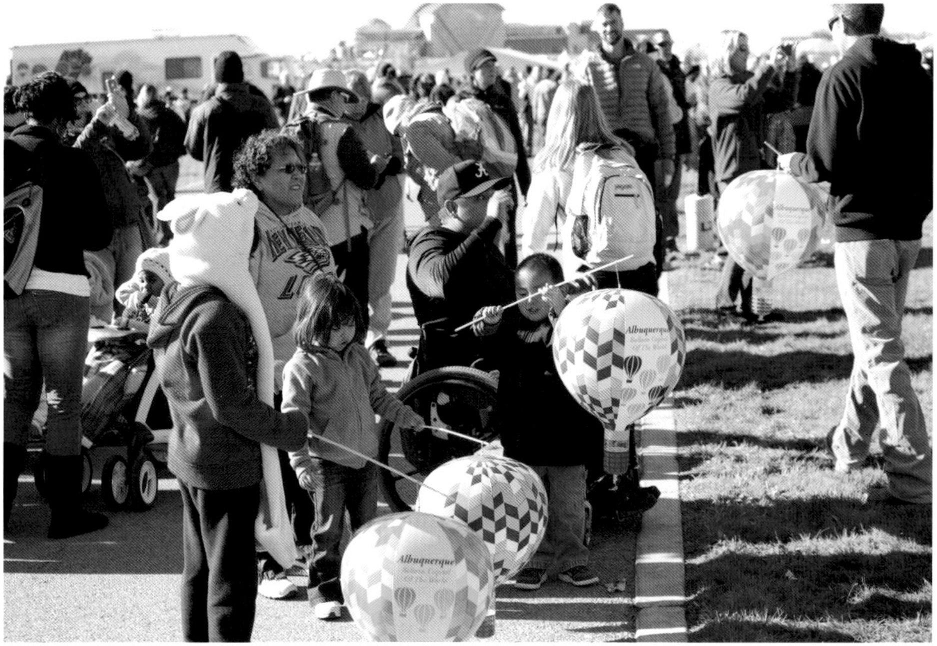

Kids enjoy balloon balloons, one of the many items for sale at Fiesta.

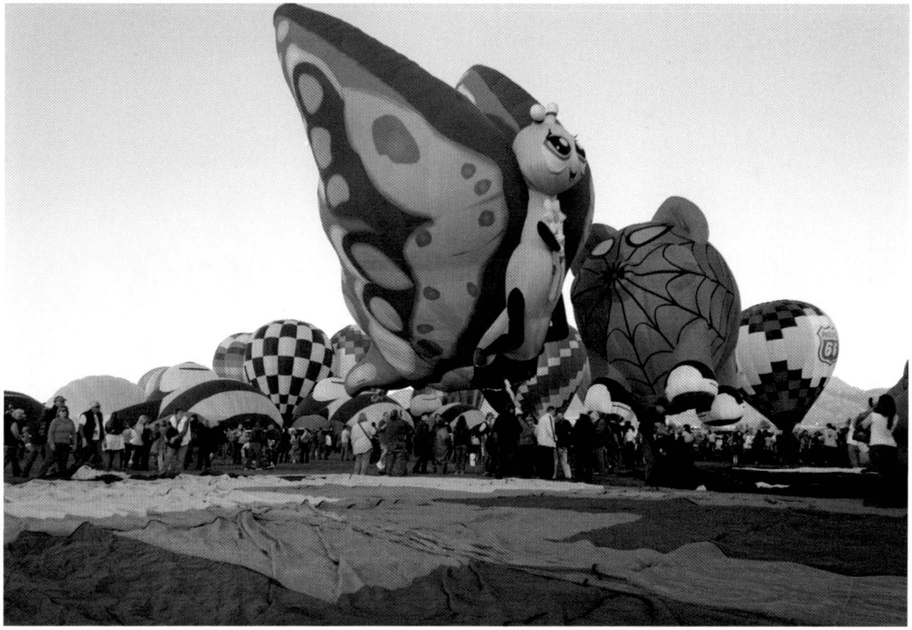

Albuquerque's "SpyderPig," a character from 2007's *The Simpsons Movie*, nuzzles against "Butterfly" from Arizona.

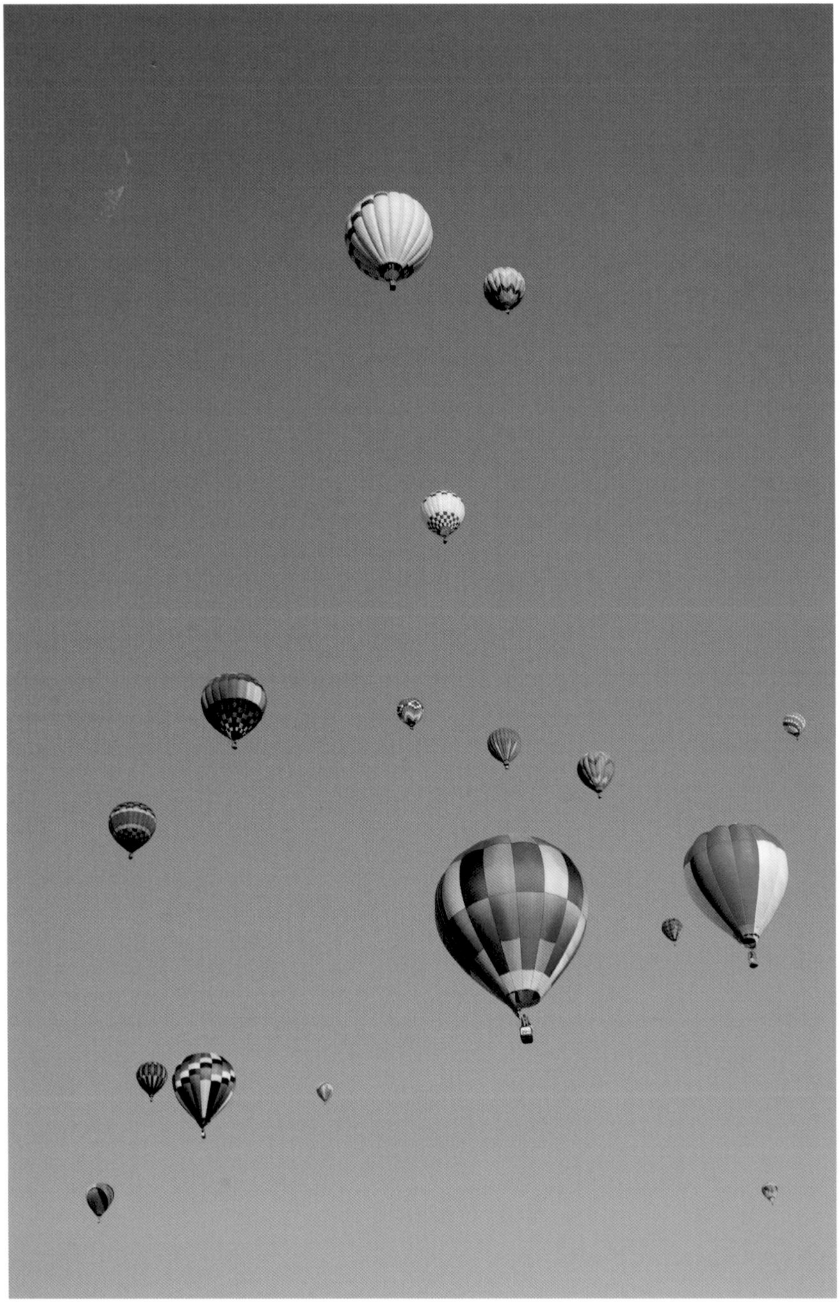
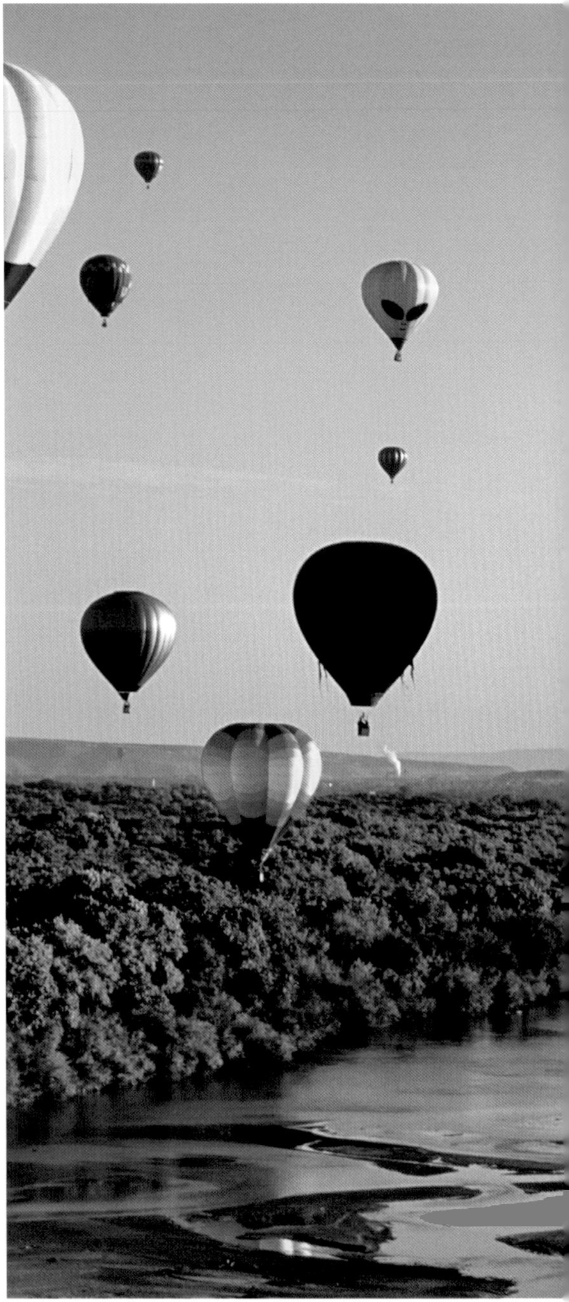

Balloons drift away from the field after a mass ascension.

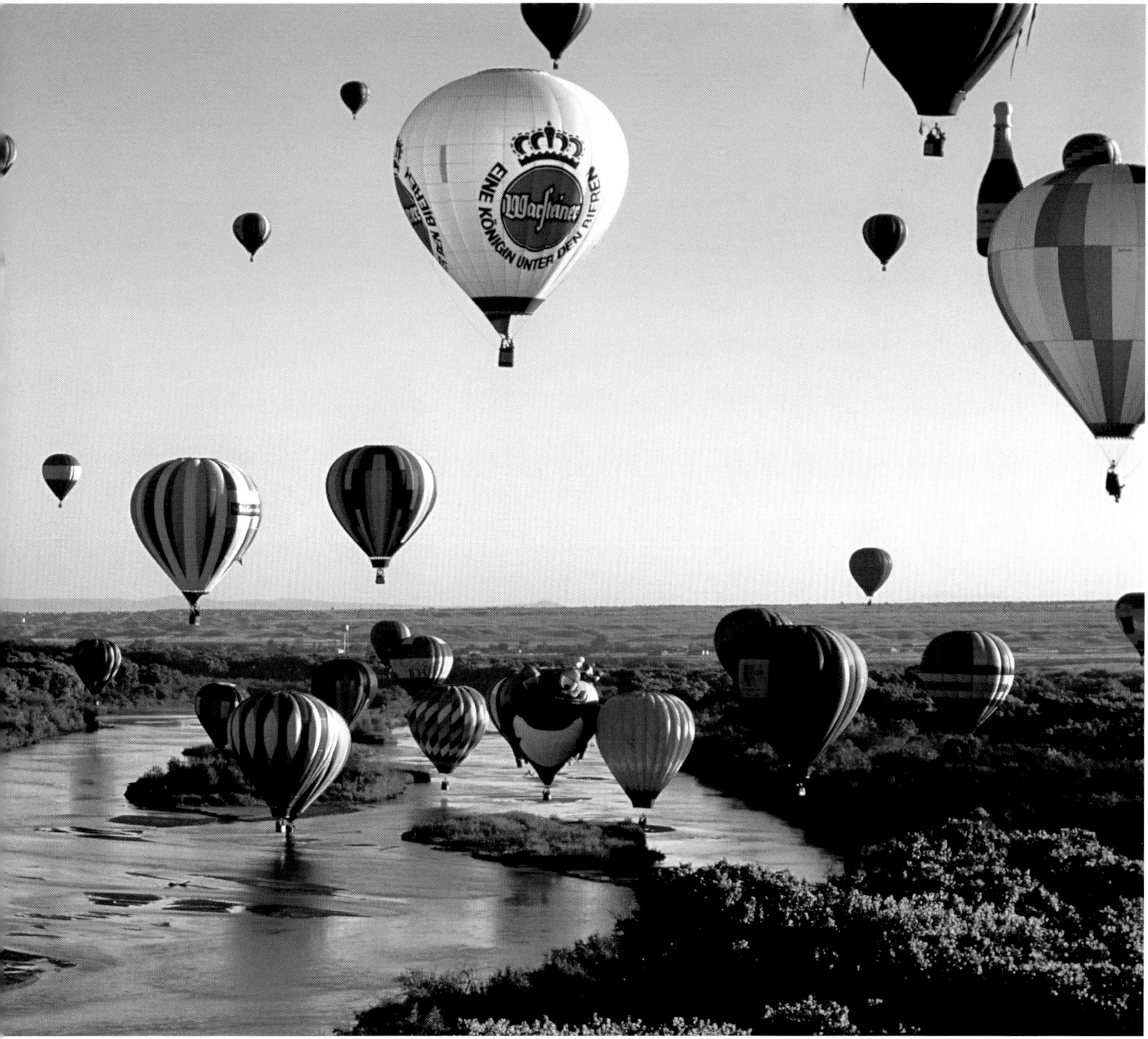

The nearby Río Grande is a favorite destination for pilots when winds permit.

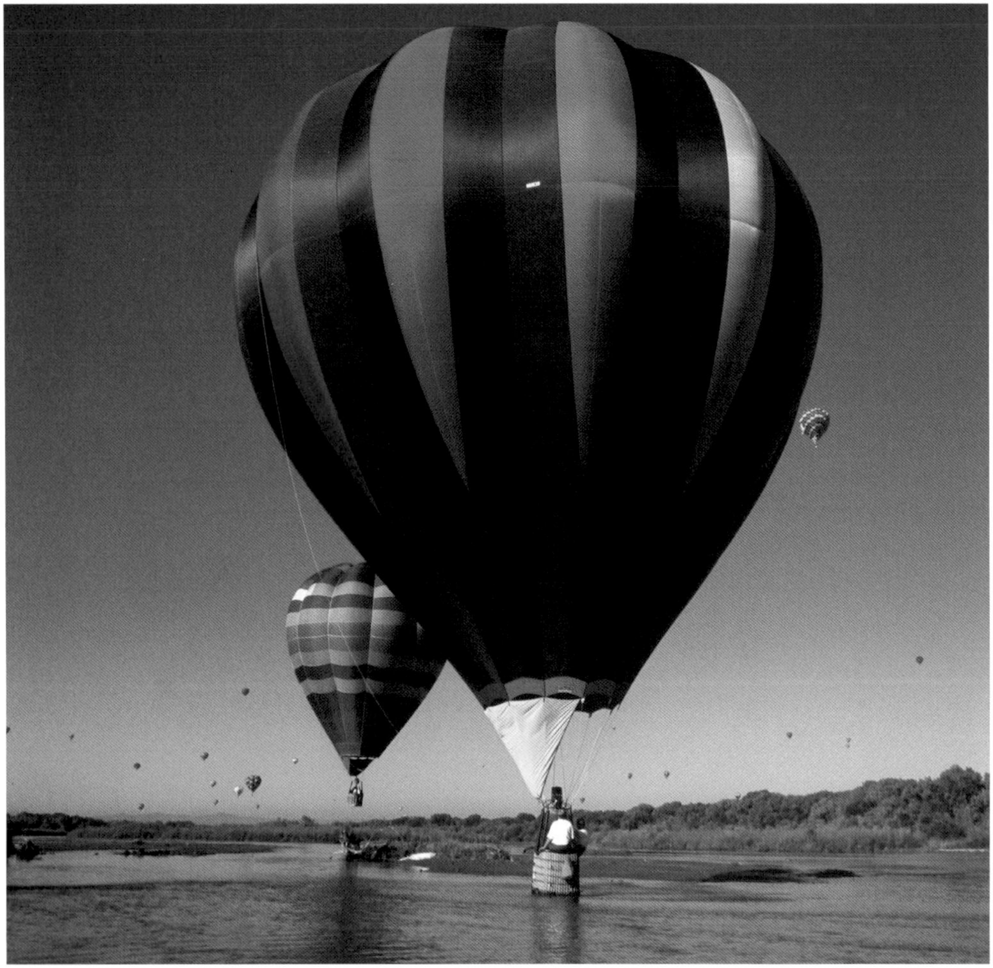

It takes a great deal of skill to touch down on water without swamping the wicker basket.

A lone balloon drifts across the face of the Sandía Mountains to the east of Albuquerque.

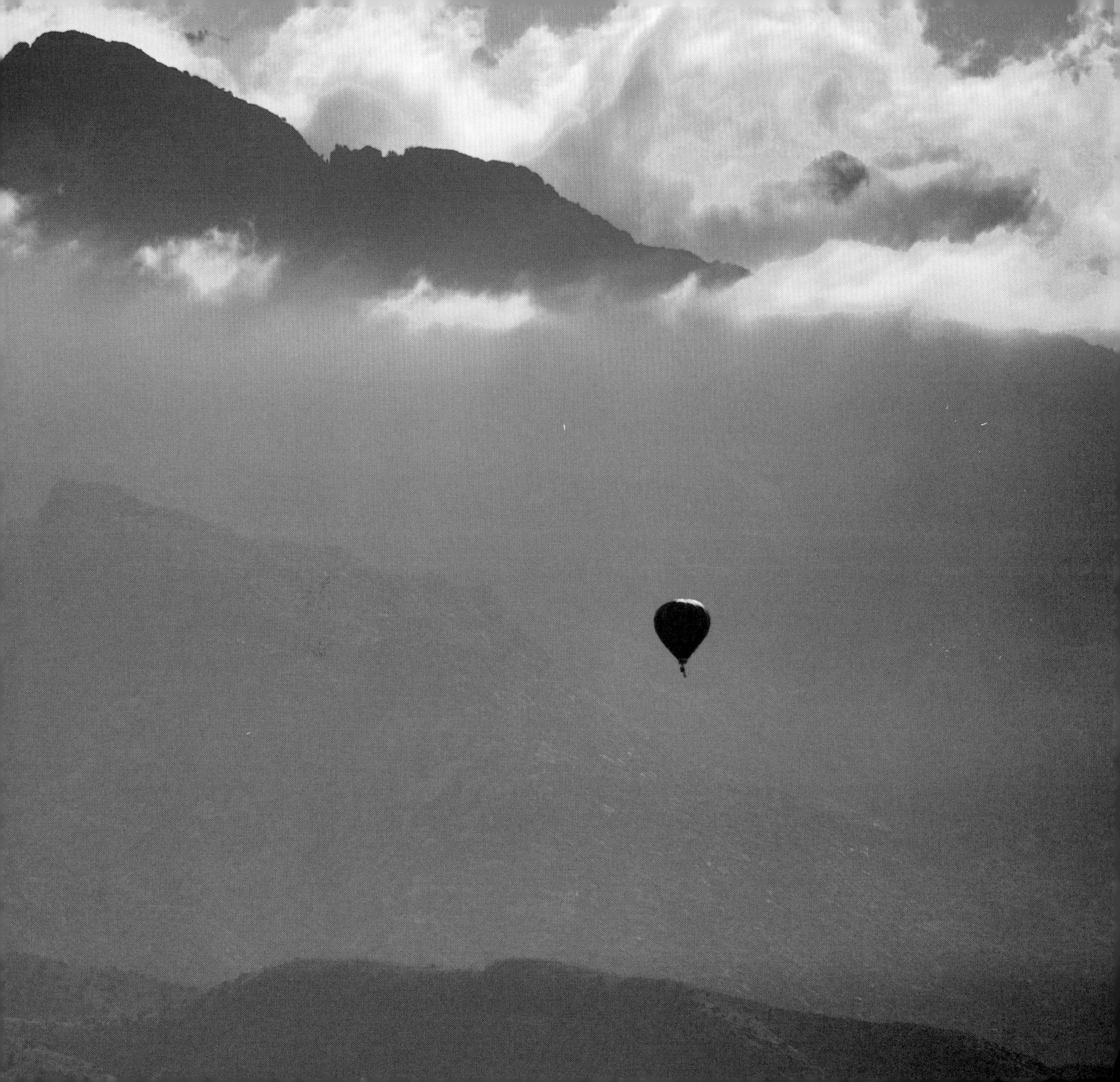

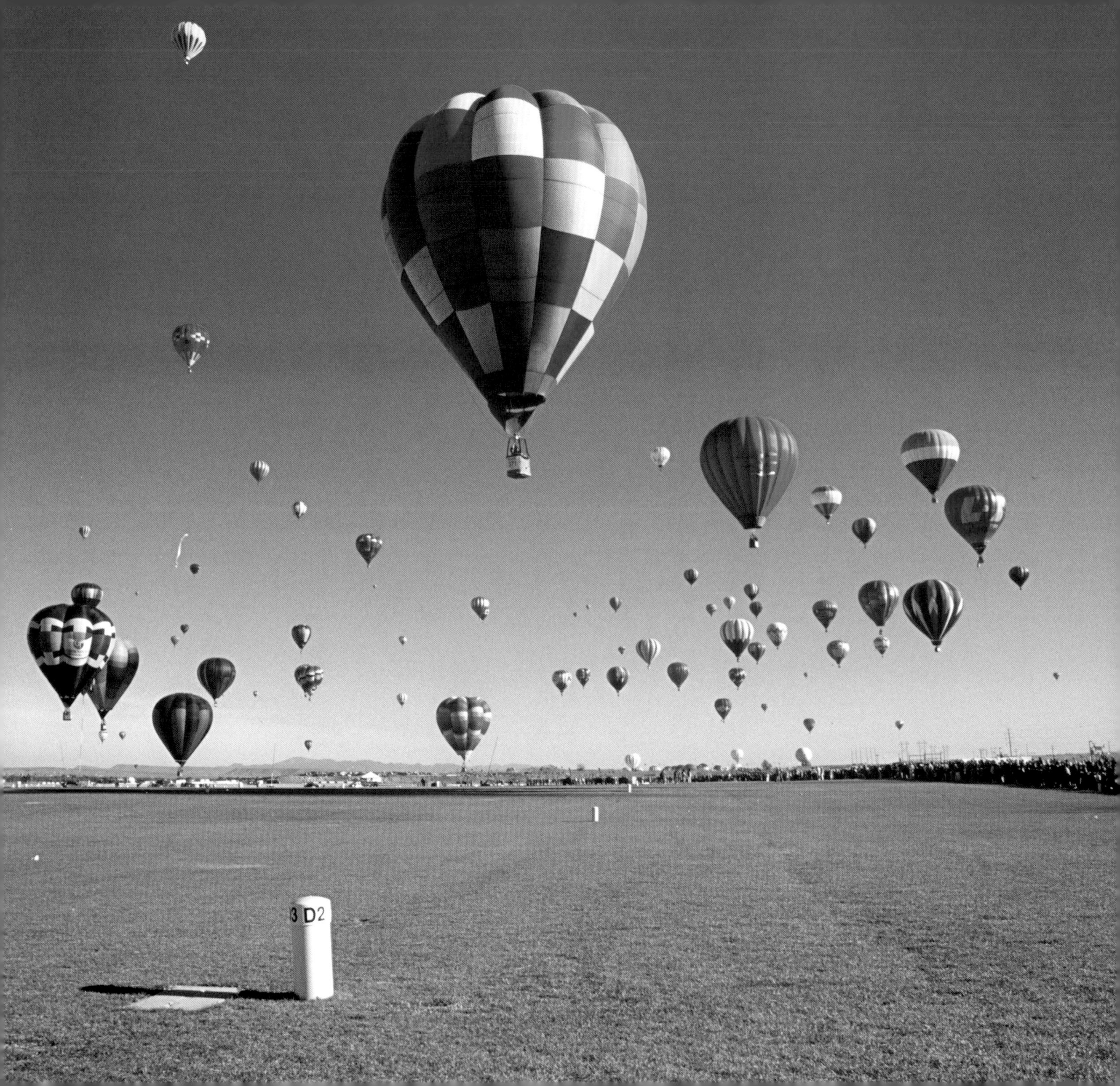
3 D2

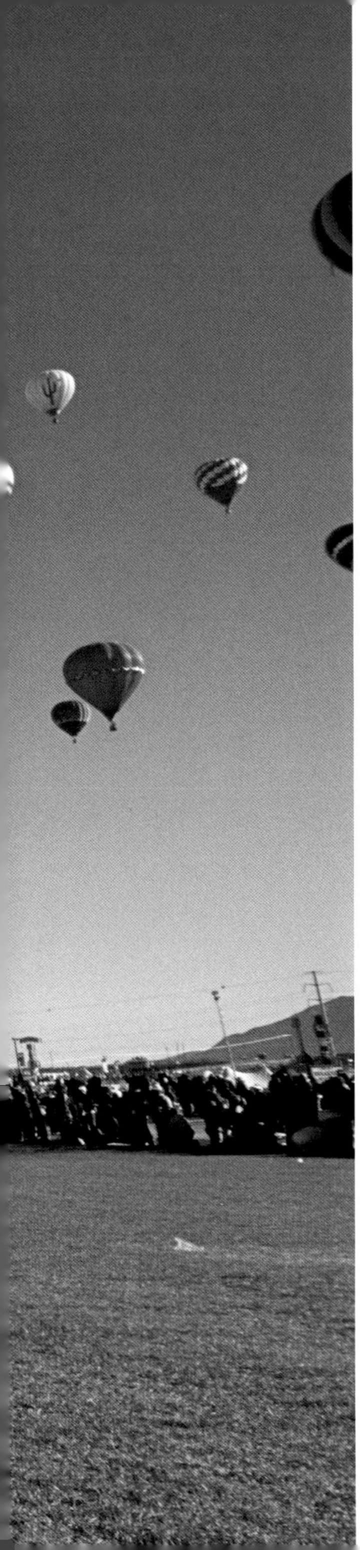

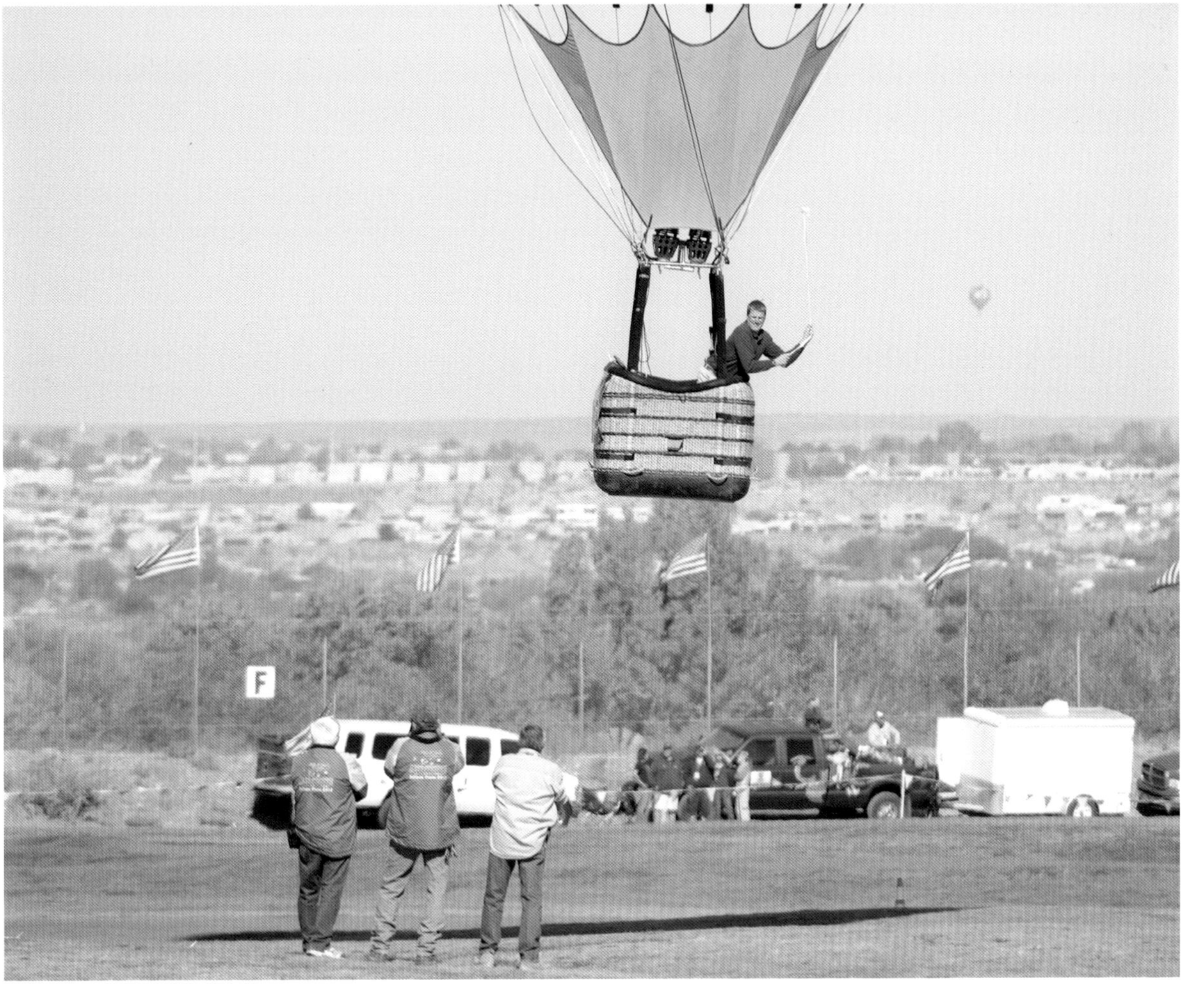

A pilot prepares to throw a bean bag at a ground target during a flying competition as judges look on.

A large part of Balloon Fiesta are the flying competitions. Pilots compete in such tasks as hitting targets on the field with bean bags and grabbing keys atop poles that start prize trucks. The field is cleared of spectators, and balloons launch off-site and fly toward the park on contest days.

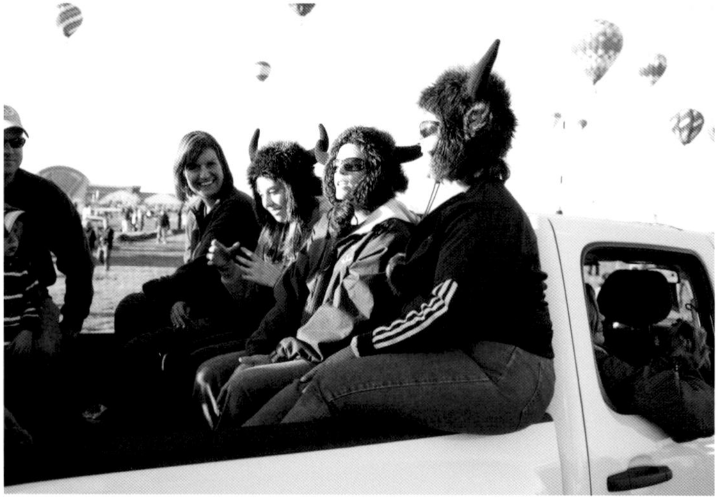

Chase-crew members head out in support of their balloon. Chase crews help pilots after they land by holding down the balloon, deflating, and packing it away. Spectators may sign up to join chase crews if they'd like to experience ballooning first hand.

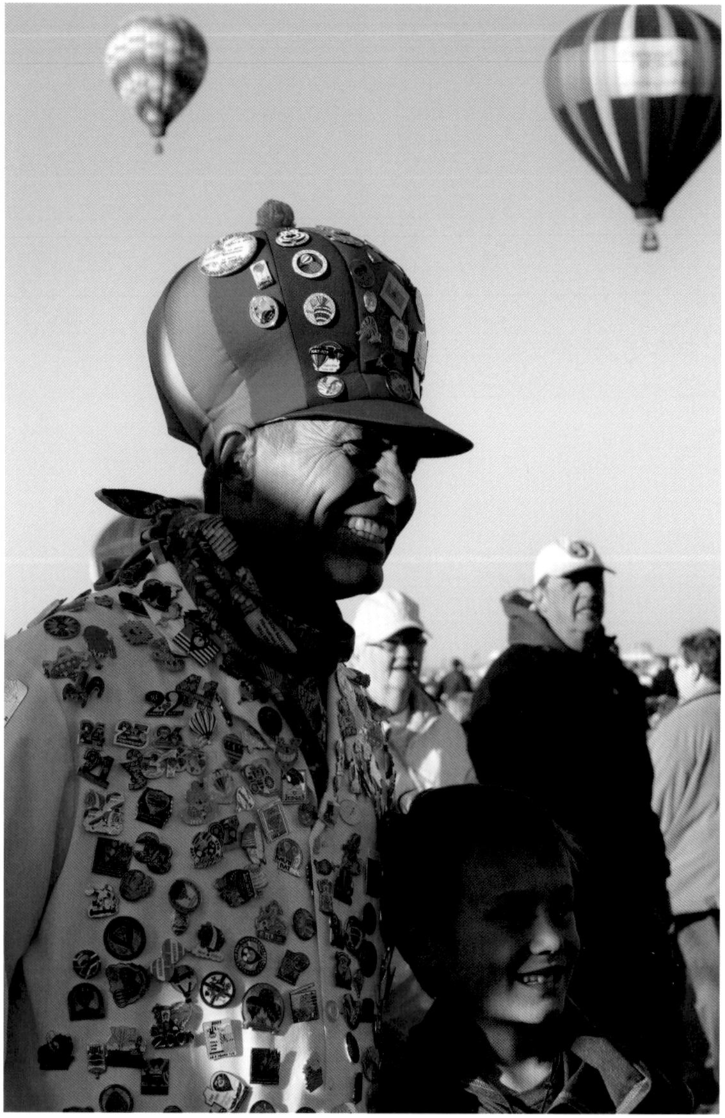

Local KOB news anchor Steve Stucker broadcasts from the balloon field during Fiesta and is known for his impressive balloon pin collection. Sid Cutter organized the first Balloon Fiesta in 1972 in support of KOB radio's fiftieth anniversary.

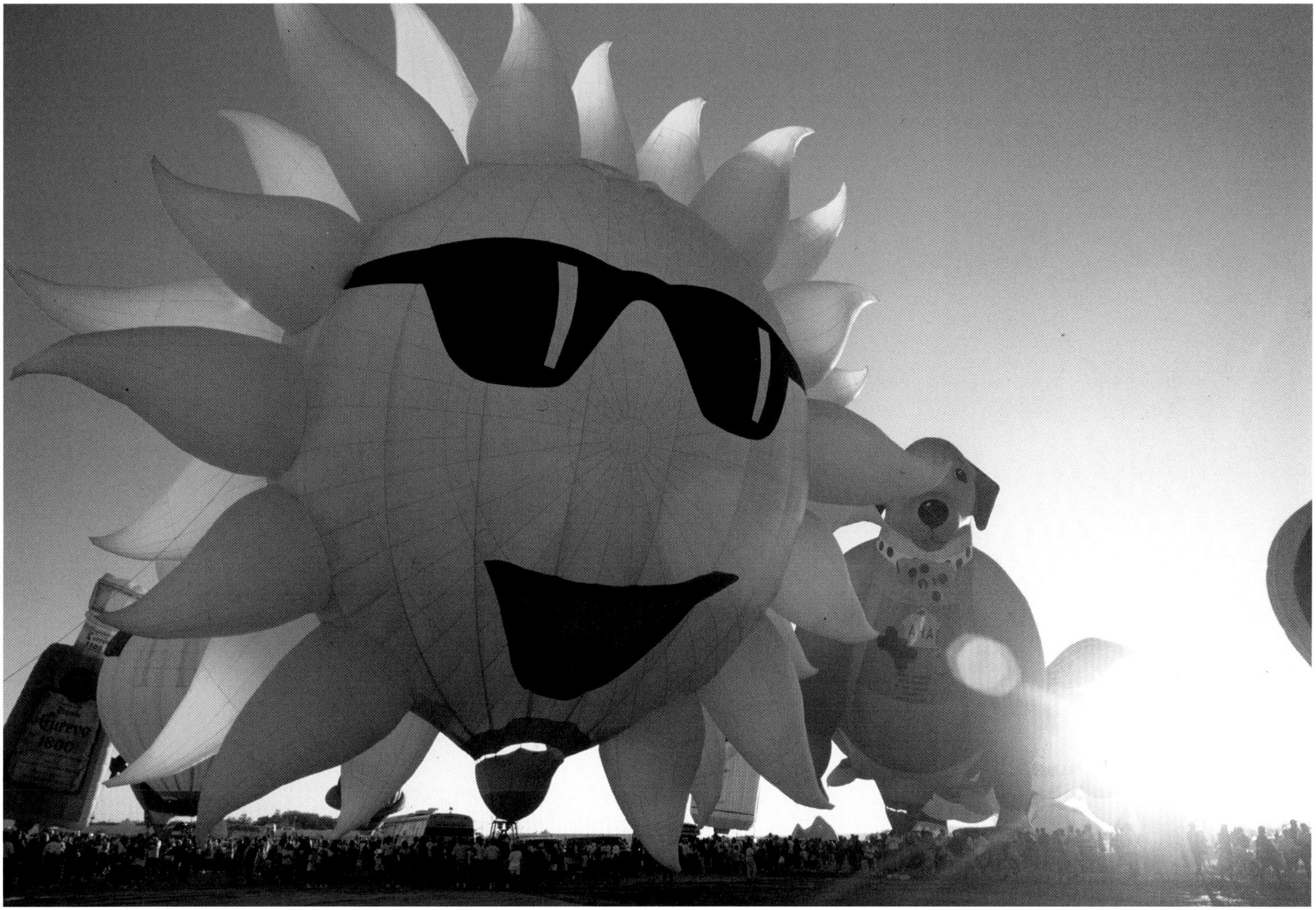

"Sunny Boy" from Ohio brightens the field.

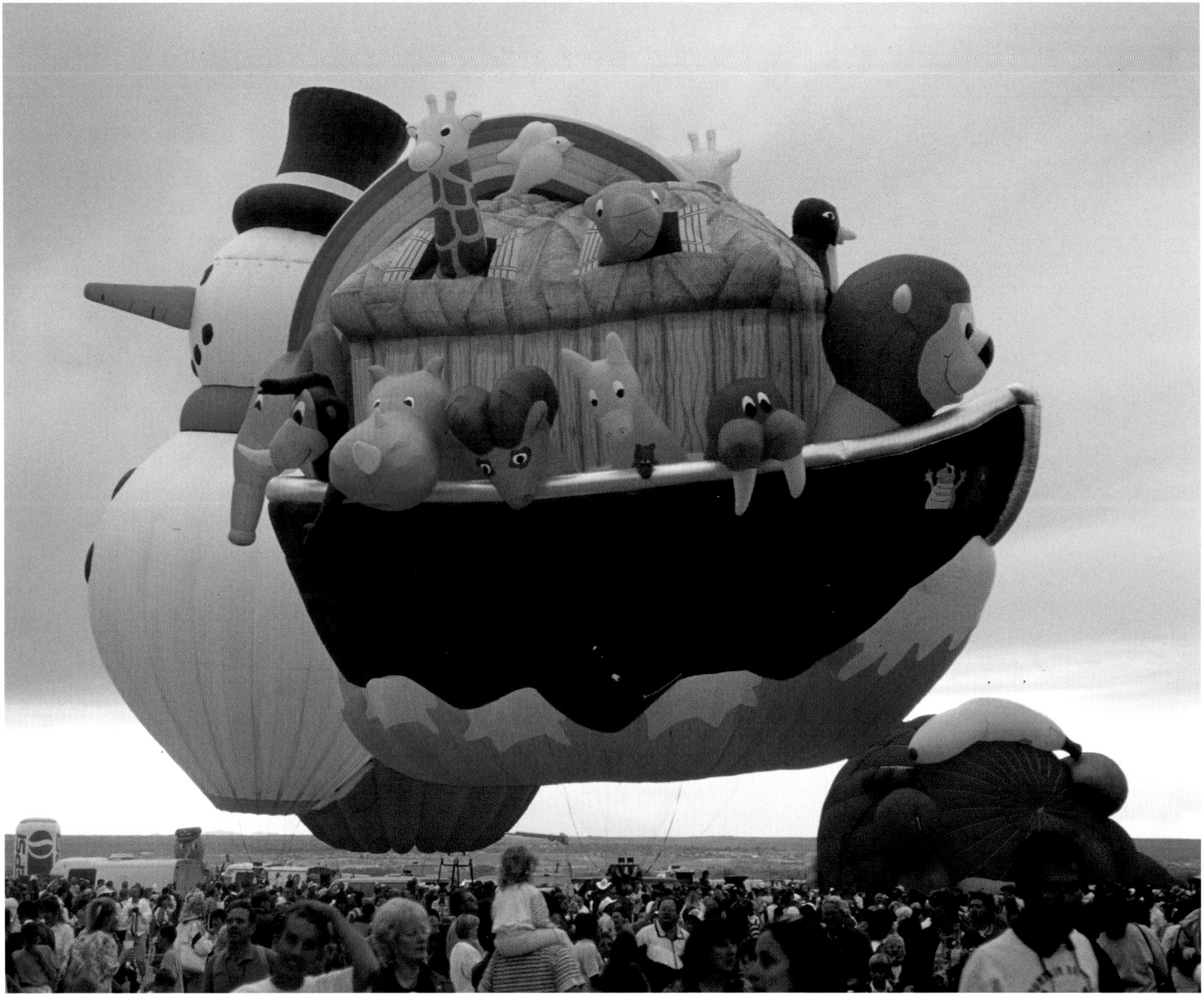

"ARKY" from Oregon inflates despite the threat of rain, or maybe because of it.

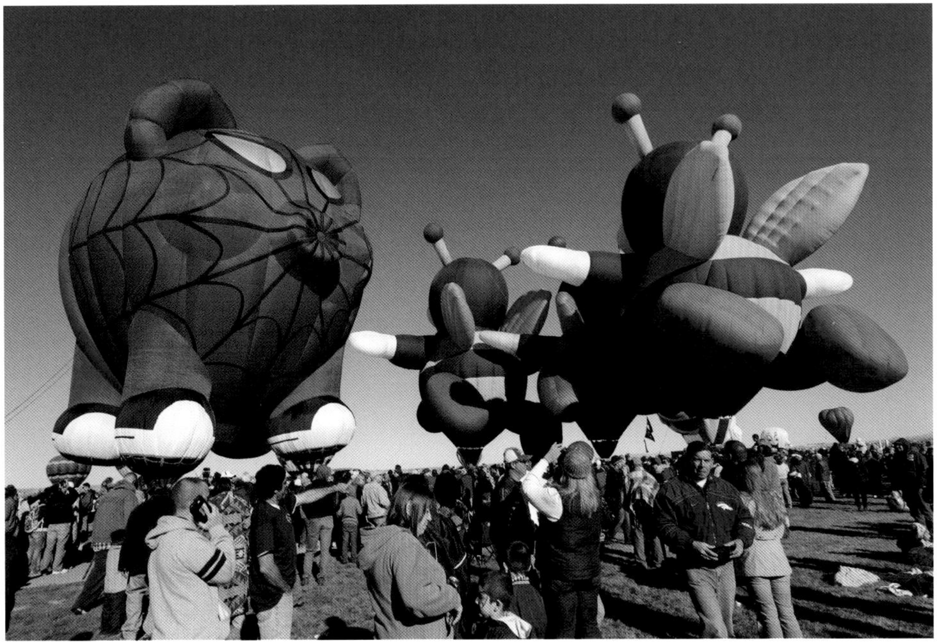

Thursday and Friday see the morning Special Shapes Rodeo, when only special shapes fly, and the evening Special Shapes Glowdeo.

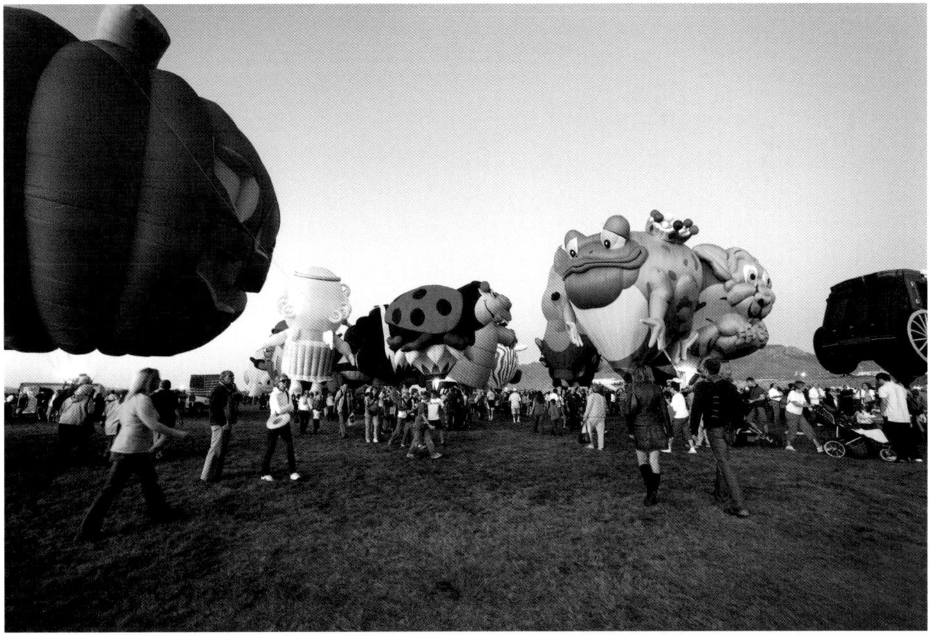

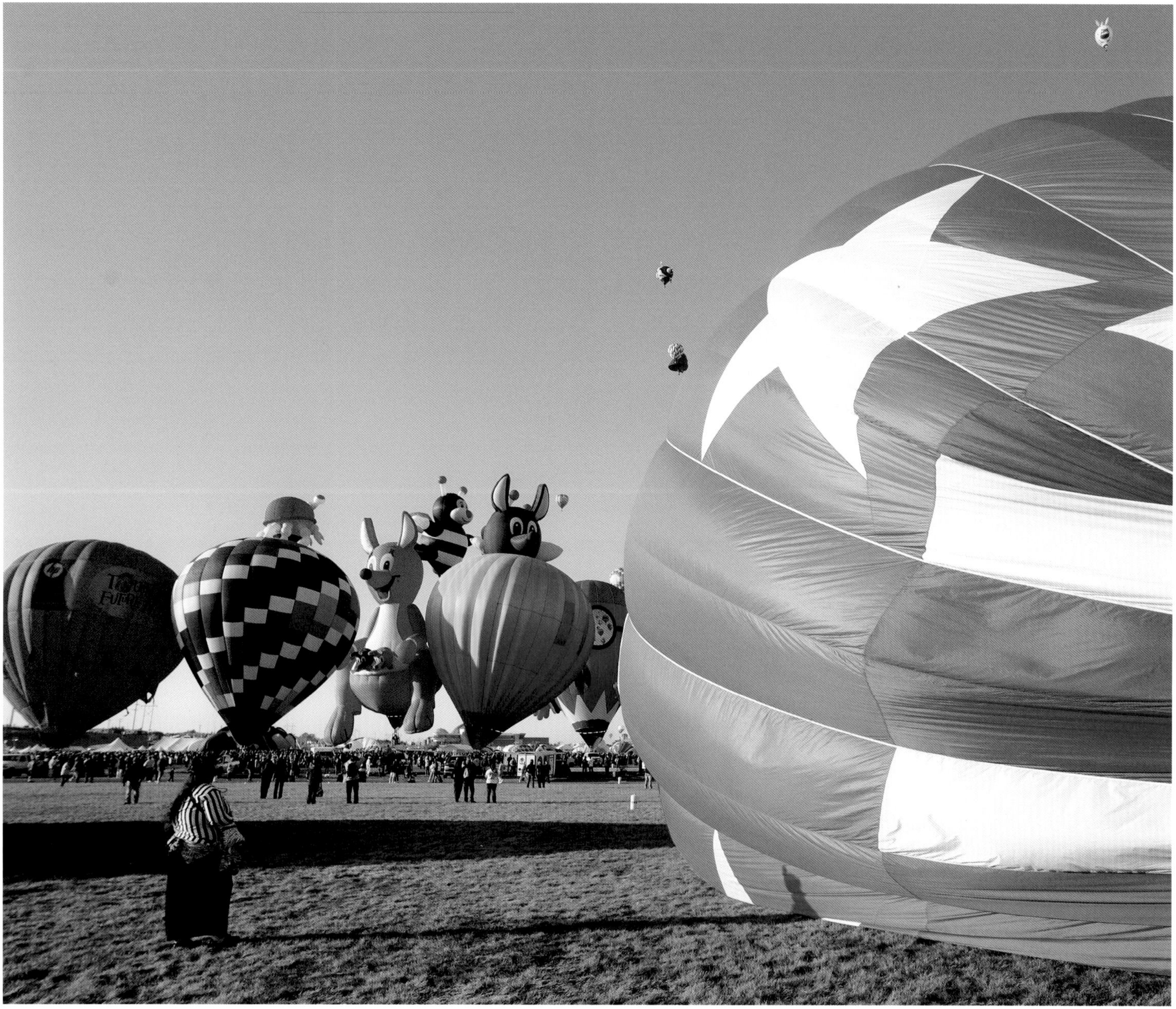

"Polly" the kangaroo special shape prepares to bound into the sky during a mass ascension.

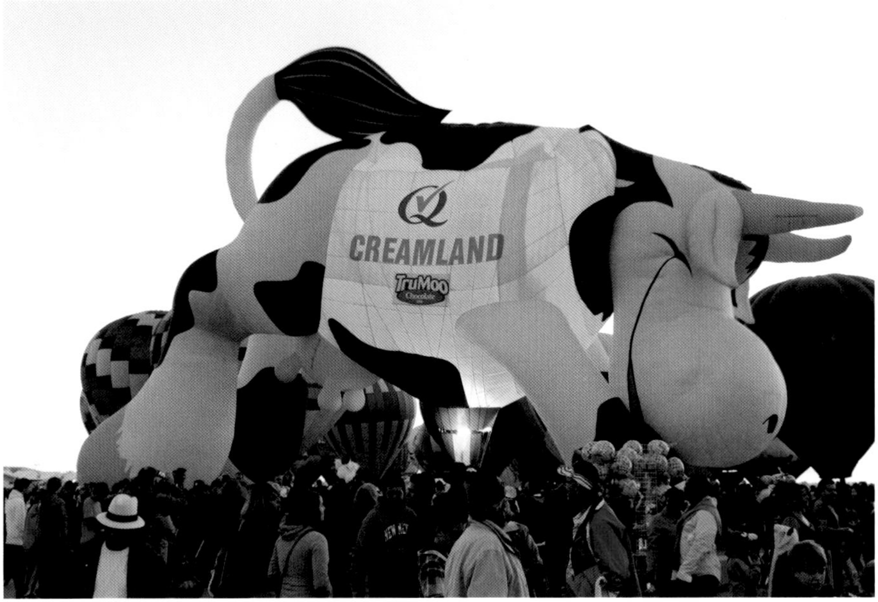

"Airabelle" glows to the udder delight of the crowd.

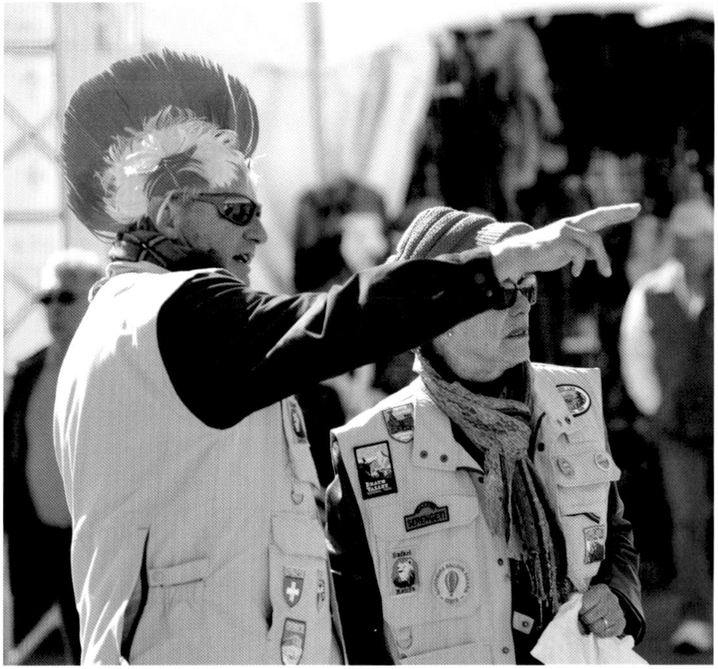

Balloons aren't the only colorful characters on the field.

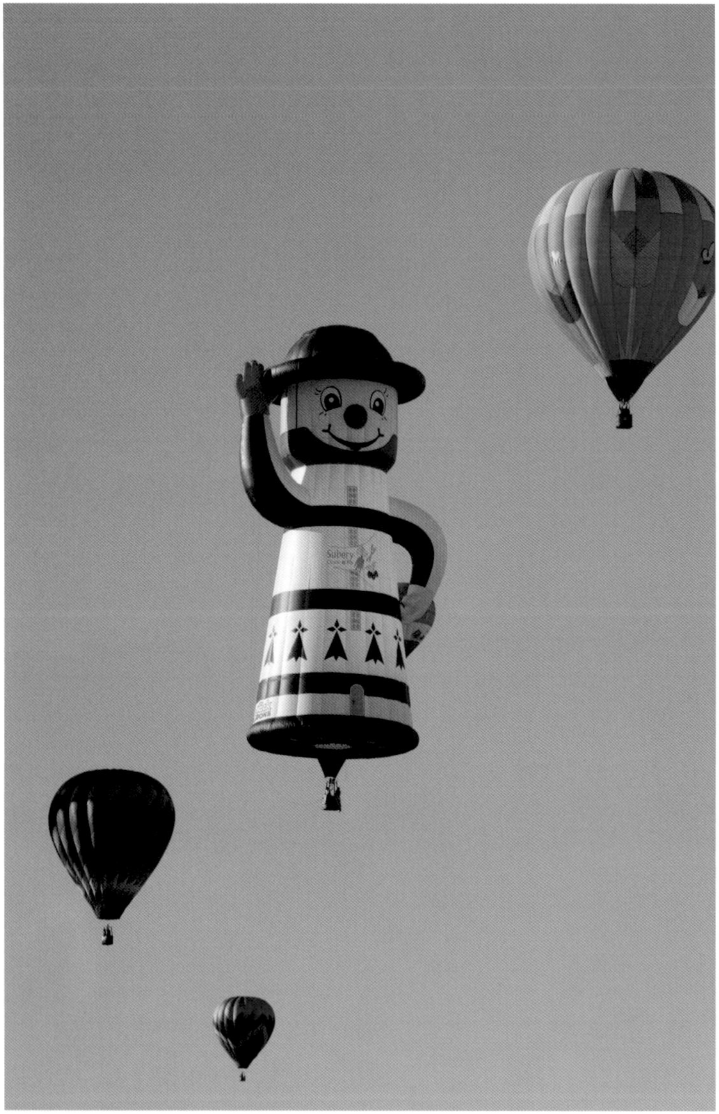

"Breizh on Board" from France guides the way through the Albuquerque sky.

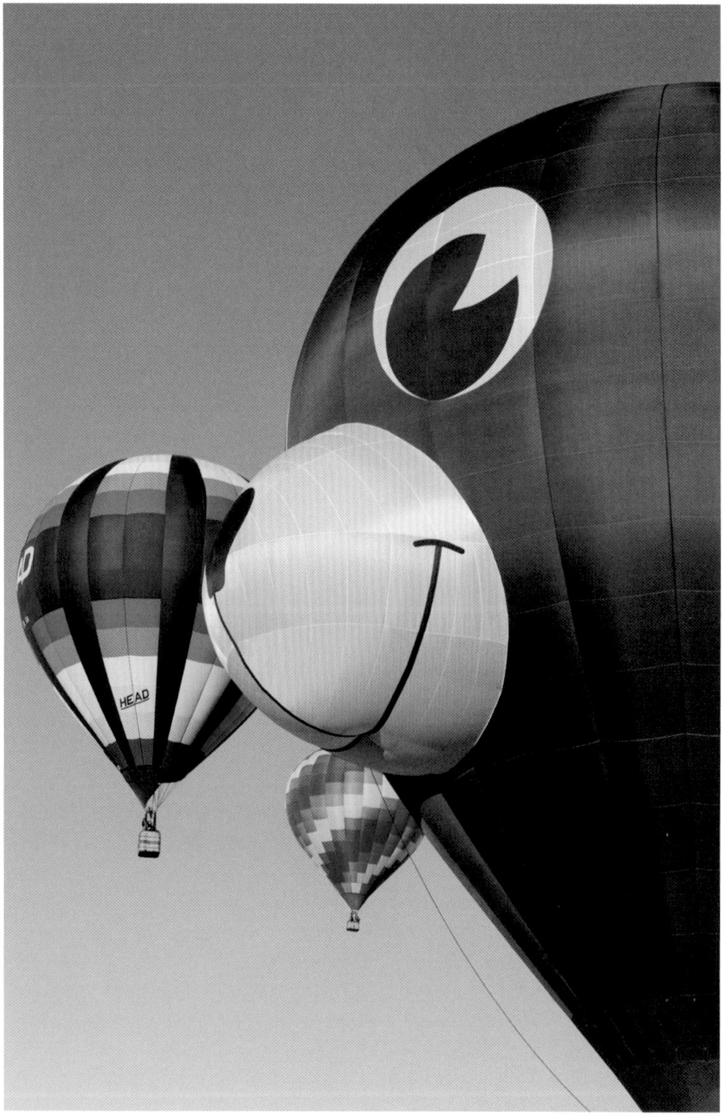

"Air Bear" keeps its eye on the sky.

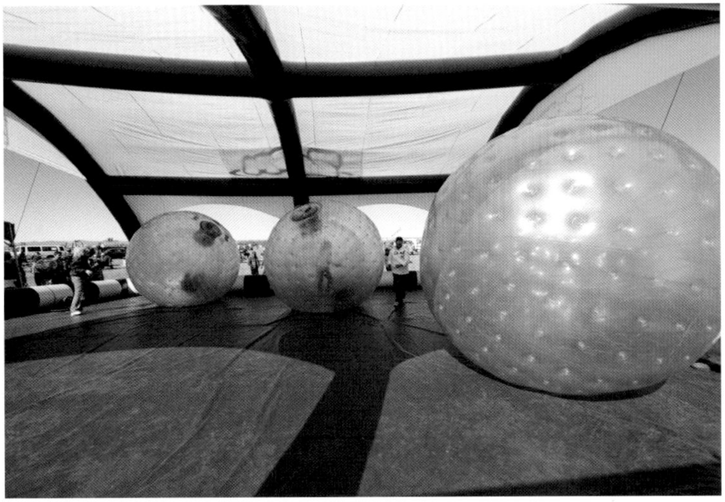

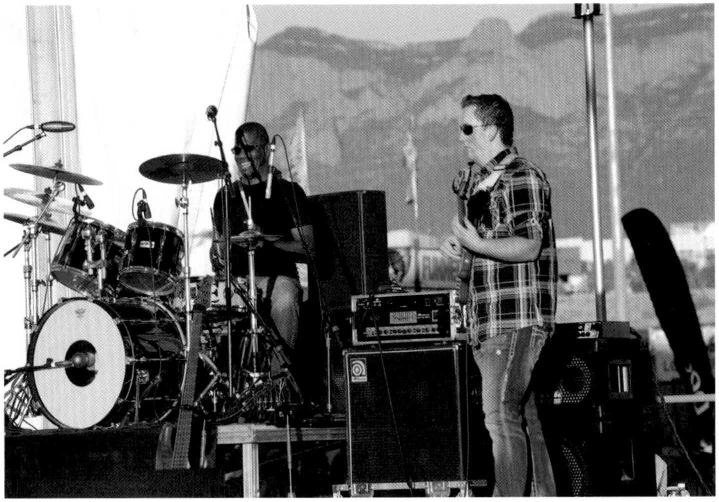

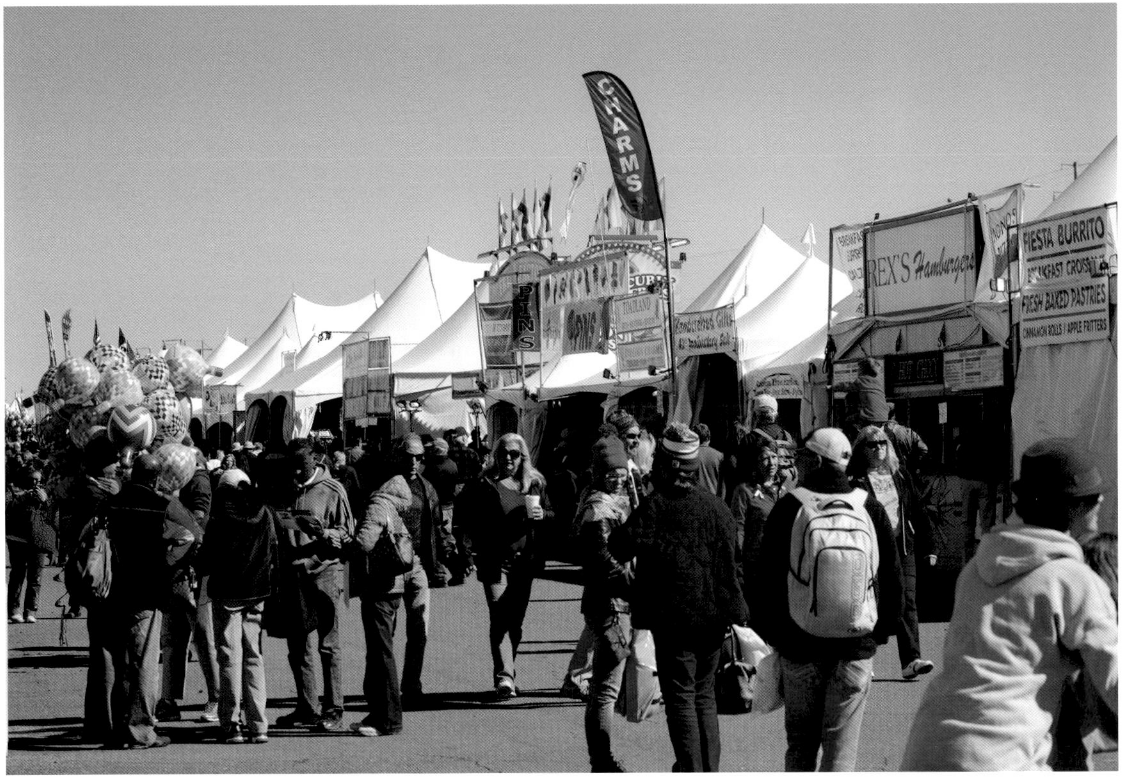

Balloon Fiesta Park's Main Street is a one-third-mile stretch of vendors, music, food, and activities worth a visit after the ballooning events.

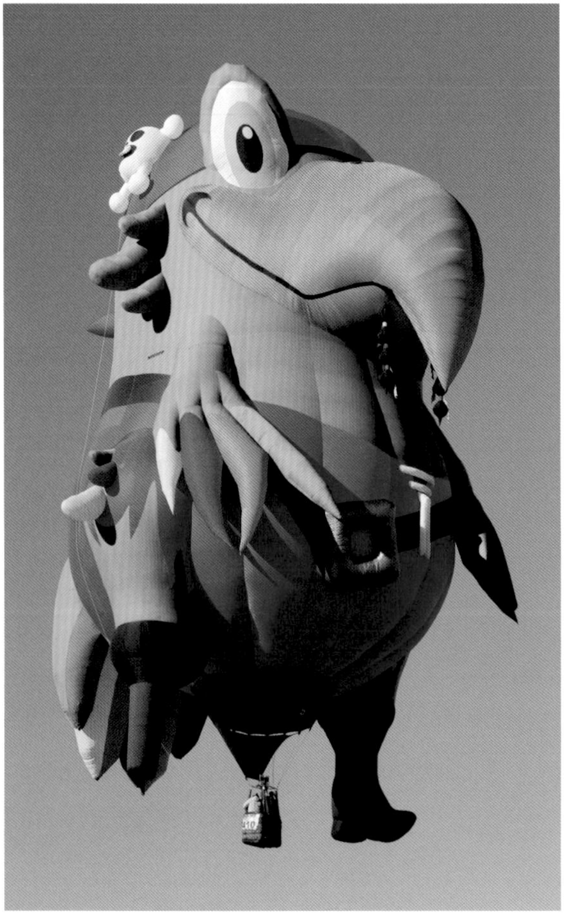

"Peg leg Pete" from Illinois.

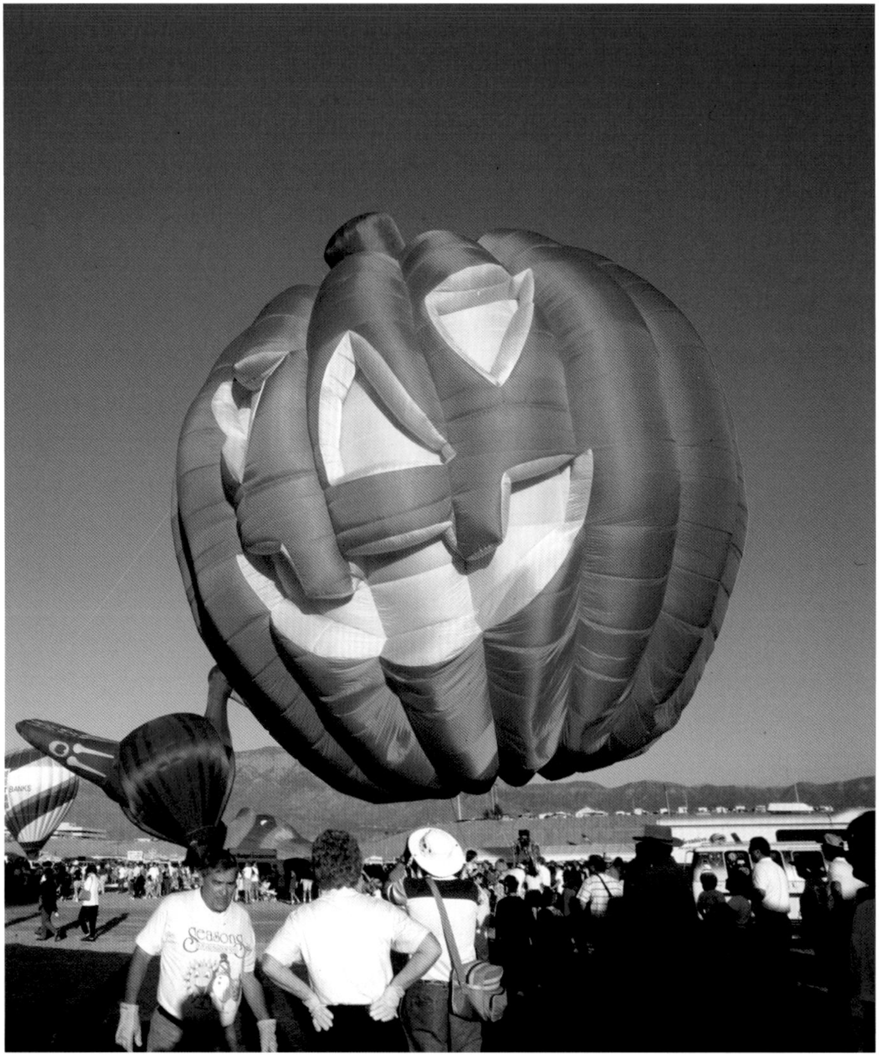

Perfect for New Mexico's October skies, "Pumpkin Head" from Wichita Falls, Texas, would make an estimated 2.7 million pies with its 100,000 cubic feet of volume.

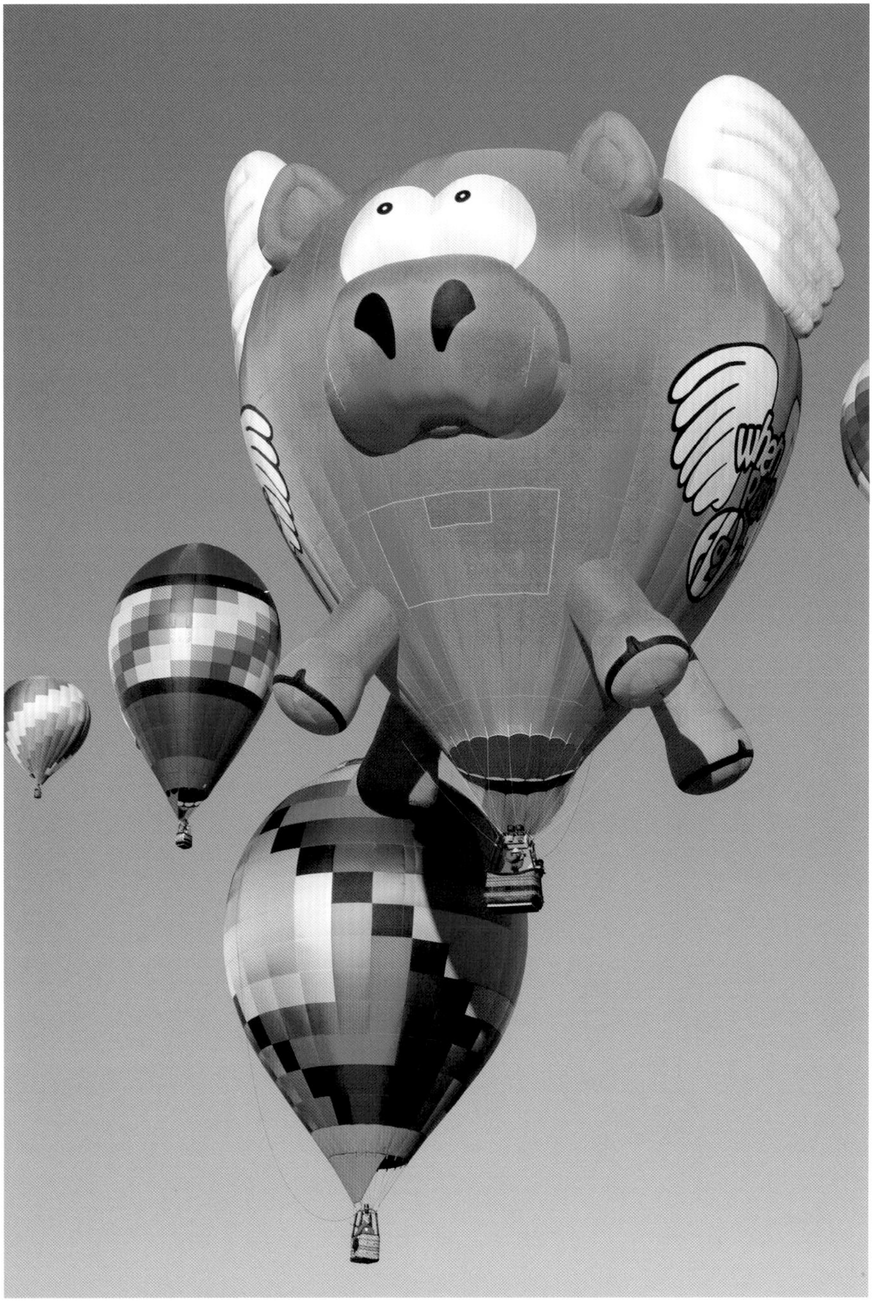

"Ham-Let" from Colorado sets out to prove a common misperception wrong.

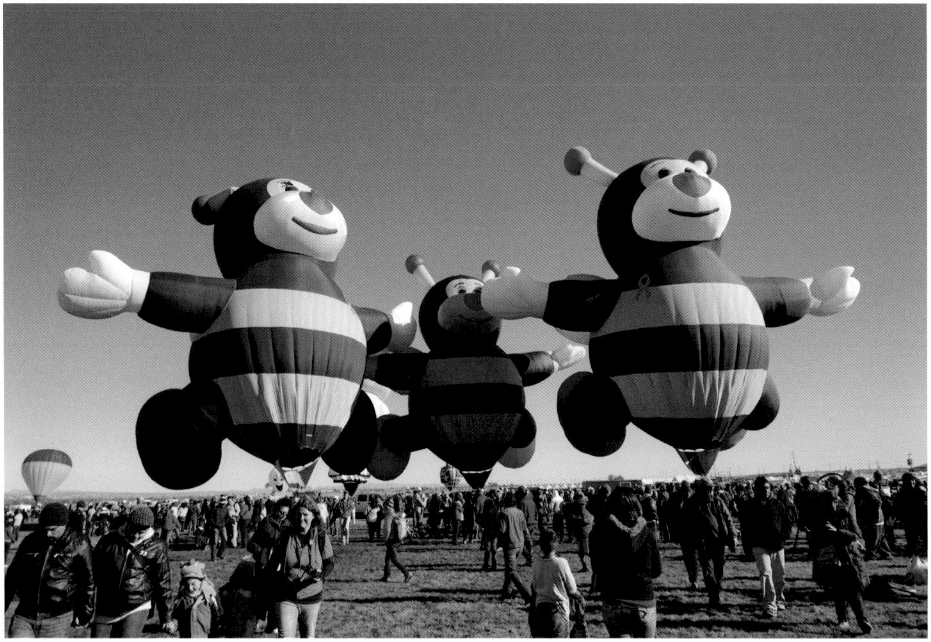

Lilly, Joey, and Joelly of the "Little Bees" always draw a crowd and cheers year after year. Michael Glen, who pilots "Little Bee Joelly," became the world's first paraplegic hot-air balloon pilot in 2006. His website is www.rollingpilot.com.

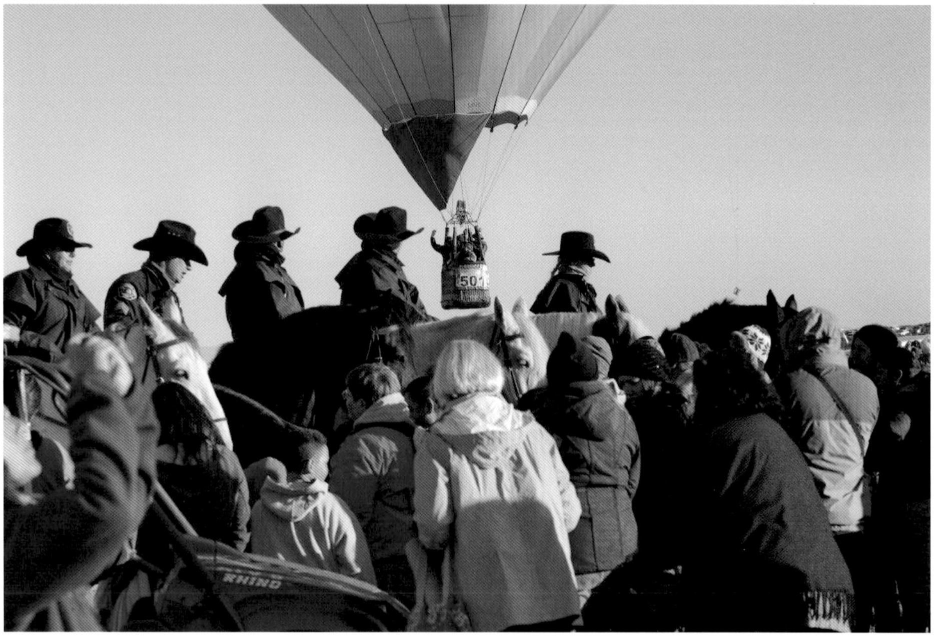

The Percheron Draft horses of the Albuquerque Police Department Mounted Unit have become a popular attraction themselves.

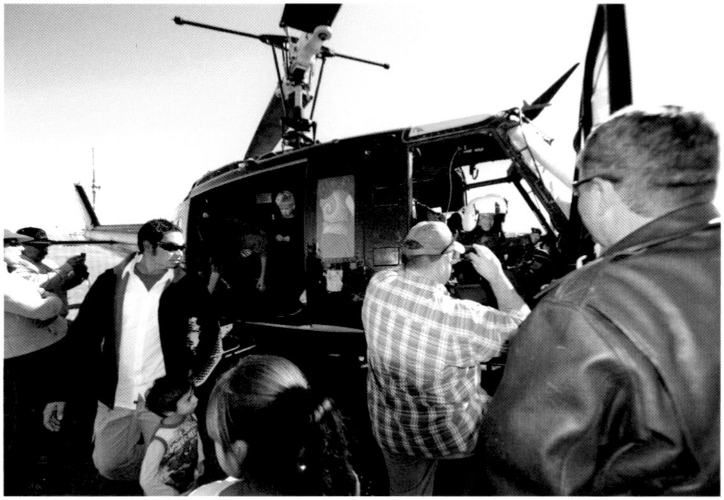

Various New Mexico law enforcement agencies land and let visitors tour their helicopters after ballooning events during the week.

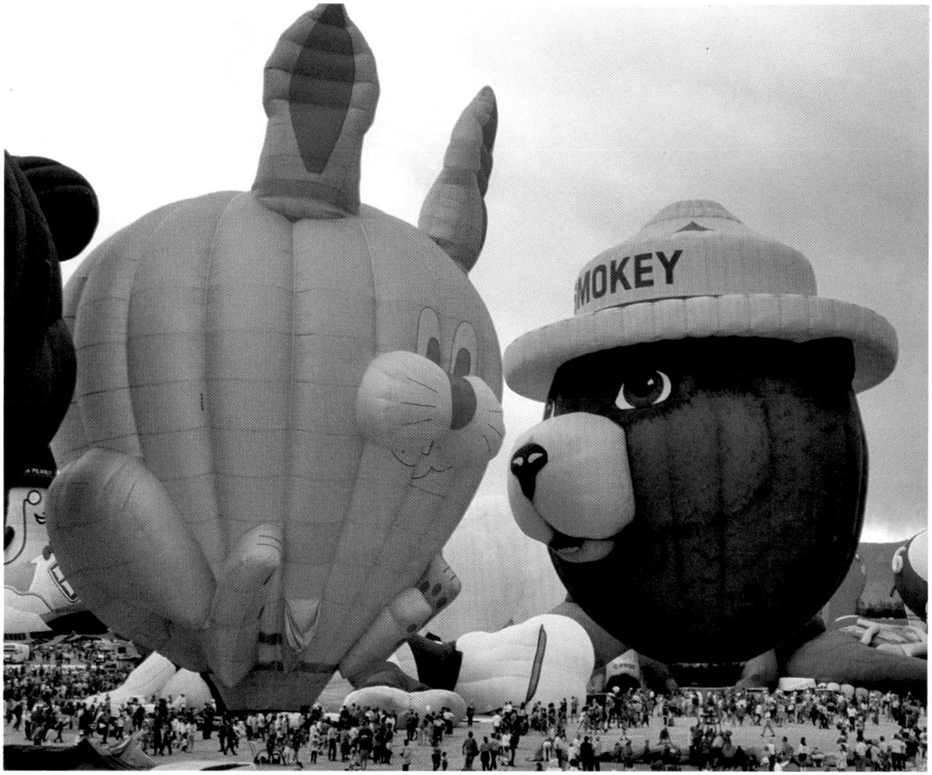

Balloons take shape for a Glowdeo.

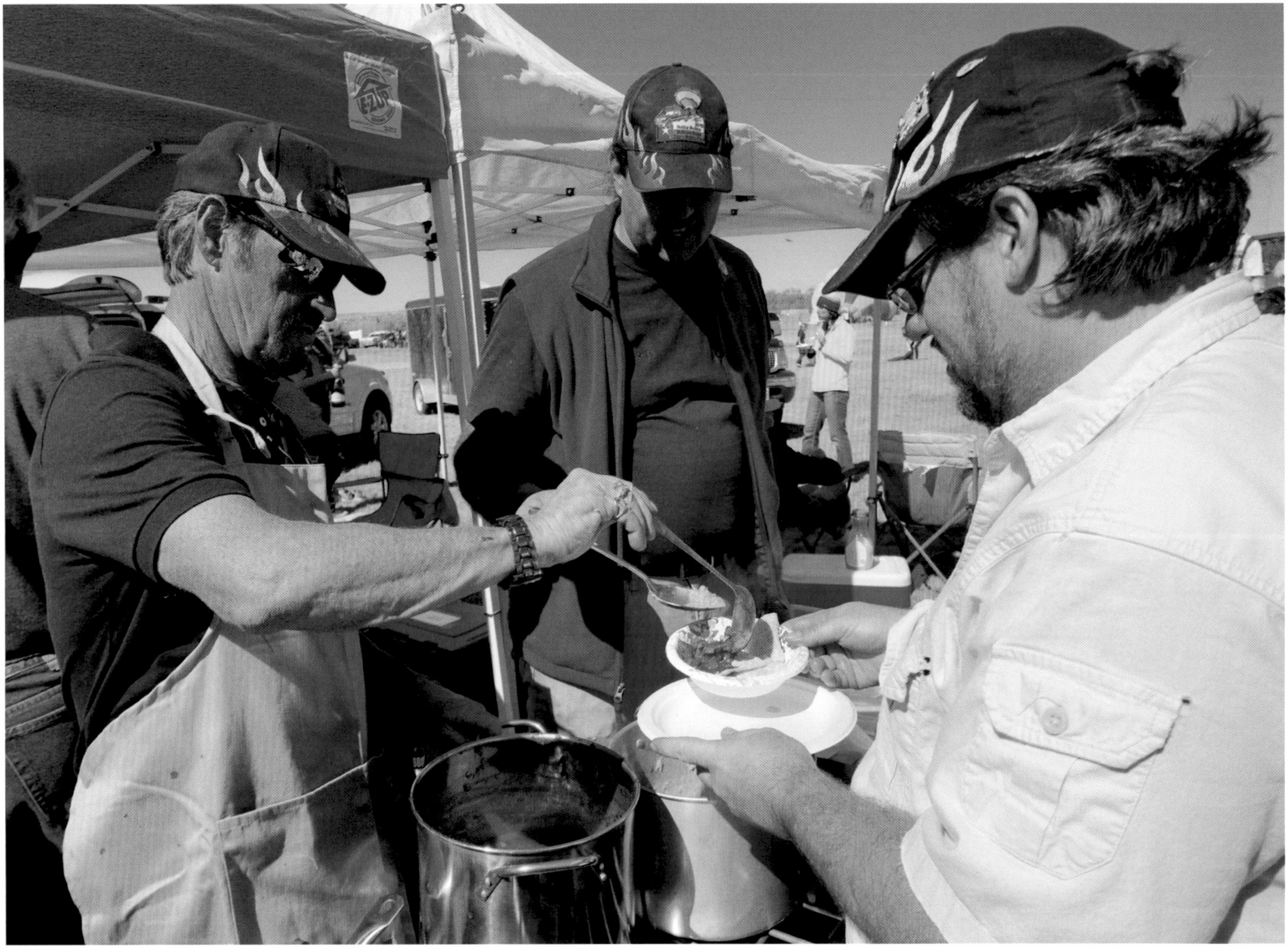

After most of the visitors have left and chase crews have retrieved their balloons and returned to the field, lunch-time tailgating on the field is a popular activity for balloon crews.

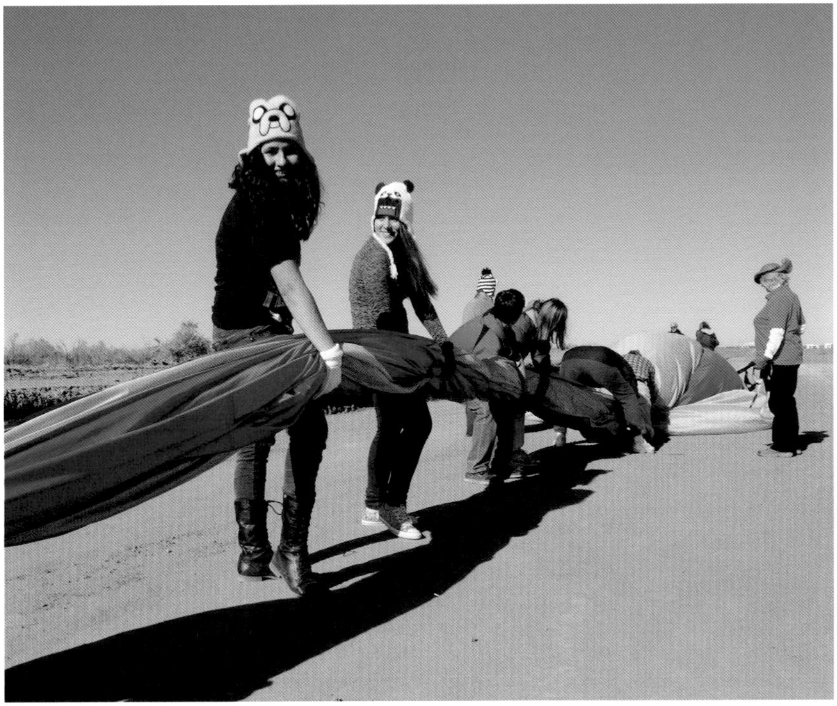

Volunteers help pack away a balloon that landed in Rio Rancho.

After a successful flight, a first-time flyer gets the balloonists' toast, in which Champaign is poured on the person's head and the Balloonist's Prayer is recited:

May the winds welcome you with softness; May the sun bless you with its warm hands; May you fly so high and so well that God joins you in laughter and sets you gently back into the loving arms of Mother Earth.

When French balloonists landed in farm fields in the late 1700s, farmers often attacked the balloons, thinking they were smoke-billowing demons, or just because they were angry that some of their crops were crushed. Balloonists quickly found that having a bottle of Champaign on board to offer as a gift avoided such conflicts.

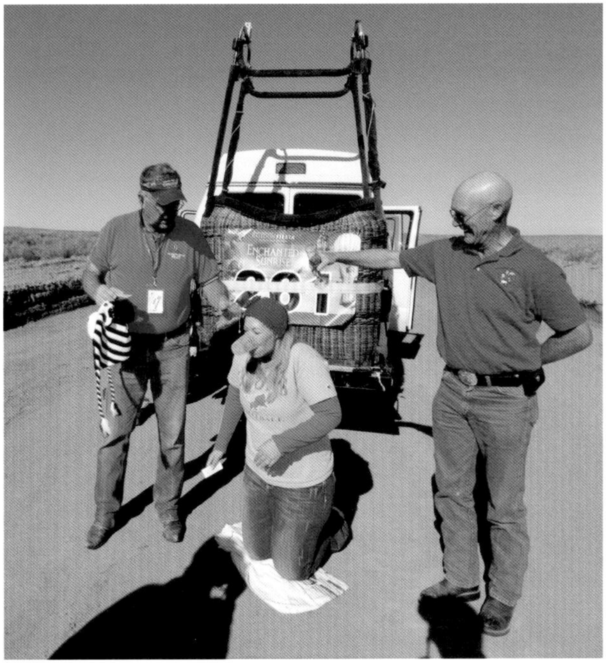

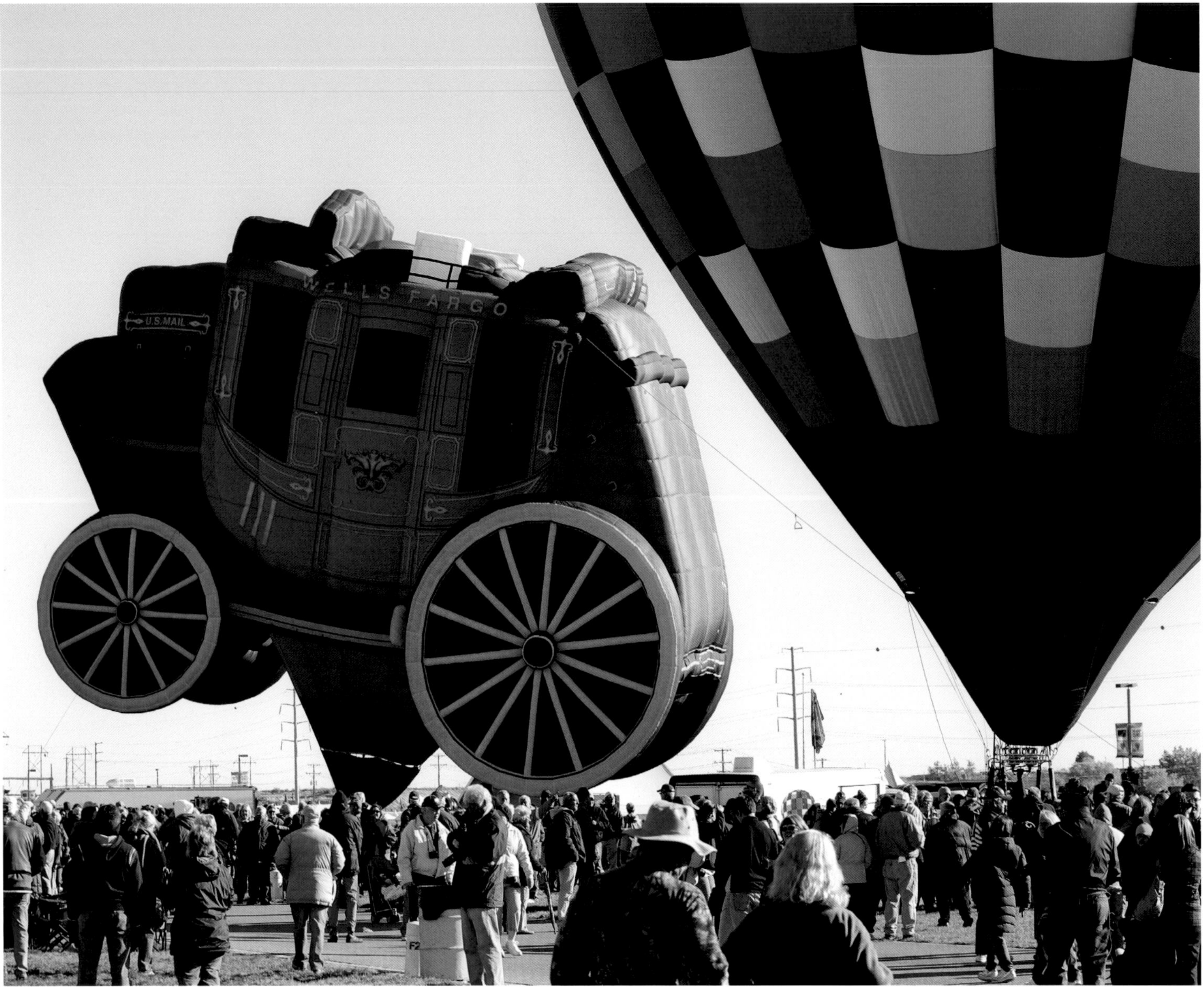

"Cent'r Stage," the balloon of Wells Fargo, banks on a great day of flying.

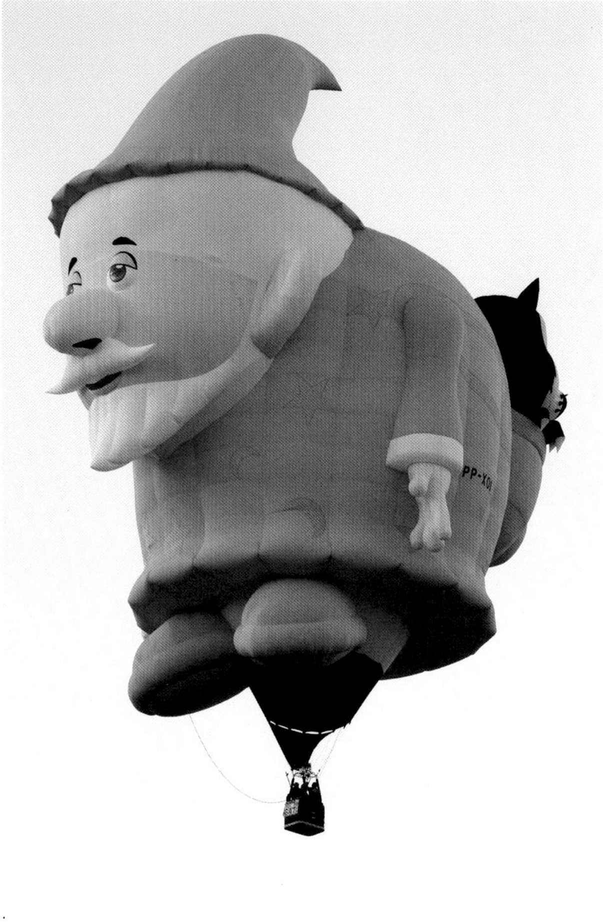

"Little Wizard" makes for a magical time at Balloon Fiesta.

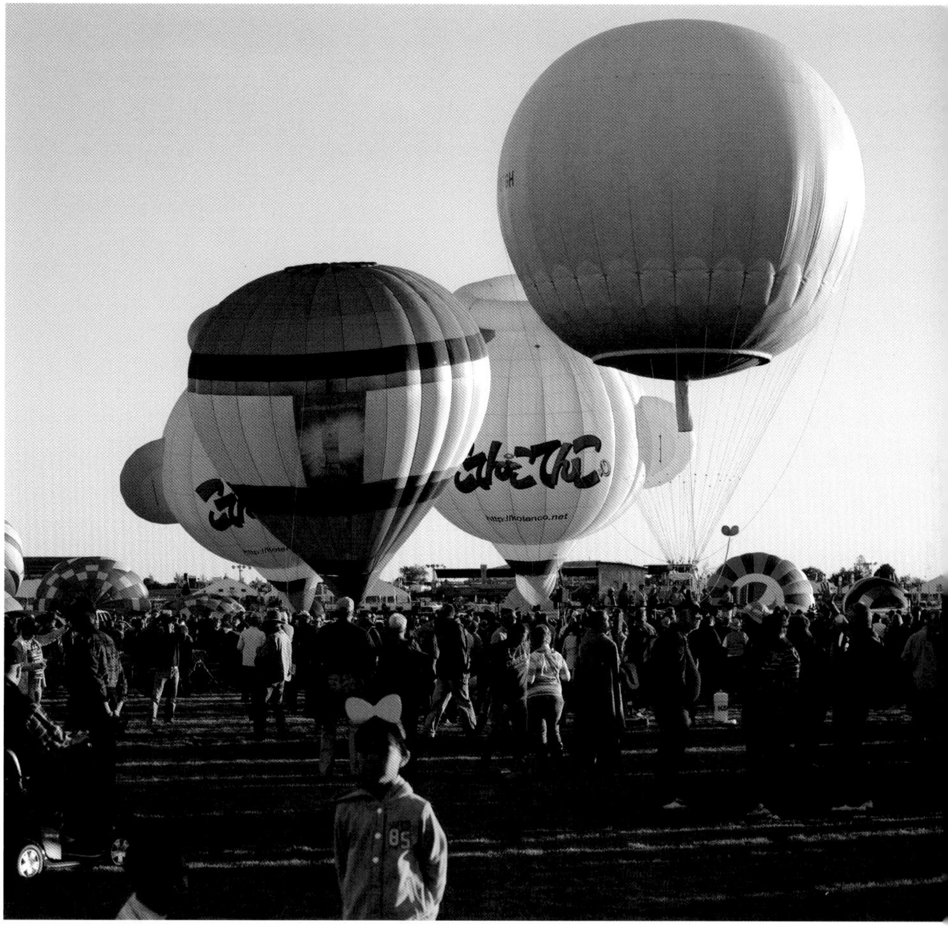

A hydrogen-filled gas balloon participating in the America's Challenge prepares to launch amid its hot-air cousins.

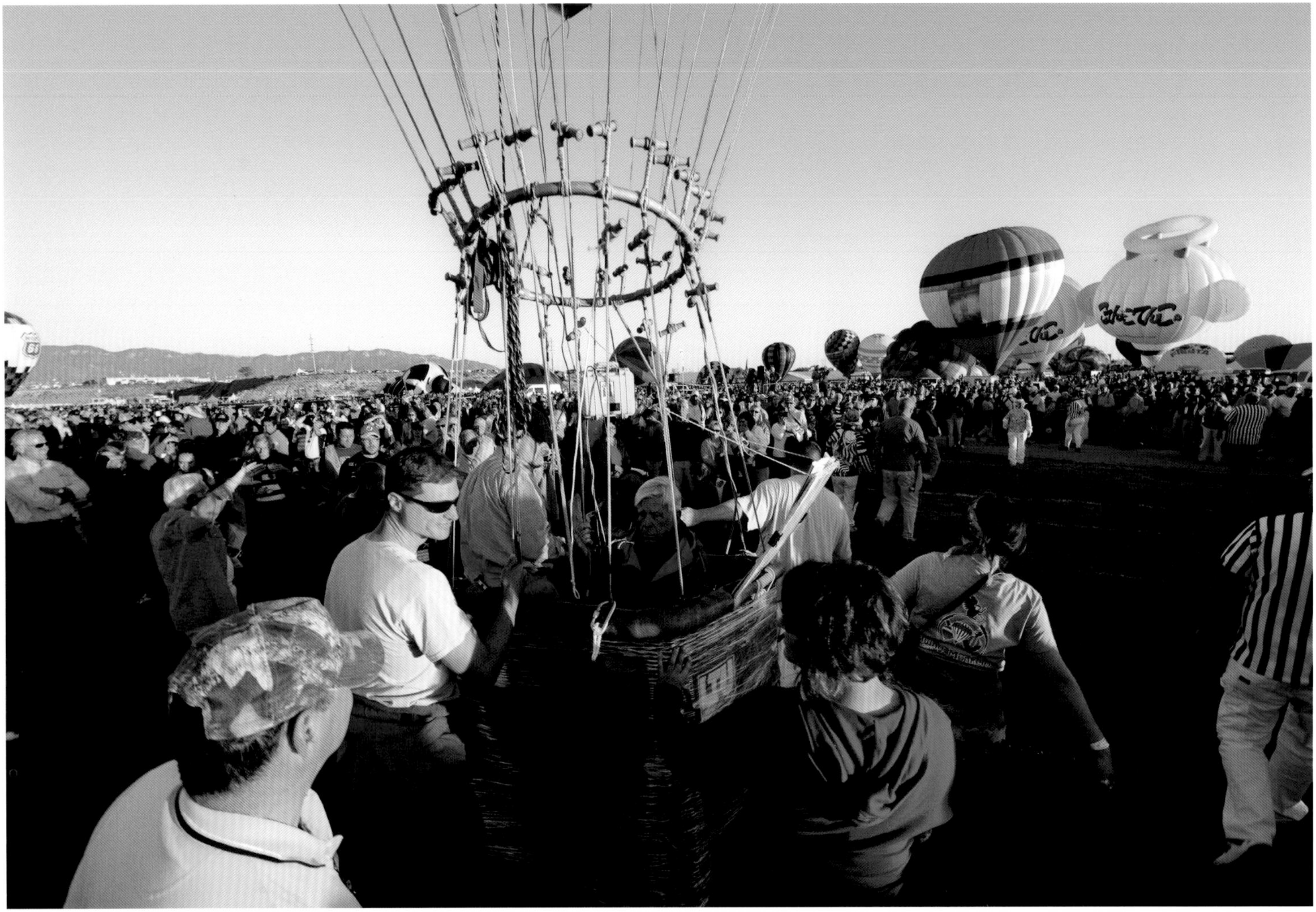

America's Challenge Gas Balloon Race was first held at the Balloon Fiesta in 1995. Gas balloonists from around the world compete to see who can fly the farthest, with some balloonists landing as far away as Canada after several days of flight. Gas balloons are completely sealed and filled with hydrogen gas. The farthest an America's Challenge competitor has flown was in 2000, when David Levin and Alan Levin flew 1,998 miles over sixty-four hours from Albuquerque.

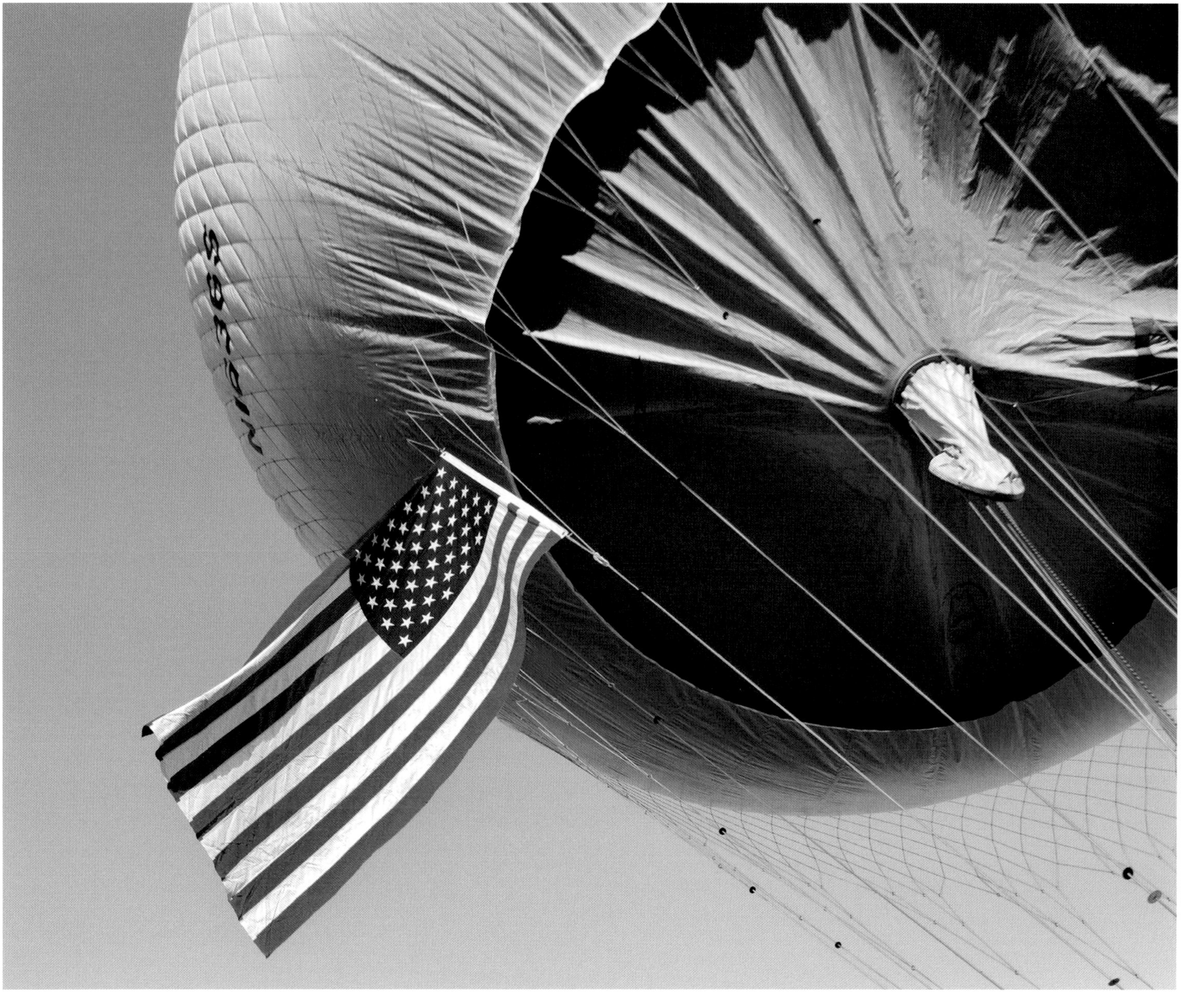

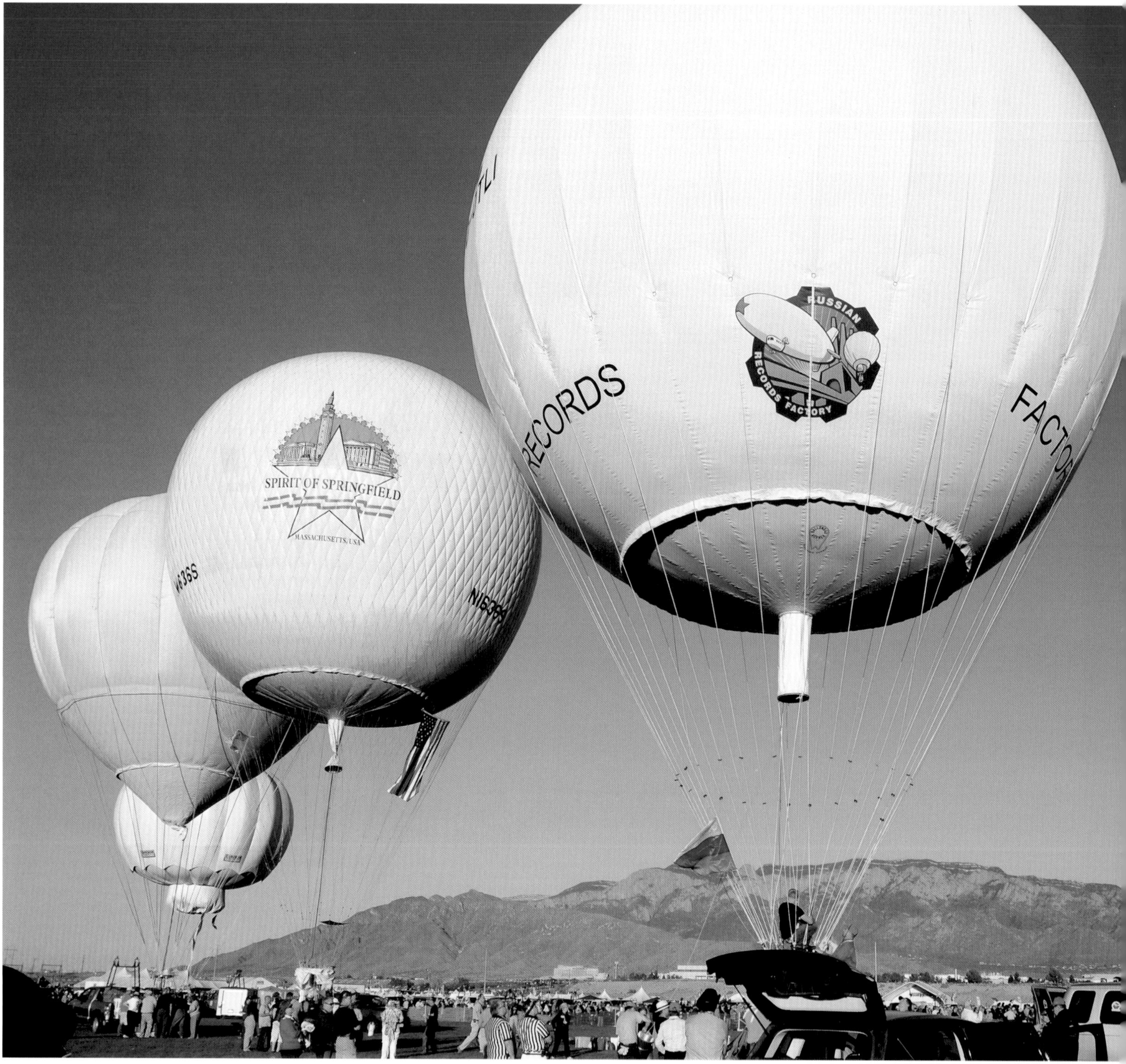
SPIRIT OF SPRINGFIELD
MASSACHUSETTS, USA
RECORDS
RUSSIAN
RECORDS FACTORY

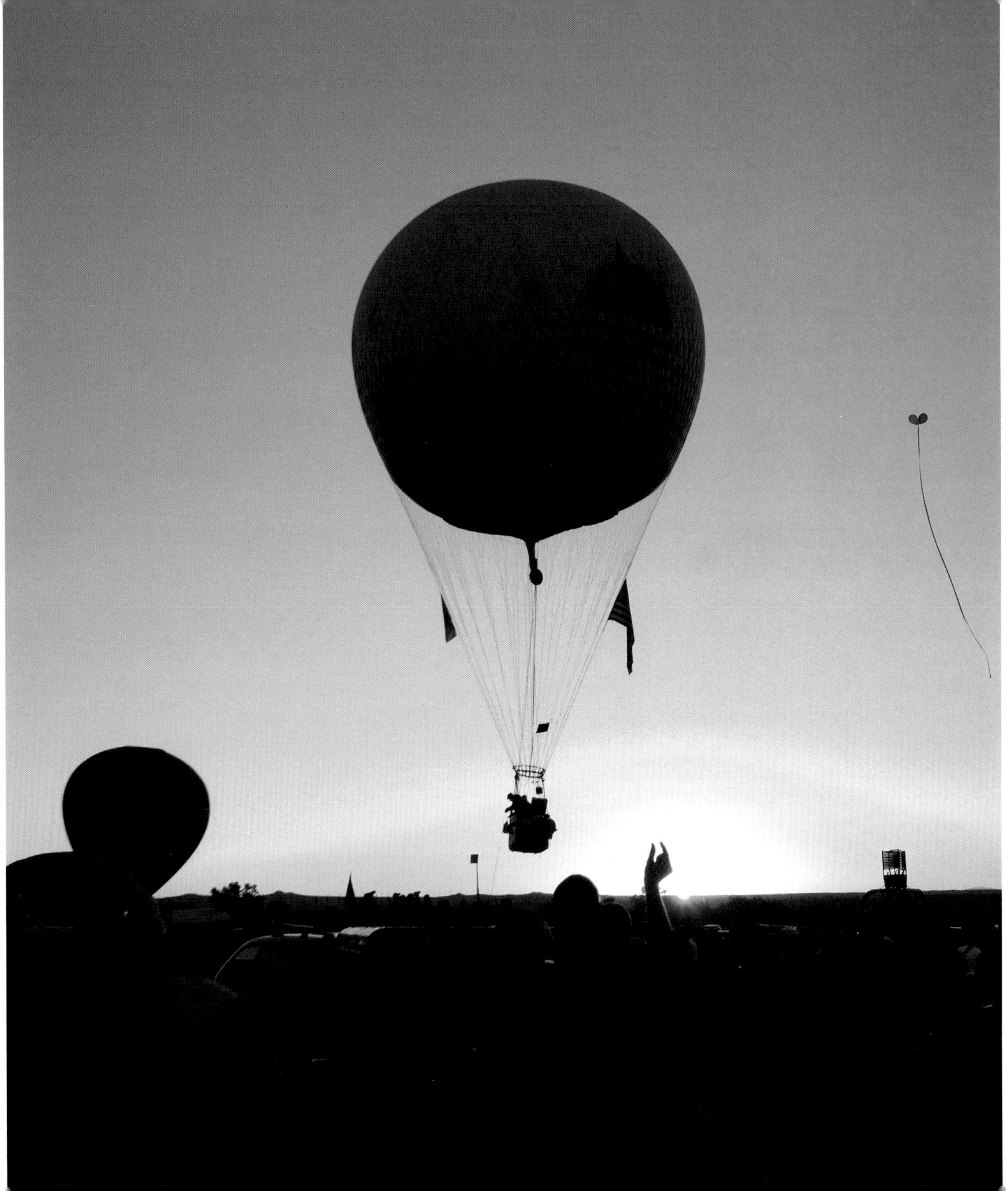

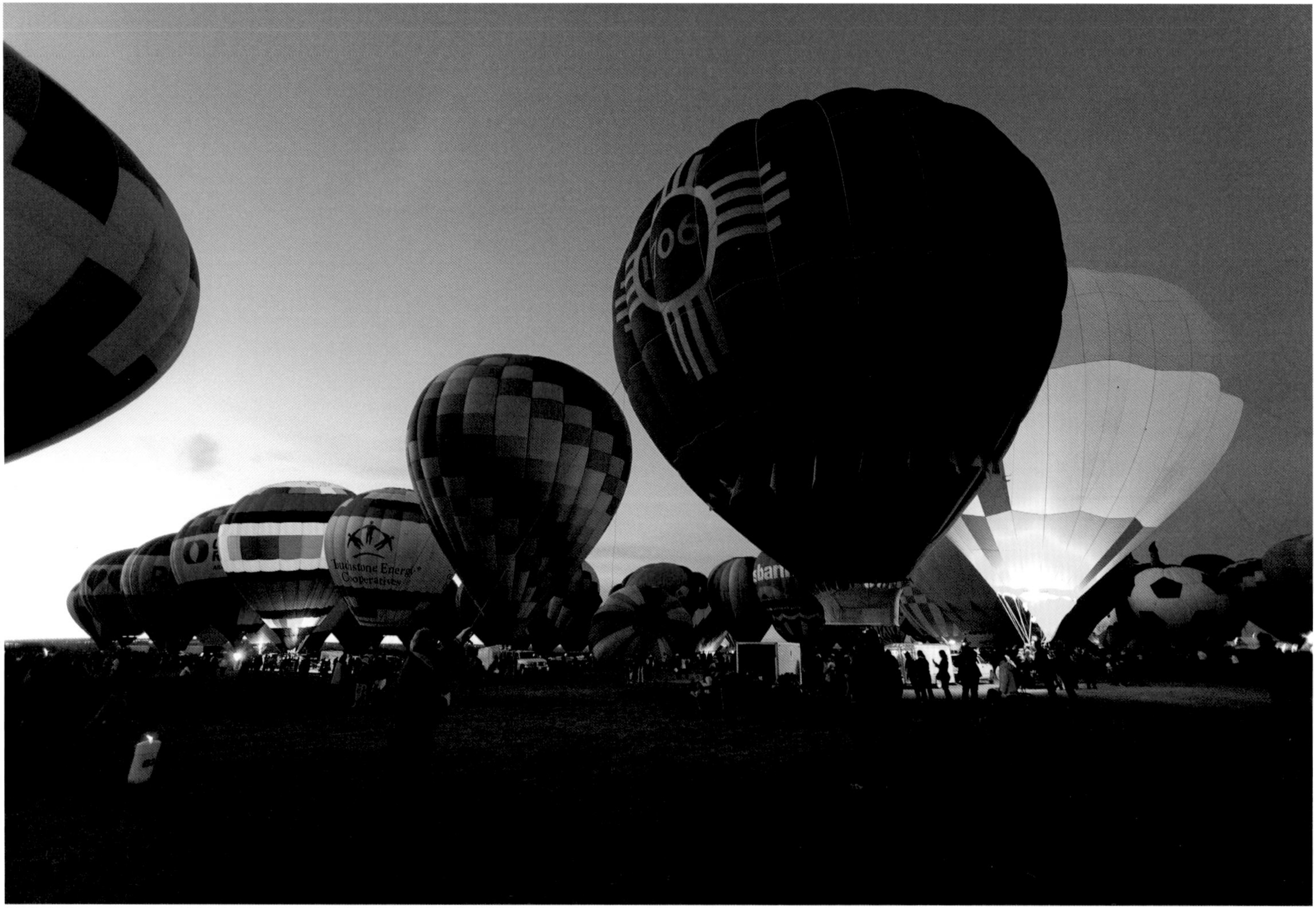

Balloons begin to glow against a dusk sky. During Balloon Glows, the craft remain tethered and synchronize their flares to countdowns. Fireworks light up the sky after the glow.

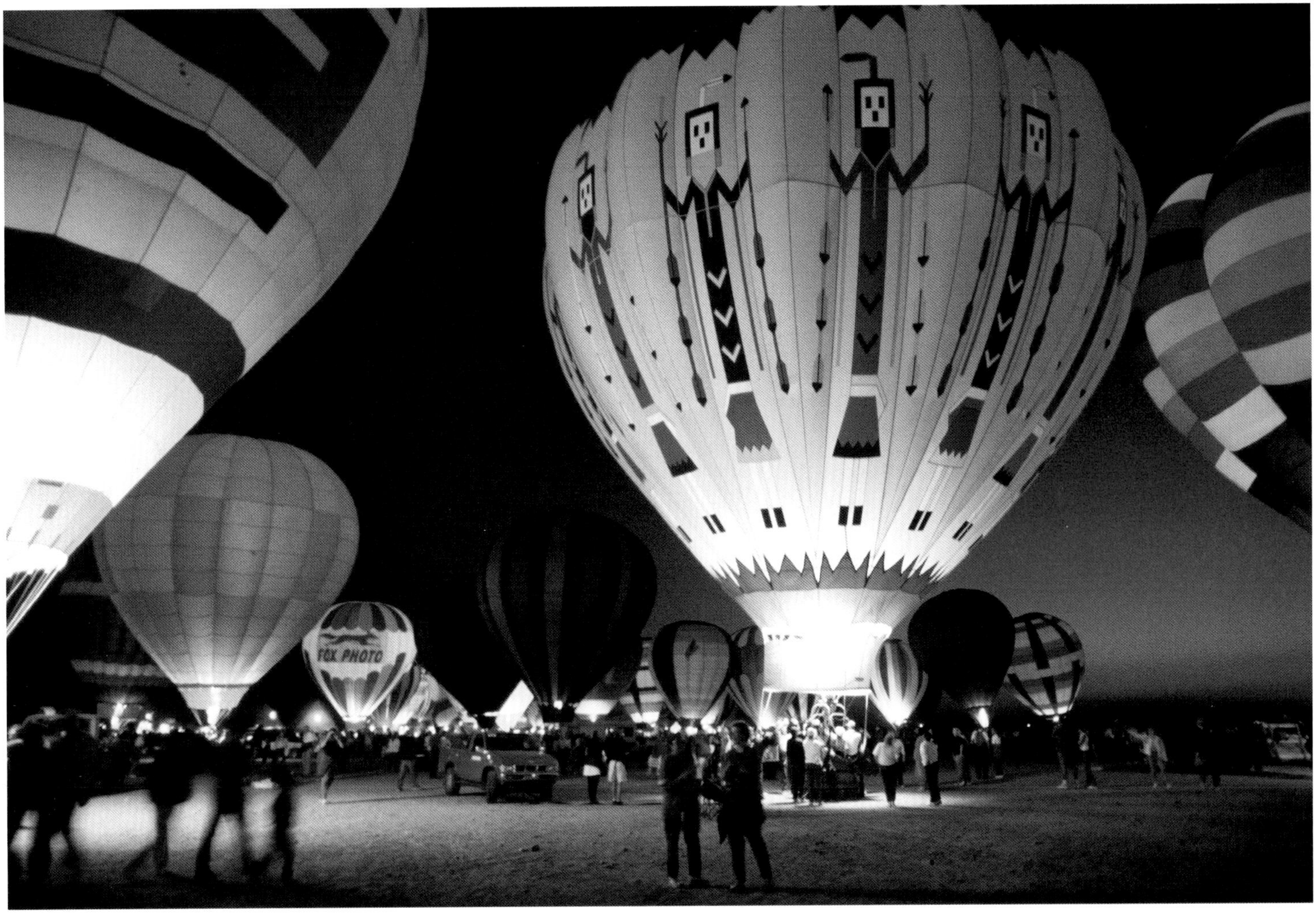
FOX PHOTO

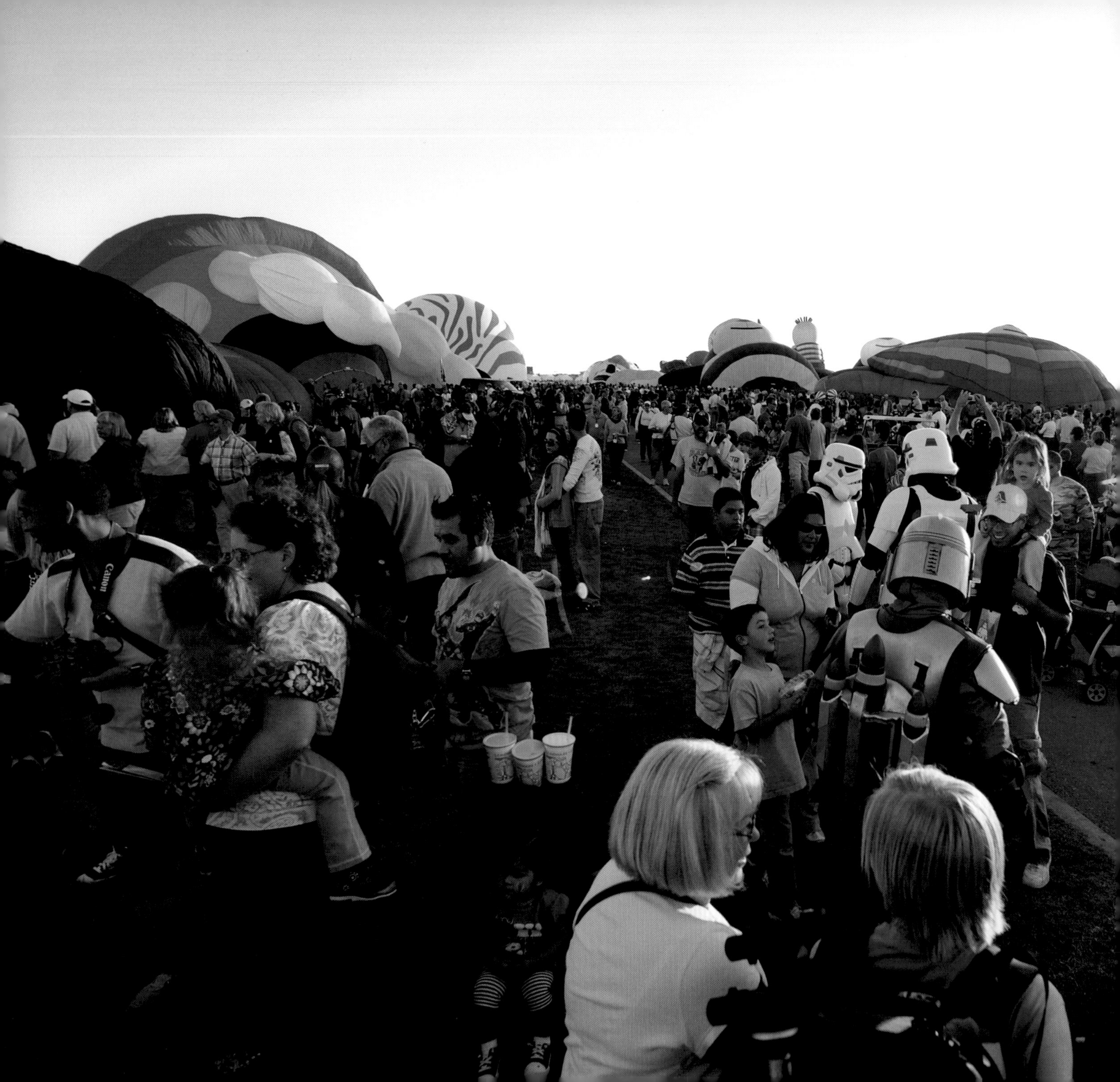
Canon

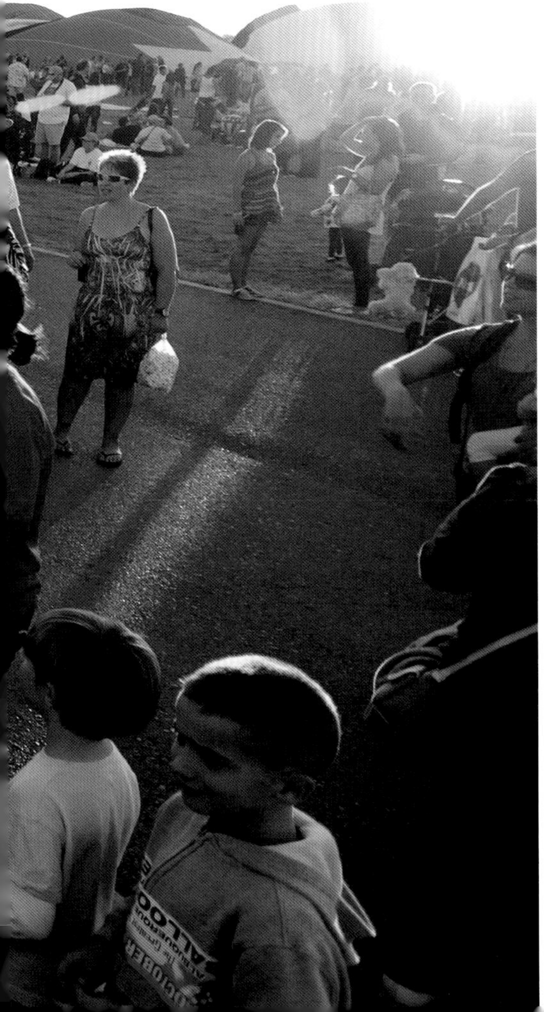

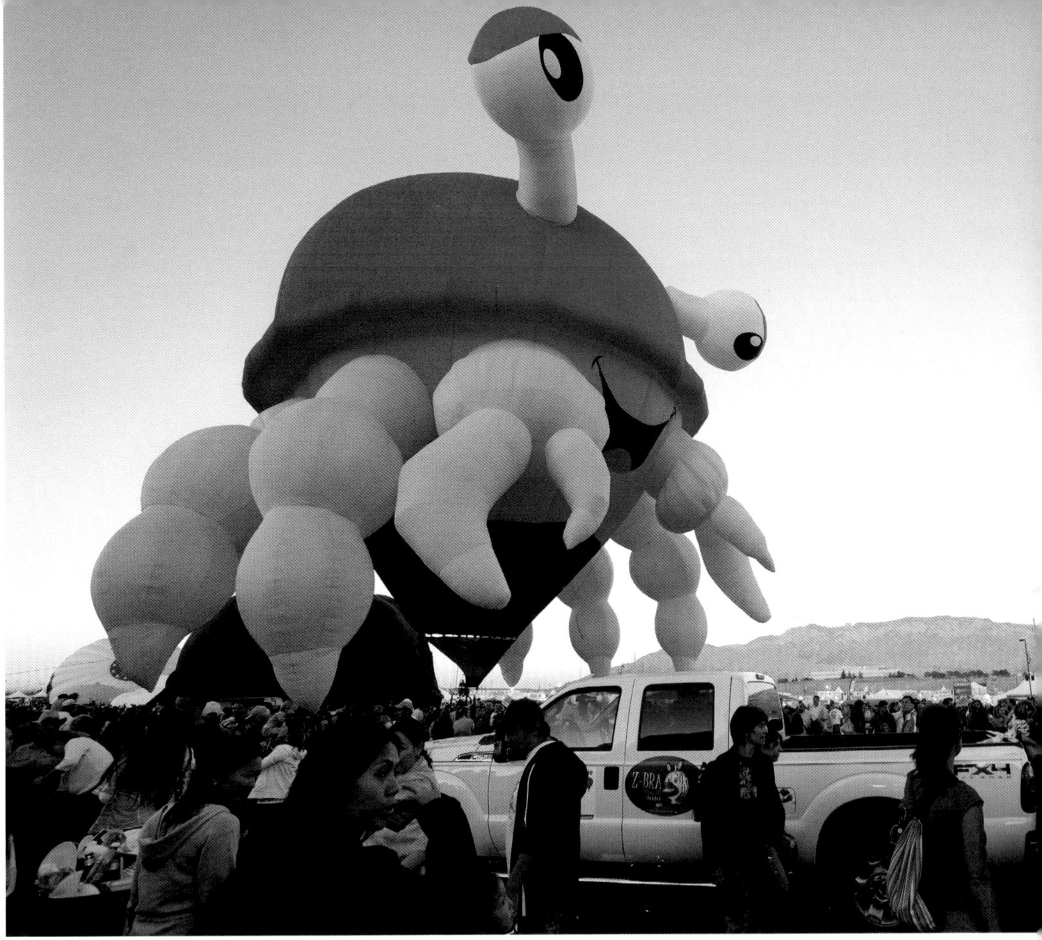

"Crazy Crab" readies for a Balloon Glow.

The sun sets as balloons inflate in preparation for a Balloon Glow.

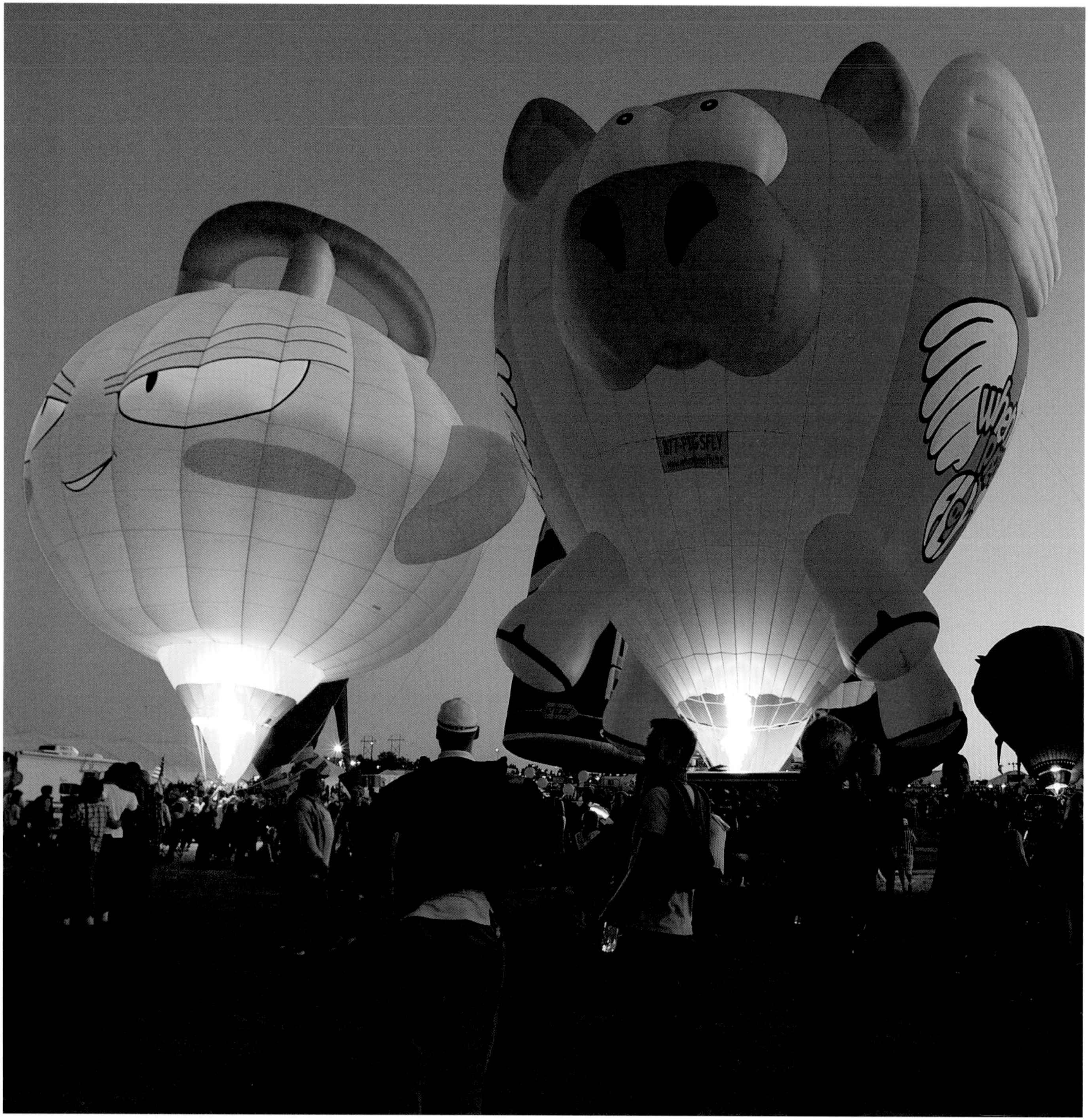

Special shapes flare during a Glowdeo. Pilots must allow enough time in between bursts for the balloon to cool to prevent unwanted take offs.

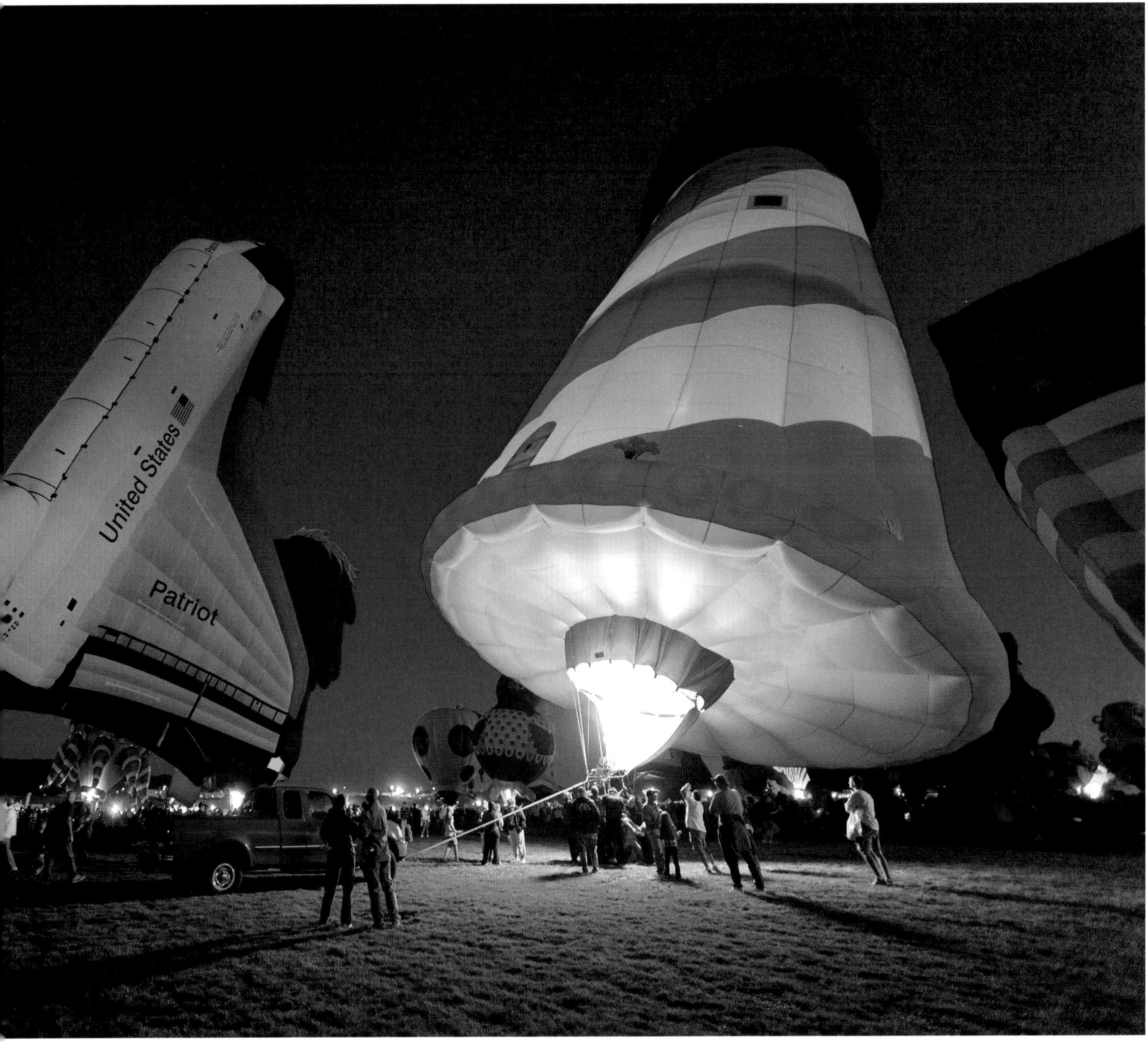
United States
Patriot

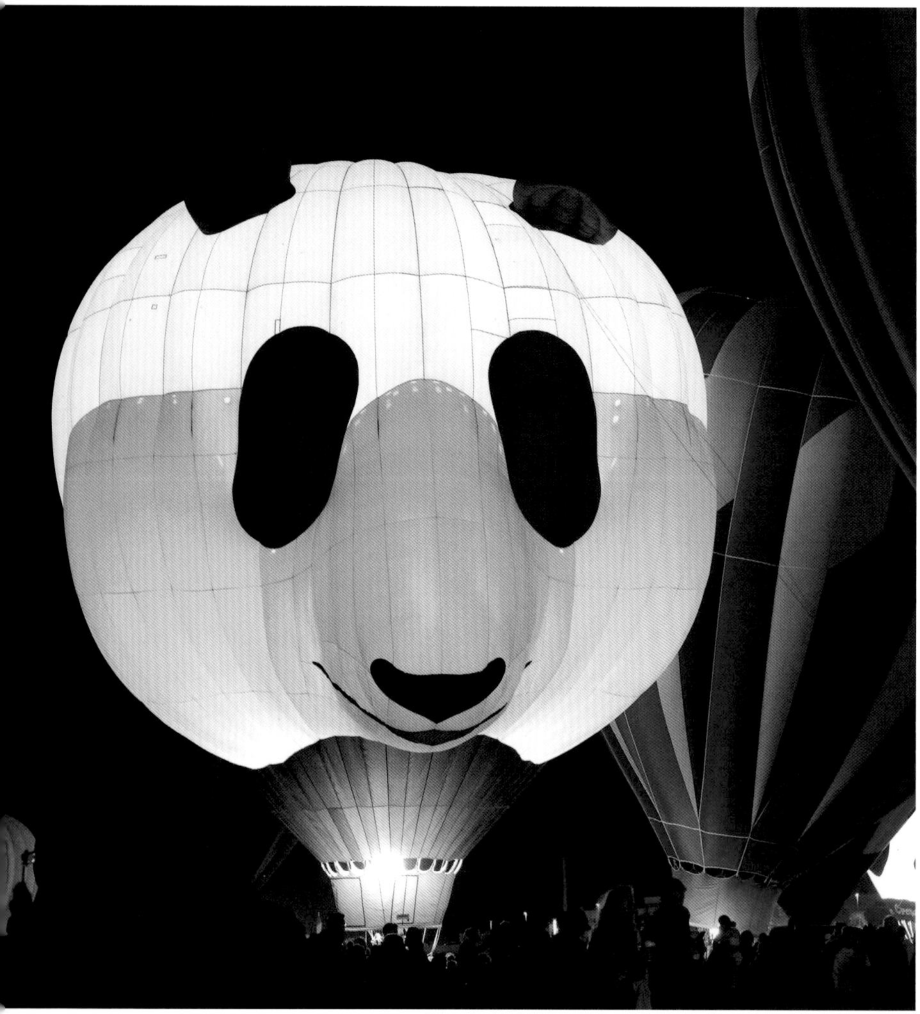

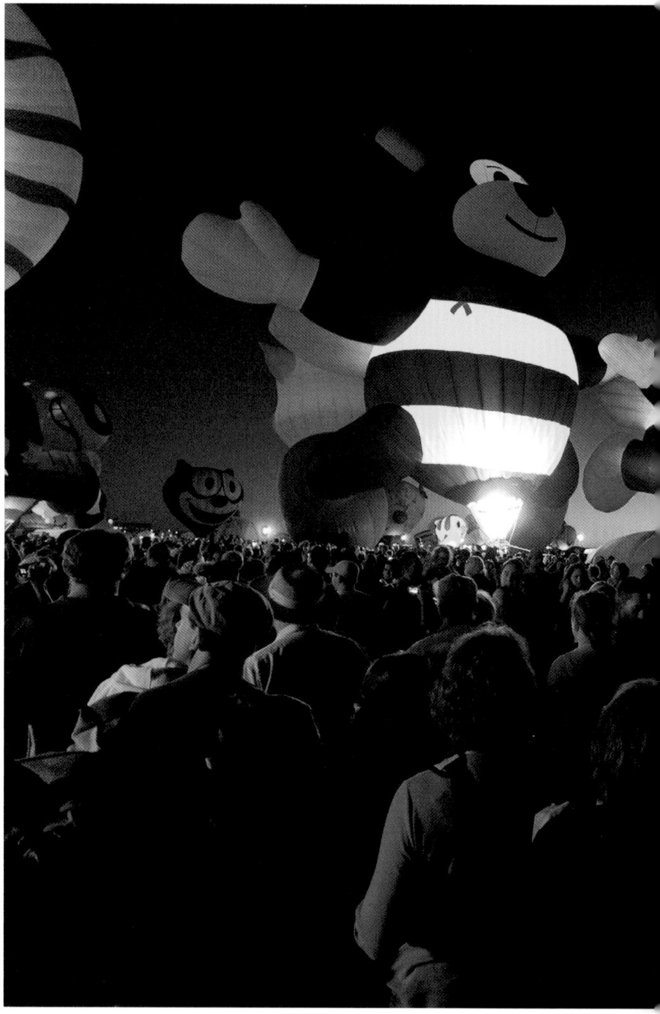

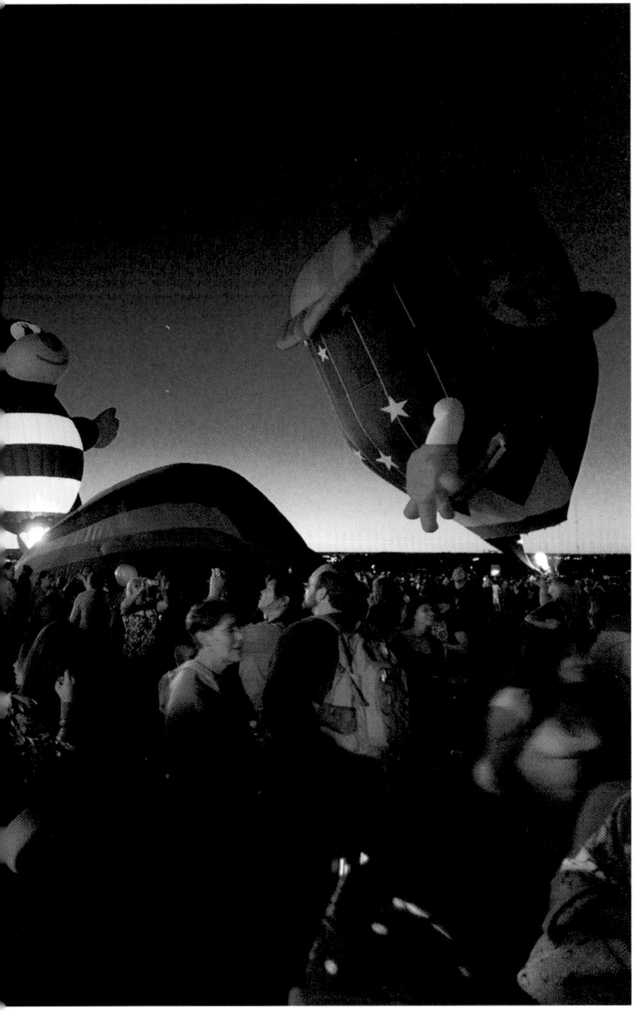

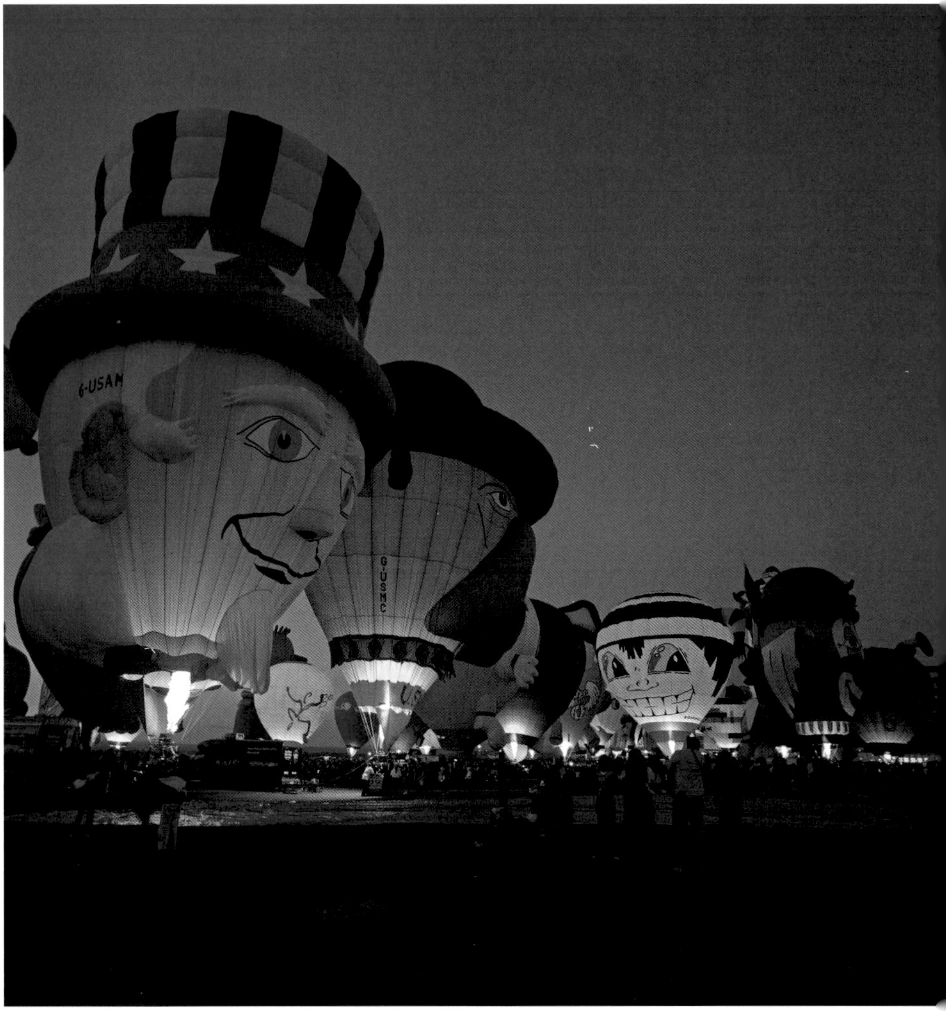
G-USAM
G-USMC

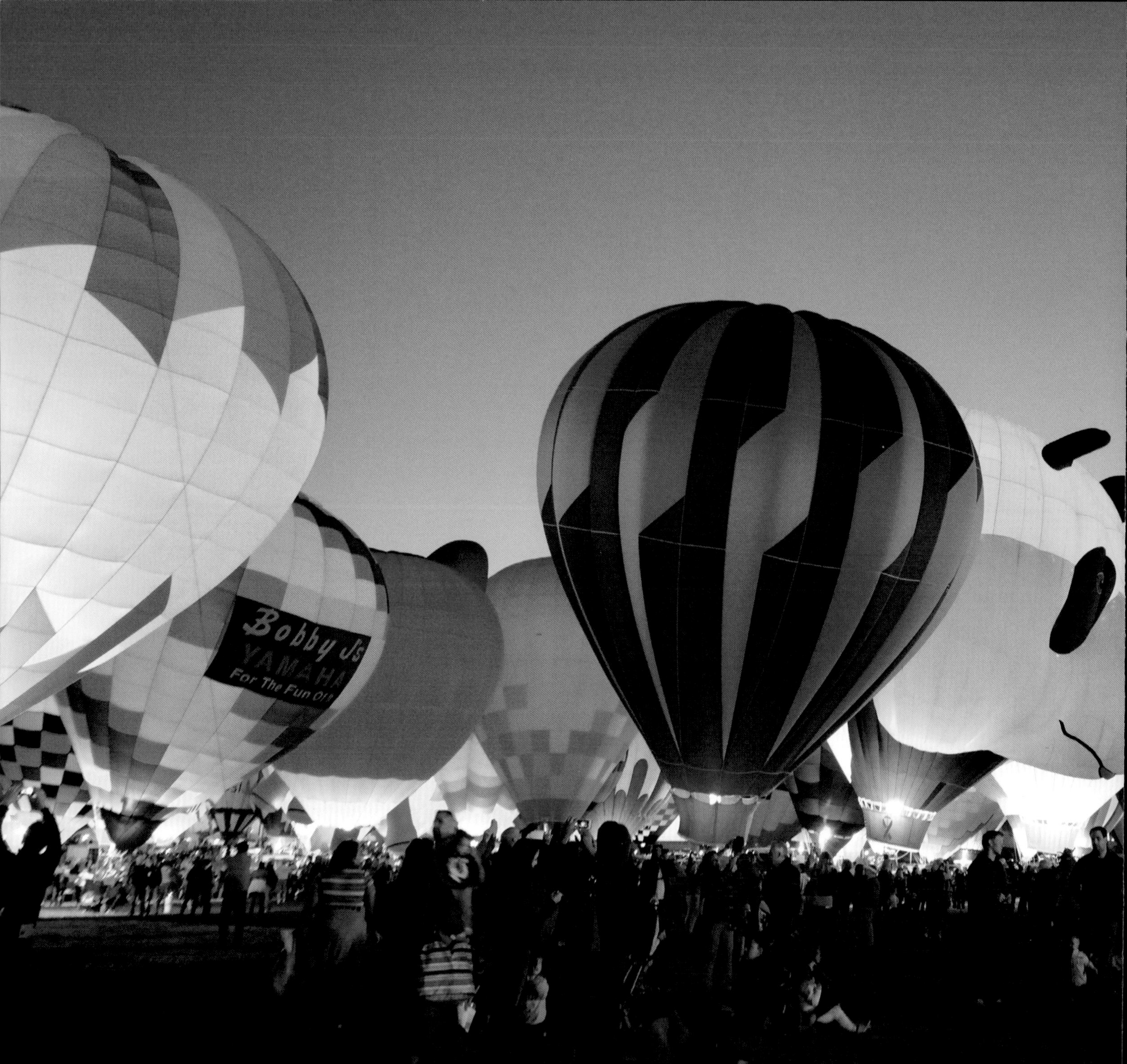
Bobby J's
YAMAHA
For The Fun Of It

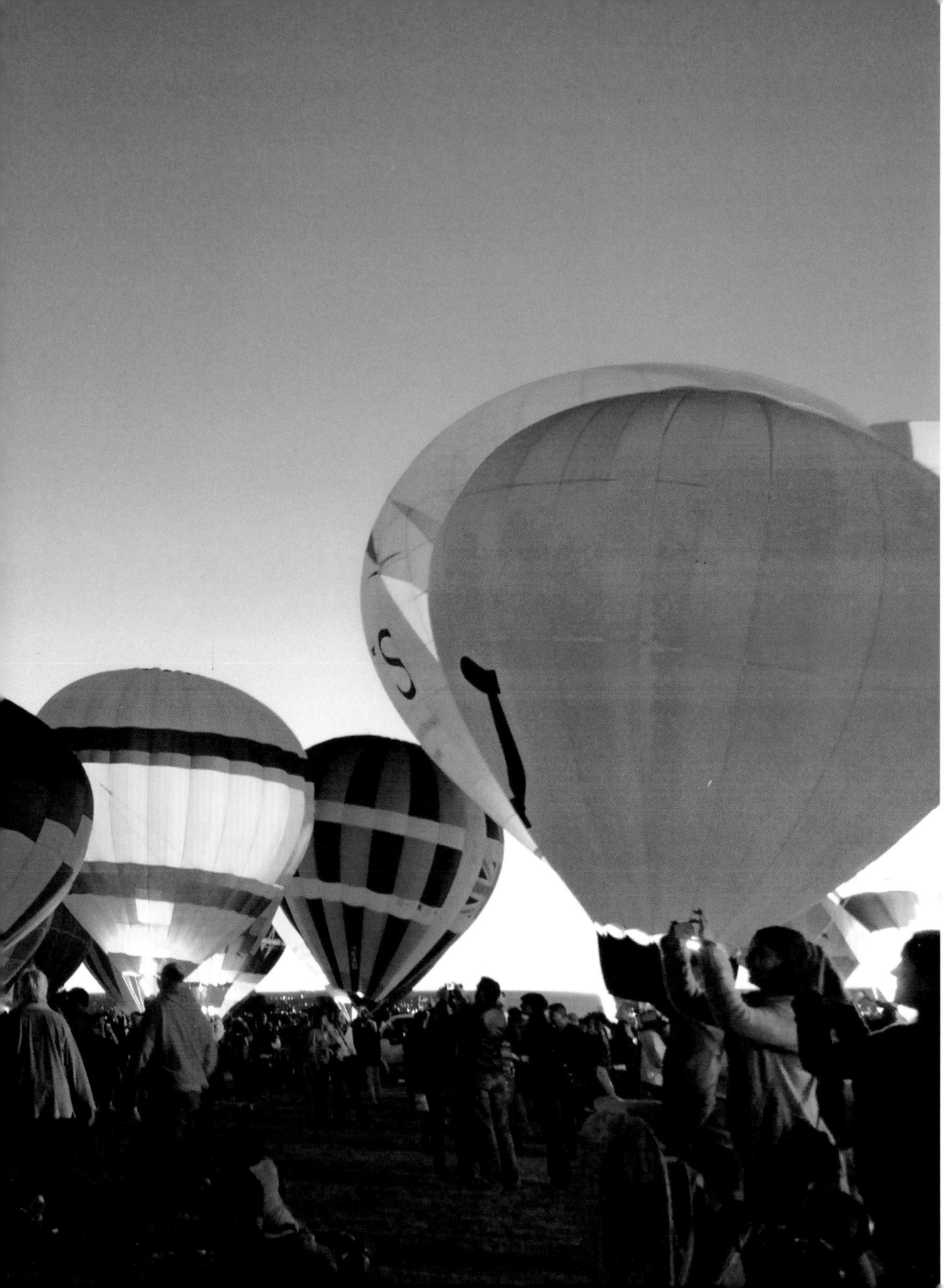

Beginning at 5:30 p.m., glows are popular events, as they draw locals who have finished their work day. Glows began in 1979 to commemorate New Mexico's seventy-fifth year of statehood. A balloonmeister coordinates either flickers, where the burners are hit several times, or "all-burns," where burners are hit for several seconds. Countdowns are announced over speakers, so the thousands of spectators can join in.

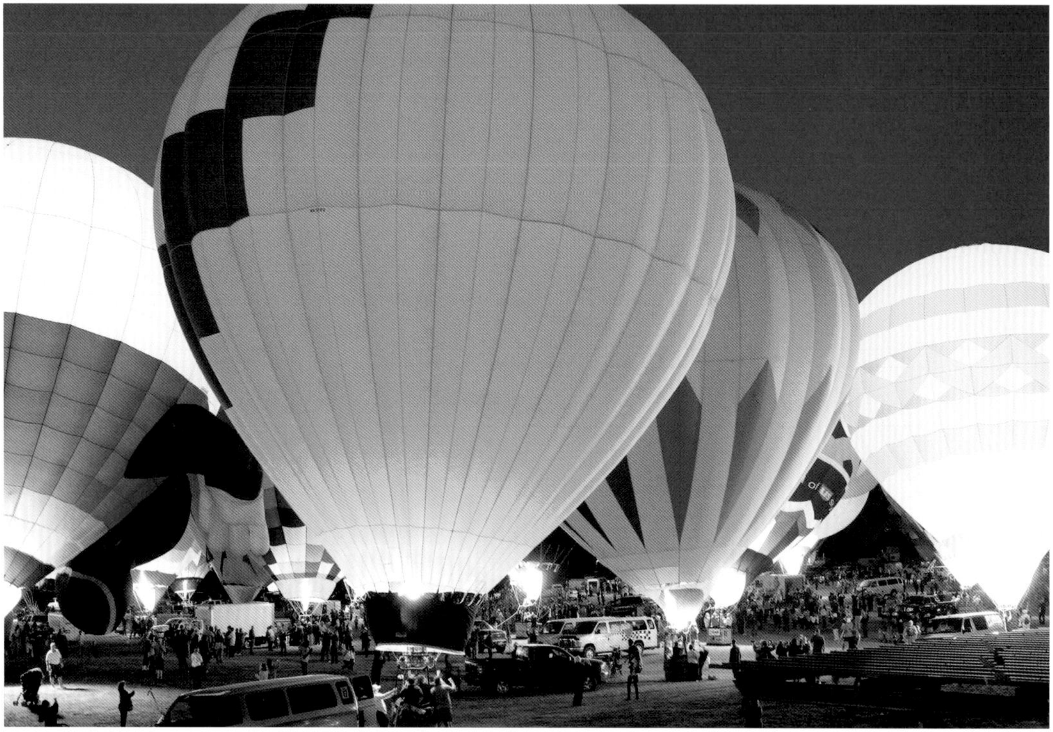

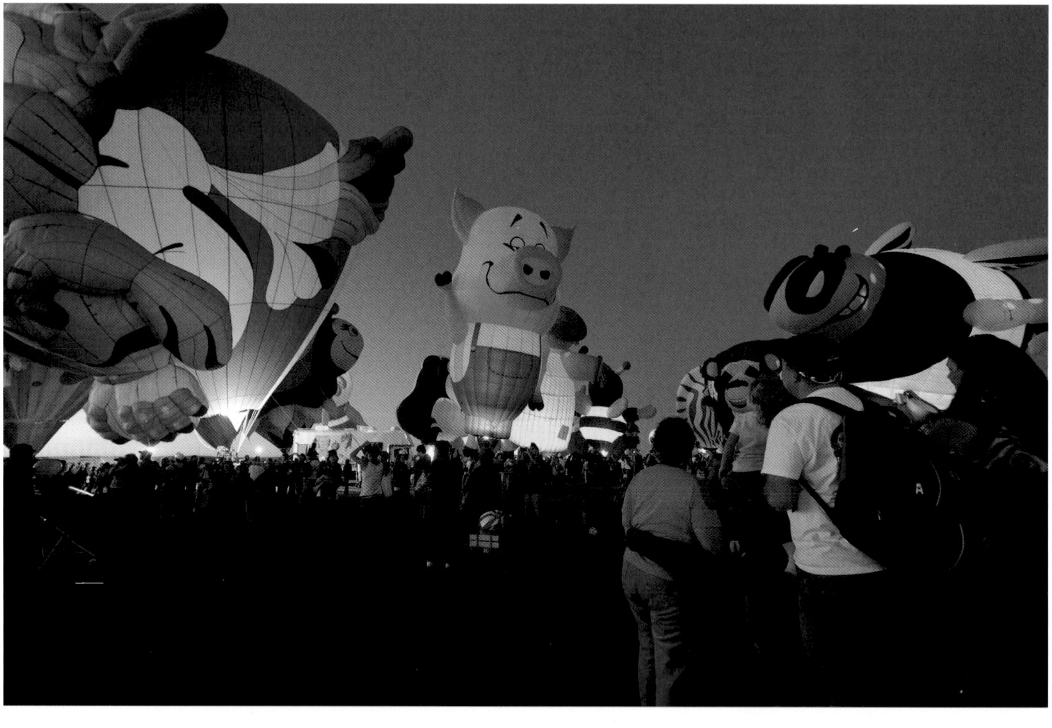

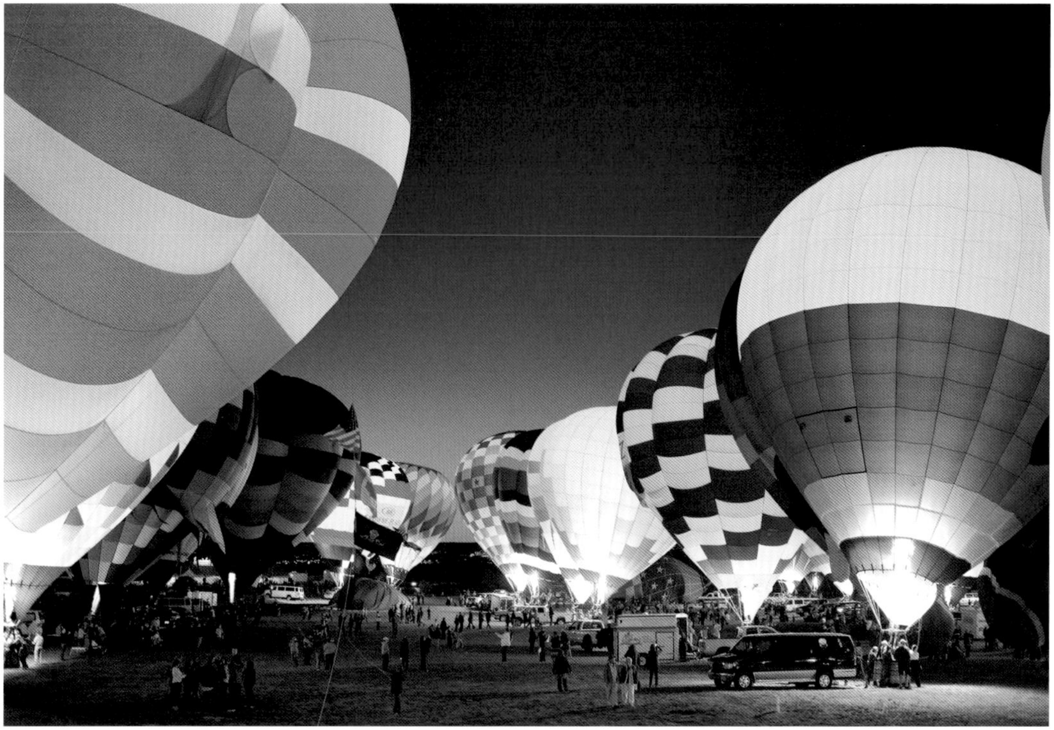

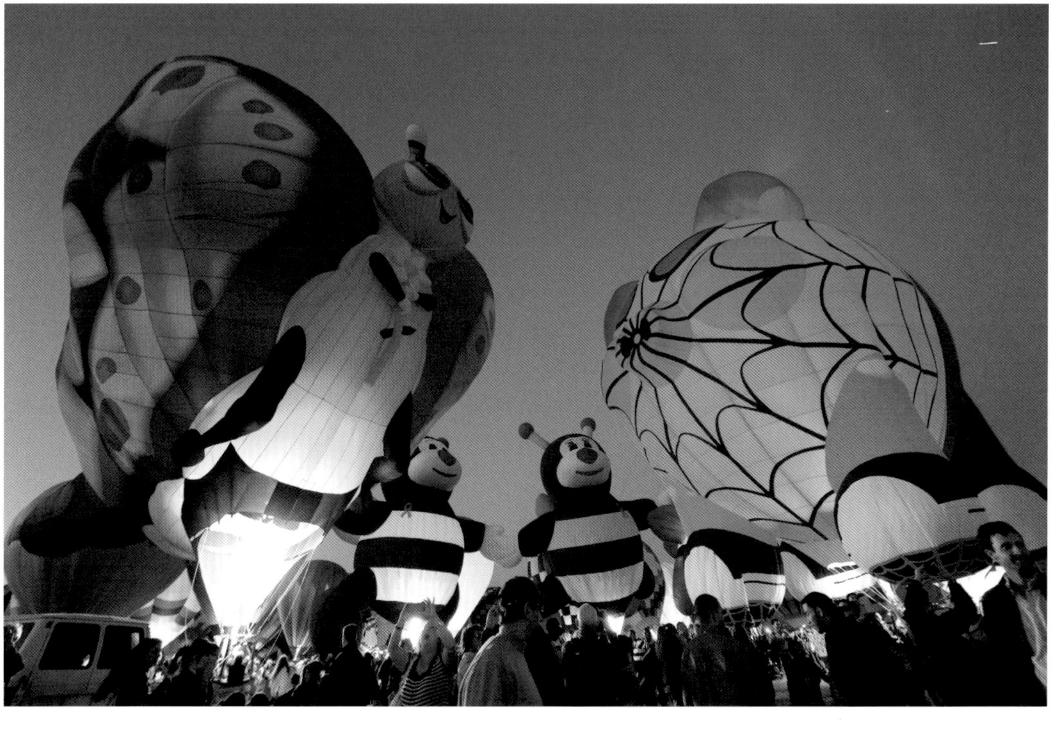

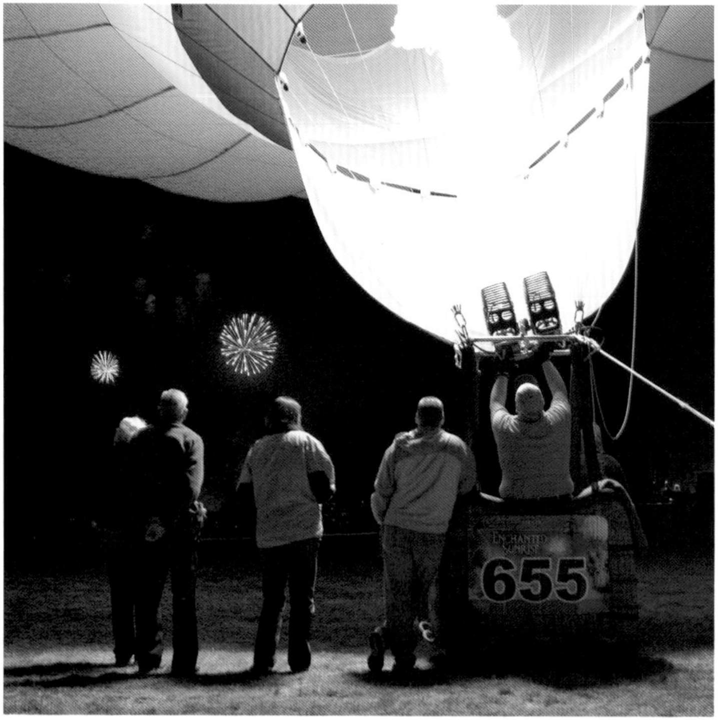
ENCHANTED
655

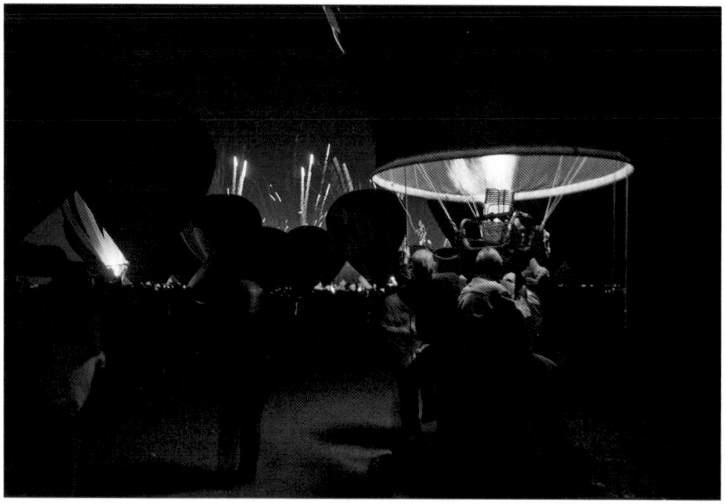

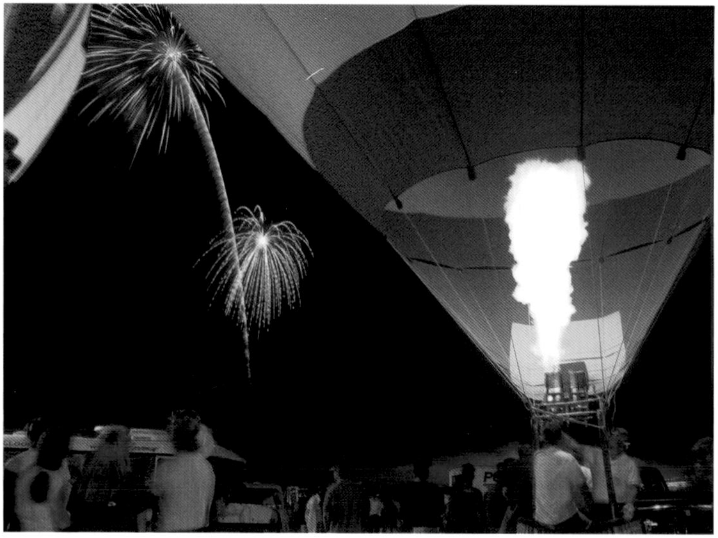

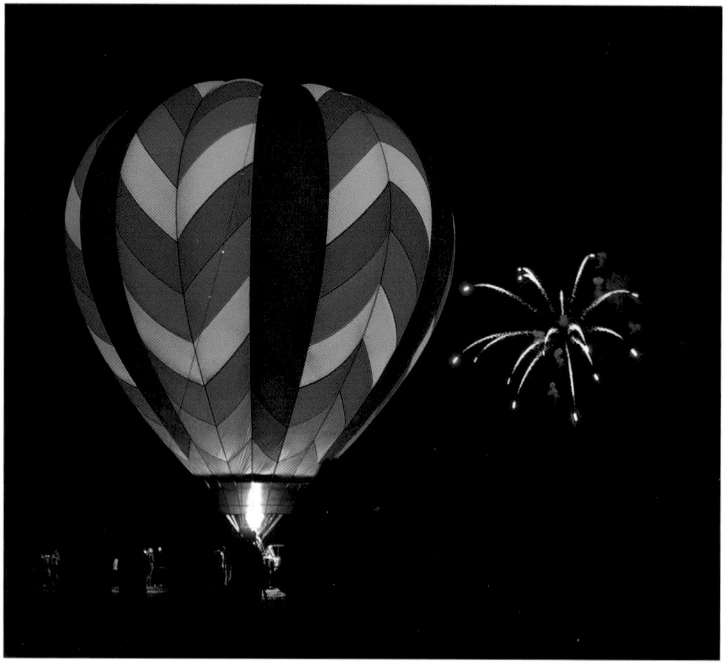

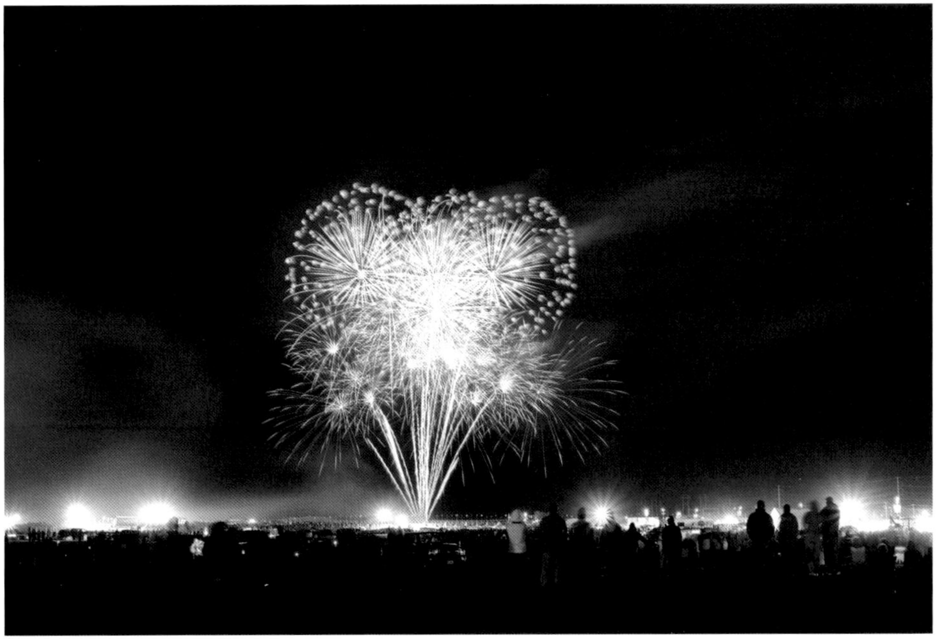

The AfterGlow Fireworks Show that follows balloon glows on Saturdays, Sundays, and Thursday and Friday are worth attending by themselves. In the event glows are cancelled due to bad weather, the fireworks go on, to the delight of the crowd.

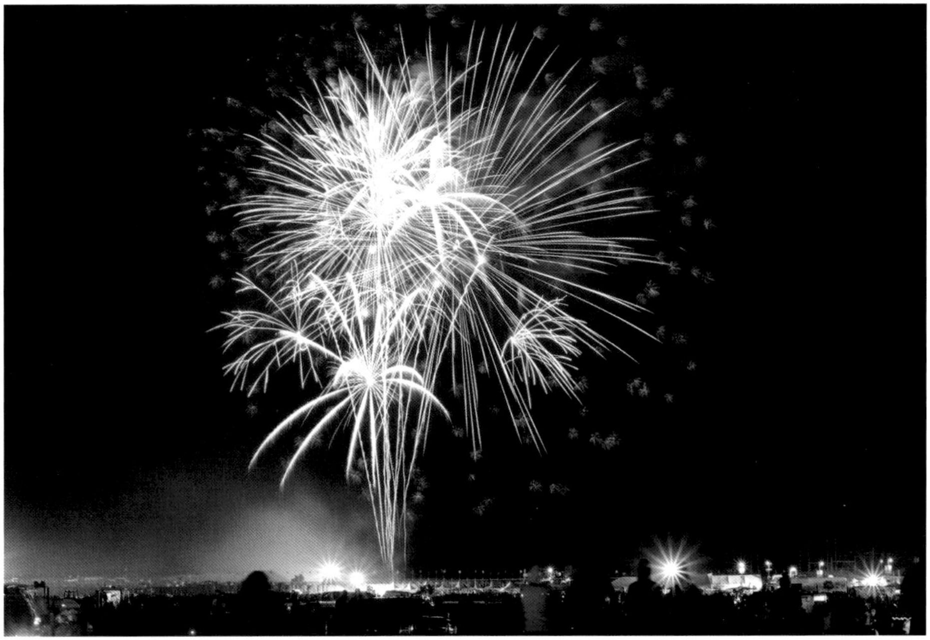

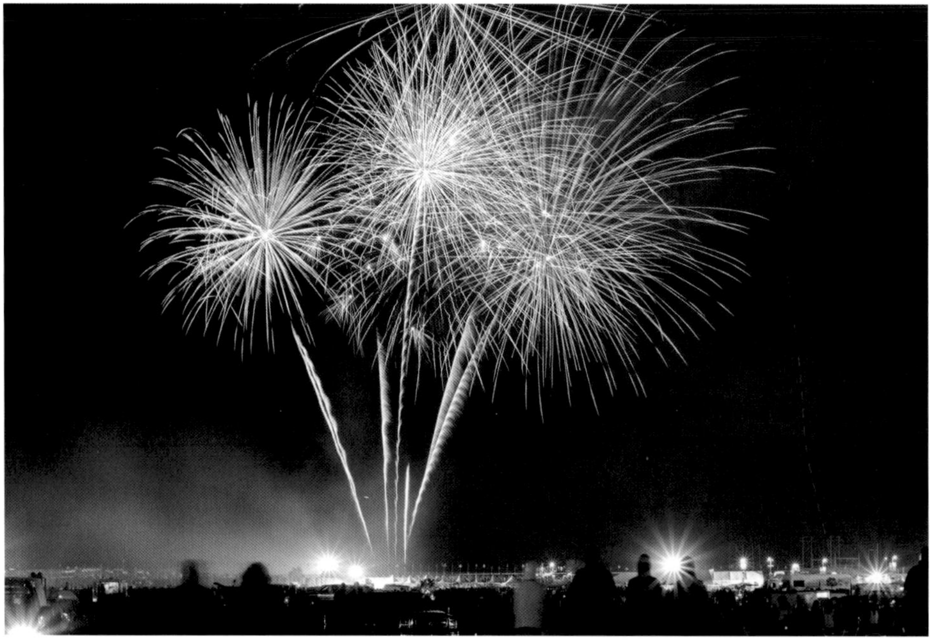

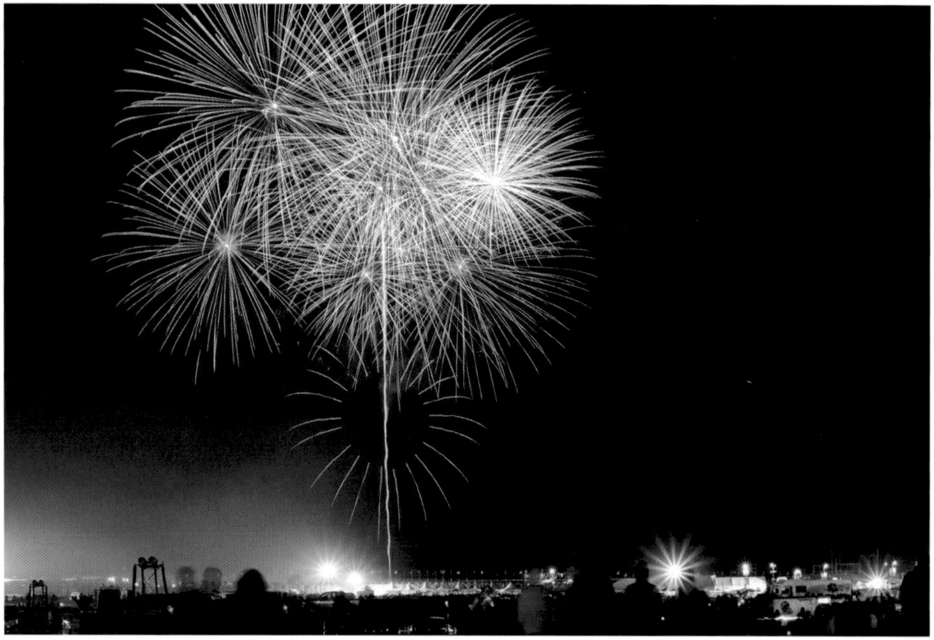

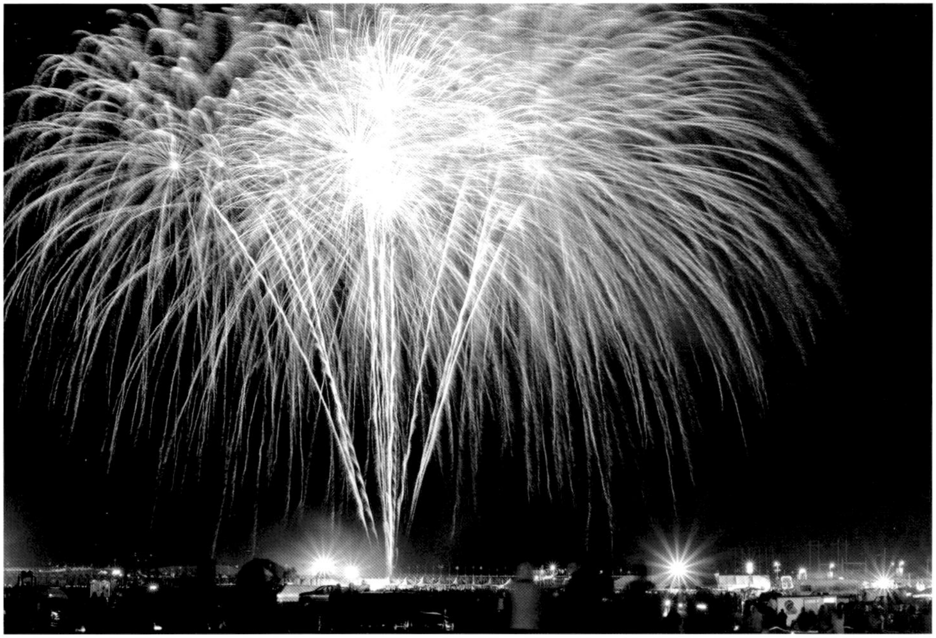

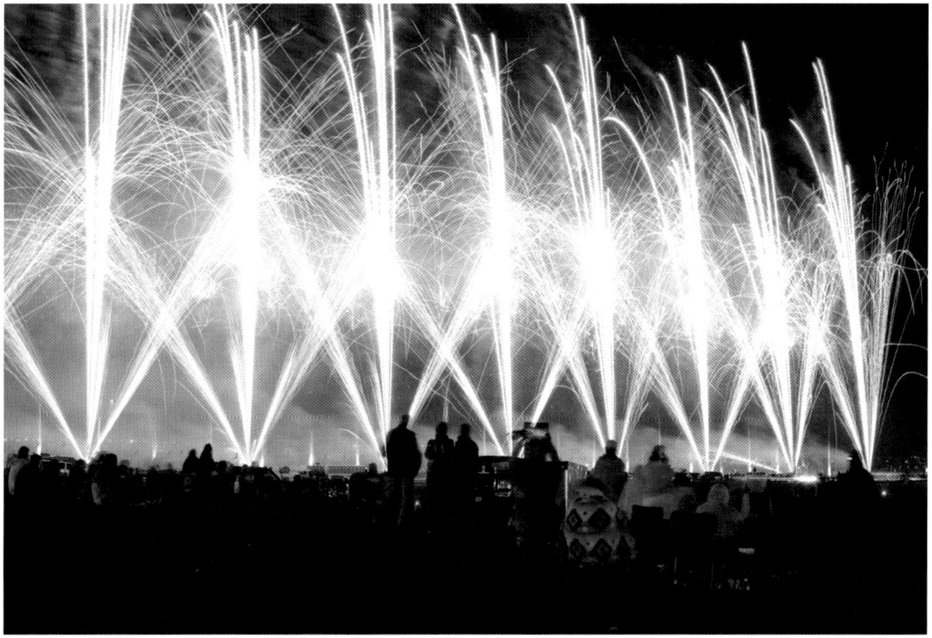

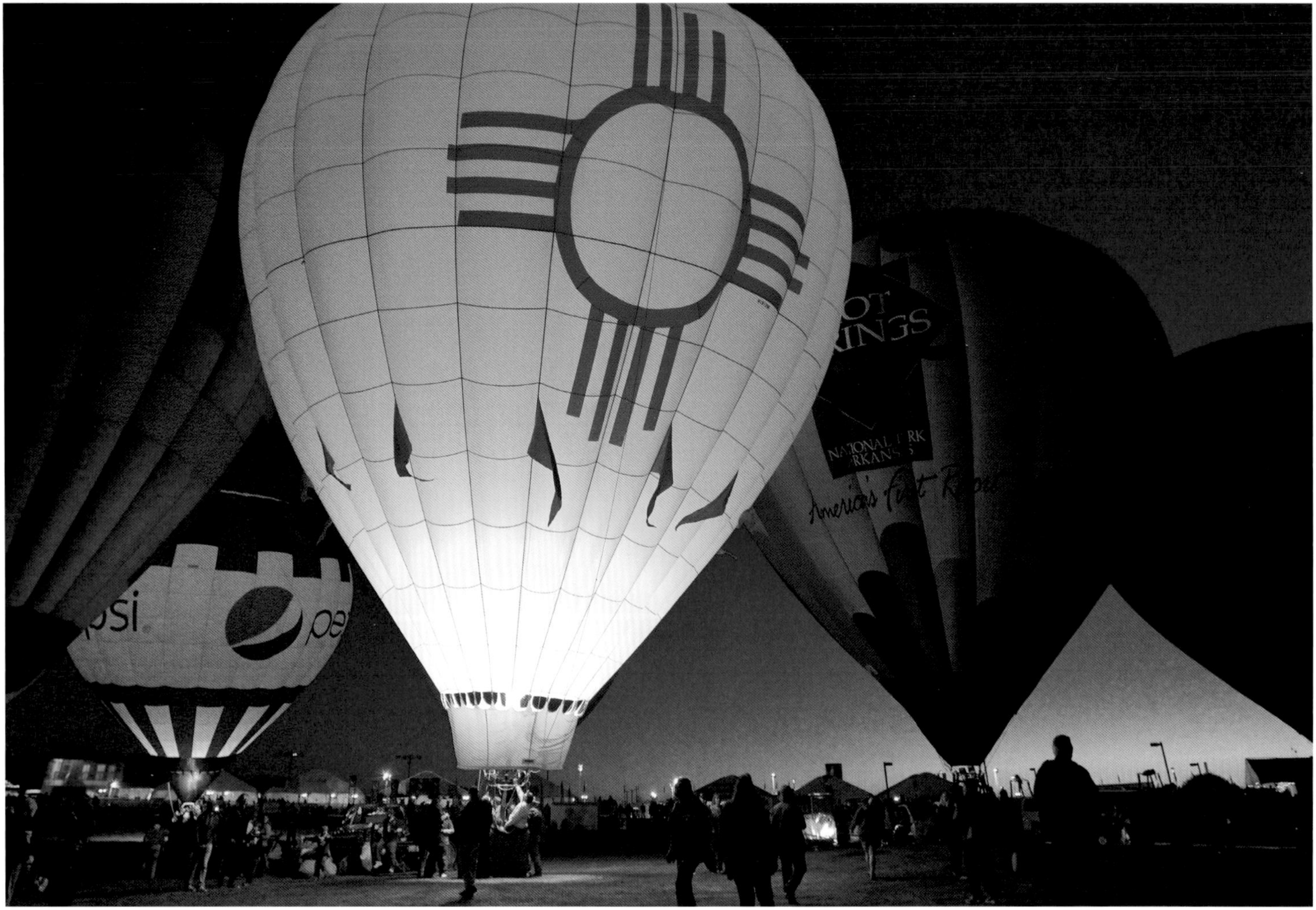

New Mexico's state symbol, the Zia, glows at the conclusion of another Albuquerque International Balloon Fiesta.

About the Author

Steve Larese is an Albuquerque-based travel journalist who is editor of *GuestLife New Mexico*, and is a correspondent who covers New Mexico for *Forbes Travel Guide* and *USA Today Travel.* He also writes about and photographs North American and Caribbean destinations and topics for such publications as *National Geographic Traveler*, *American Way*, *Interval World*, *New Mexico Journey*, *Southwest Fly Fishing*, *Cape Cod Life*, *Oklahoma Today*, and many other regional and national publications. His books include *Southwest Reflections: Grand Canyon & the Four Corners*, *Durango Perspectives*, *Santa Fe Reflections*, and *The Best Recipes from New Mexico's B&Bs.* Though Larese travels extensively for assignments, he feels most at home exploring the cultures and landscapes of the American Southwest. His website is stevelarese.com.